MARKET LEADER

Course Book

D0139171

INTERMEDIATE
BUSINESS ENGLISH

David Cotton   David Falvey   Simon Kent

Longman

FINANCIAL TIMES
World business newspaper.

the book

Grammar reference: page 134   **Writing file:** page 142   **Activity file:** page 150

	Discussion	Texts			Case study
Unit 9 Money page 70	Do a quiz and discuss attitudes to money	Reading: Three sto… market speculatio… Listening: An inter… a bank director			Angel Investments: Raise the money to finance a new invention Writing: report
Unit 10 Ethics page 78	Discuss ethics at work Rank a list of unethical activities	Reading: The mos… corrupt countries – *Times* Listening: An interview with a senior manager	… *honesty* and *dishonesty* Narrating		Profit or principle: Decide if a manager has acted unethically and what action to take Writing: letter
Unit 11 Change page 86	Discuss attitudes to change in general and at work Rank stressful situations	Reading: A CEO's views on managing change Listening: An interview with an independent management consultant	Words for describing meetings Reporting	Meetings	Metrot: Agree on changes at a company that has been taken over Writing: action minutes
Unit 12 Strategy page 94	Define strategy and discuss who should be involved in making strategy	Reading: The advantages and disadvantages of a merger Listening: An interview with the head of a worldwide organisation	Words for talking about business strategies Dependent prepositions	Decision-making	Texan Chicken: Work out a strategy to save a failing fast food company Writing: press release
Unit 13 Cultures page 102	Discuss the importance of cultural awareness in business	Reading: Doing business across cultures – *Financial Times* Listening: An interview with an expert on cultural awareness	Modal verbs	Social English See also: The social-cultural game on pages 148 and 149	Visitors from China: Plan a visit by a Chinese manufacturer Writing: fax
Unit 14 Leadership page 110	Discuss the qualities of good leadership	Reading: Profile of a leading chief executive Listening: An interview with a leading chief executive	Words to describe character Relative clauses	Leading a team	Orbit Records: Discuss ideas to save a failing music retailer Writing: letter
Unit 15 Competition page 118	Do a quiz on how competitive you are	Reading: Strategies to gain a competitive advantage Listening: An interview with a senior executive about competition	Words and expressions for talking about competition Talking about the future	Negotiating	City Plaza Hotel: Work out a new competitive strategy for a hotel Writing: report
Unit 16 Quality page 126	Discuss different ways of measuring quality	Reading: New style quality – *The Financial Times* Listening: Two interviews about defective products	Words for talking about quality control and customer services Prepositions of time	Complaining on the telephone	Western Airport: Work out an action plan following complaints form passengers Writing: memo

Audio scripts: page 158 **Glossary of business terms:** page 168

What is Market Leader and who is it for?

Market Leader is an intermediate level business English course for business people and students of business English. It has been developed in association with the *Financial Times*, one of the leading sources of business information in the world. It consists of 16 units based on topics of great interest to everyone involved in international business.

If you are in business, the course will greatly improve your ability to communicate in English in a wide range of business situations. If you are a student of business, the course will develop the communication skills you need to succeed in business and will enlarge your knowledge of the business world. Everybody studying this course will become more fluent and confident in using the language of business and should increase their career prospects.

The authors

David Falvey *(left)* has 20 years' teaching experience in the UK, Japan and Hong Kong. He has also worked as a teacher trainer at the British Council in Tokyo, and is now Head of the English Language Centre and Principal lecturer at London Guildhall University.

David Cotton *(centre)* has 30 years' experience teaching and training in EFL, ESP and English for Business, and is the author of numerous business English titles, including Agenda, World of Business, International Business Topics, and Keys to Management. He is also one of the authors of the best-selling Business Class. He is currently a Senior Lecturer at London Guildhall University.

Simon Kent *(right)* has 12 years' teaching experience including three years as an in-company trainer in Berlin at the time of German reunification. He is currently a lecturer in business and general English, as well as having special responsibility for designing new courses at London Guildhall University.

What is in the units?

Starting up

You are offered a variety of interesting activities in which you discuss the topic of the unit and exchange ideas about it.

Vocabulary

You will learn important new words and phrases which you can use when you carry out the tasks in the unit. A good business dictionary, such as the *Longman Business English Dictionary* will also help you to increase your business vocabulary.

Discussion

You will build up your confidence in using English and will improve your fluency through interesting discussion activities.

Reading

You will read authentic articles on a variety of topics from the *Financial Times* and other newspapers and books on business. You will develop your reading skills and learn essential business vocabulary. You will also be able to discuss the ideas and issues in the articles.

Listening

You will hear authentic interviews with business people. You will develop listening skills such as listening for information and note-taking.

Language review

This section focuses on common problem areas at intermediate level. You will become more accurate in your use of language. Each unit contains a Language review box which provides a review of key grammar items.

Skills

You will develop essential business communication skills such as making presentations, taking part in meetings, negotiating, telephoning, and using English in social situations. Each Skills section contains a Useful language box which provides you with the language you need to carry out the realistic business tasks in the book.

Case study

The Case studies are linked to the business topics of each unit. They are based on realistic business problems or situations and allow you to use the language and communication skills you have developed while working through the unit. They give you the opportunities to practise your speaking skills in realistic business situations. Each Case study ends with a writing task. A full writing syllabus is provided in the Market Leader Practice File.

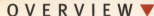

UNIT 1 Globalisation

> *We are not a global business. We are a collection of local businesses with intense global coordination.*
>
> Percy Barnevik, Swedish business leader

Starting up

Discuss these questions.

1 What do you think *globalisation* means?

2 Do you think globalisation is a recent trend?

3 What global companies can you think of? What industries are they in?

4 Do global companies do more harm than good?

Listening
For and against globalisation

▲ Stephen Haseler

A Stephen Haseler is Professor of Government at London Guildhall University. Before you listen, match the words below with their definitions.

1 infrastructure   a) important subjects that people discuss

2 issues   b) money paid by the government to people in need, for example, the unemployed

3 profitability   c) basic facilities and services of a country, for example, water, power, roads

4 welfare benefits   d) a movement of large sums of money out of a country

5 flight of capital   e) the ability of a business to make money

B  1.1 **Listen to the interview and answer these questions.**

1 Is Stephen Haseler generally in favour of globalisation or against it?

2 Which of the points below does Stephen Haseler make?

Advantages

• Globalisation increases the power of governments.

• Globalisation increases competition among companies.

• Competition between China, India and the West will increase employment everywhere.

Disadvantages

- Globalisation could lead to big employment problems in the West.
- Globalisation lowers people's living standards.
- Globalisation prevents governments from controlling their welfare systems.
- Globalisation creates cross-cultural problems, for example, between India, China and the West.

C Complete the text below with these phrases from the interview. Use a good dictionary to help you.

> give-and-take   gather pace   rule the roost

In some countries, international companies ....[1] and strongly influence governments' actions. Stephen Haseler thinks there should be ....[2] between companies and governments. In the future, the process of globalisation will ....[3] and the power of companies could increase.

Reading 1
Going global

A Discuss these questions.

1 What do you know about Boeing?
2 Where is its head office?
3 What do you think *in-plant* and *out-plant* mean?

B Now read the article and check your answers.

C Which of these statements are true? Correct the false ones.

1 Boeing employees seem to be rather conservative and inward-looking.
2 The chairman of Boeing believes the company must make changes.
3 Boeing used to be in the train business.
4 The chairman thinks that Boeing is the most global company in the world.
5 The chairman wants people to identify Boeing as a US company.

PHILIP CONDIT, CHAIRMAN OF BOEING, TALKS ABOUT THE PROBLEMS OF TURNING BOEING INTO A GLOBAL COMPANY

Flight plan from Seattle

By Michael Skinner

In the last thirty years, Philip Condit says, not much has changed. The problem, he says, is not just that employees at Boeing think of other countries as being exotic. They take the same attitude to anywhere in the US outside Seattle, where the company has its headquarters and its most important factories. Boeing staff talk about something as being 'in-plant' or 'out-plant'. In-plant means Seattle. Out-plant means one of the group's other locations, such as Wichita, Kansas.

Condit, who became Boeing's chairman in February, wants to change all that. Over the next 20 years, he wants Boeing to become a global rather than a US company. Boeing employees could be forgiven for thinking that being a Seattle company has served them well enough. Boeing is the world's most successful aircraft maker.

Condit believes, however, that Boeing cannot stand still. There are too many examples in aviation and other sectors of what has happened to companies that have tried to do that.

Last year, in a speech to managers, he described his vision of what the group would look like in 2016, its centenary year. He told them that Boeing would be an aerospace company. It would not repeat earlier mistakes such as attempting to enter the train or boat-building business.

Second, he said, Boeing would be a 'global enterprise'. This would mean increasing the number of countries of operation. He is impressed, he says, by the way in which oil companies have benefited from losing national images. 'BP is probably the most global company in the world. It is interesting to see that in the US its nationality has begun to disappear. Almost everybody in the US says BP and not British Petroleum. It is a local kind of company.' Royal Dutch/Shell is another group which manages to present itself as a local company in the countries in which it operates.

Would he be happy if 20 years from now people did not think of Boeing as being a US company? 'Yes,' Condit says, 'I believe we are moving towards an era of global markets and global companies.'

From the *Financial Times*

FINANCIAL TIMES
World business newspaper.

Vocabulary
Entering new markets

A When a company globalises, it tries to choose the best method to enter its overseas markets. Match the methods below to the definitions. Use a good dictionary, such as the *Longman Business English Dictionary*, to help you.

1	acquisition	a)	a company partly or wholly owned by a parent company
2	joint venture	b)	giving someone the exclusive right to sell products in a certain area
3	consortium	c)	selling the right to a manufacturer's trademark, usually in a foreign market
4	franchising	d)	buying or taking over another company
5	licensing	e)	a person or company who cooperates with a foreign company who wishes to enter the market
6	local partner	f)	two or more companies join temporarily to carry out a large project
7	subsidiary	g)	a group of companies in similar businesses working together

B Complete these sentences with some of the methods listed above.

1 Wal-Mart, a US retail chain, entered the Mexican market by setting up a 50-50 .... with a local Mexican retailer.

2 When the Japanese tyre group Bridgestone entered the US market, it made an .... , buying the local production base of Firestone.

3 If a company wishes to enter the Chinese market, it usually looks for a .... who will cooperate in setting up a joint venture.

4 If a company is short of capital to expand overseas, it may prefer to have .... or .... agreements with local businesses.

Language review
Comparing

> Complete the table with the comparative and superlative forms of these adjectives: *successful, rich, global, early, big*. Add others.
>
> | One syllable | Add -er or -est. | rich, richer, richest |
> |---|---|---|
> | One syllable ending vowel+consonant | Double the last letter, and add -er or -est. | |
> | Two syllables ending in y | Change y to i, and add -er or -est. | |
> | Two or more syllables | Put more or most in front. | |
>
> Some other ways of comparing are:
> - as … as   The new photocopier is **as** unreliable **as** the old one.
> - much -er than   His boss is **much** older **than** him.
> - compared to /   Their economy looks quite healthy **compared to /**
>   in comparison to   **in comparison to** ours
>
> page 134

A Correct the grammatical mistakes in these sentences.

1 Prague has become central Europe's ~~glamourest~~ *most glamorous* city.

2 Most tallest office towers in the world are in Kuala Lumpur.

3 Cleveland is now one of the most cleanest cities in North America.

4 In Buenos Aires foreign bankers are as common than coffee house poets.

5 The London Underground is worst than the Tokyo Underground system.

6 Ireland is not as larger as Sweden.

7 The London Stock Exchange is very older than the Singapore Exchange.

8 Their prices are very high in compared to ours.

p. 155

B 🎧 1.2 **Complete this extract from a radio programme with the correct comparative or superlative forms of the adjectives in brackets. Then listen and check your answers.**

A survey has come up with some interesting information about the cost of living in our major cities.

Tokyo is still *the most expensive* [1] (expensive) city in the world. Osaka is second and Moscow third, on a par with Hong Kong. Many European cities have gone down the rankings because their exchange rates have become .... [2] (weak) against the US dollar. Moscow's exchange rate has also become .... [3] (weak), but Russia has a much .... [4] (high) inflation rate than many European countries. So prices in Moscow are among .... [5] (high) in Europe. But there is one advantage of living in Moscow. The underground is excellent – very cheap and much .... [6] (comfortable) than the one in London.

New York is .... [7] (expensive) US city. This is because the US dollar is .... [8] (strong) than many other currencies. Some European countries that used to be far .... [9] (expensive) than New York are now much .... [10] (cheap).

London is the 10th .... [11] (expensive) city in the world, according to the survey. A year ago, London was 5%-10% .... [12] (cheap) than many French and German cities. This is no longer so. Now London is 15% .... [13] (dear) than the German and French cities mentioned in the survey. However, London is a good city to live in. Business people said that London was .... [14] (exciting) of all the major cities in the world. Londoners also claim that it is .... [15] (clean) than it used to be, and .... [16] (safe) than many other European cities.

If you're hard up, don't go to Oslo – it's Europe's .... [17] (expensive) city. Meals at restaurants cost a fortune and drinks are very pricey.

C **A business executive who travels a lot gives a personal response to the radio programme extract above. Complete the text below with the words in the box.**

~~different~~	as	similar	just	rather
not	much	compared	less	same

Well personally, I've had some *different* [1] experiences. For a start, I can't agree that Moscow is .... [2] expensive as Hong Kong. I've always found Moscow .... [3] expensive. The price of certain items may be about the *same* [4] as in Hong Kong, but I know the hotels are *not* [5] as expensive. I agree that the Moscow Underground is really good .... [6] to the London Underground and is definitely .... [7] more comfortable. I always walk in London .... [8] than use the Underground. Also, some other Northern European cities are *just* [9] as expensive as Oslo. In general, I find that prices in Sweden and Denmark are *similar* [10] to those in Norway.

D **Make comparisons about *one* of the following:**

1 Your city or country with another city or country you know well.

2 Your company with another company in the same sector.

3 Your present job with another job you had in the past.

Reading 2
Phone rage

A Globalisation has helped to make the telephone an essential business communication tool. Before you read the article, discuss these questions.

1 Do you like using the phone?

2 What makes you angry on the phone?

3 What are the special problems of telephone communication compared to face-to-face communication?

B Read the article and find the answers to these questions.

1 What do people find most annoying on the phone?

2 What three reasons for the rise in phone rage are given? Do you agree?

3 Are telephone techniques improving?

4 What do you think is meant by *remote working*?

Bad line on behaviour

WHAT DRIVES YOU to lose your temper on the telephone? Being kept waiting, being connected to voice mail or being passed on to someone else are all common flashpoints. But what infuriates people most of all is talking to someone who sounds inattentive, uncon-
cerned or insincere, according to a survey published today.

The study by Reed Employment Services, a recruitment company, found that nearly two-thirds of people feel that 'phone rage' – people losing their temper on the telephone – has become more common over the past five years. More than half the respondents, who were from 536 organisations, said that they themselves had lost their tempers on the phone this year.

The reasons for this are threefold, according to Reed. People are much more likely to express anger over the phone, rather than in writing or face-to-face. Moreover, telephone usage has been rising steeply over recent years. Increasing numbers of transactions take place entirely by phone, from arranging insurance to paying bills.

In addition, people's expectations have risen. Nearly three-quarters of respondents to the Reed survey said they are more confident that their problems can be solved over the telephone than they were five years ago.

Companies are taking steps to improve their staff's telephone answering techniques. The survey found
that 70 per cent of organisations require their staff to answer the telephone with a formal company greeting. In 43 per cent of organisations, staff have to give their own names when they answer the telephone.

But a third of organisations do not give any training, or they train only their receptionists. That may not be enough, the report says. As companies move towards 'remote working', the need for the right tone of voice extends to every level of the organisation.

From the *Financial Times*

FINANCIAL TIMES
World business newspaper.

C Discuss ways of improving employees' telephone skills.

D Write some guidelines on using the telephone at work.
For example, *Always give your name*.

Skills
Managing telephone calls

A 🎧 1.3 Listen to five telephone conversations.

1 Which of these adjectives best describes the person who receives the call? Why?

| inefficient | impatient | aggressive | bored | unhelpful |

2 How could you improve each call?

3 How important is intonation on the telephone? Why?

B We often need to spell names and addresses on the telephone.
Complete the table with the letters of the alphabet, according to the way they are pronounced.

/eɪ/	/iː/	/e/	/aɪ/	/əʊ/	/uː/	/ɑː/
A	B	F	I	O	Q	R

Useful language

Answering the phone
Hello, John Waite speaking.
Good morning, Datatech Ltd.

Making contact
I'd like to speak to Zofia Janik.
Could I have the sales
   department please?

Messages
Would you like to leave
   a message?
Can I leave a message?

Identifying yourself
This is/My name's Julio Blanco.

Making excuses
I'm sorry, he's in a meeting.
I'm afraid she's not available.

Stating your purpose
I'm calling about your invoice.
I'm returning his call.
The reason I'm calling is ...

Checking
Could you spell that?
Can I read that back to you?

Asking for information
Could I have your name?
Can I take your number?

Showing understanding
Right.
OK. That's fine.

Promising action
I'll make sure he gets
   the message.
I'll tell her when she gets back.

Ending a call
Thanks for your help. Goodbye.
Thanks for calling.

Saying telephone numbers
*Say numbers separately. Pause between groups. Say **oh** for **o** in the UK. Say **zero** for **o** in the USA.*

0 2 0	7 3 2 5	4 2 6 1
oh two oh	seven three two five	four two six one

C Answer these questions about the business call below.

1 Is the conversation grammatically correct? ✓
2 Is the conversation appropriate? ✗
3 How can you improve it?

Person receiving the call	Caller
Yes?	Give me Donna Weston.
She's not here.	Well, take a message. It's Eva Wartanowicz. Tell her to phone me back later this afternoon.
What's your name again?	Wartanowicz.
OK. And your number?	It's 01863 483 2189.
OK. I'll tell her.	Bye.
Bye.	

D Work in pairs. Role play these telephone calls.
Use phrases from the Useful Language box above.

1 A buyer from the Italian engineering firm Donatelli SpA calls the Production Manager of Rod Engineering Ltd about a recent order. Rod Engineering have sent the wrong parts.

2 A Personnel Manager calls the Reception Manager of the Belvedere Hotel to arrange accommodation for a Swedish visitor.

Buyer from Donatelli turn to page 150.
Production Manager turn to page 152.
Read your role cards then make the call.

Personnel Manager turn to page 157.
Reception Manager turn to page 155.
Read your role cards then make the call.

CASE STUDY

Fortune Garments

Background

This week, the international fashion group Fortune Garments is holding its first global conference in Barcelona, Spain. Fortune Garments, one of Hong Kong's oldest trading groups, makes high quality, clothing. It has become a global company: it has over 3000 suppliers in 17 countries, and employs staff from all over the world in its head office and factories. It is expanding rapidly in foreign markets with sales of over $US 1.8bn.

Fast delivery, innovative design, and reliable quality are essential for success in the fashion business. Fortune Garments' Chairman, Michael Chau, is proud that his company can usually accept a major order and deliver the goods to a customer within four weeks. However, globalisation has brought problems in the company's overseas plants, and this is having a bad effect on its share price. A journalist from the *Eastern Economist Review* suggested recently that the company could become the target of a takeover if it didn't sort out its problems soon.

Managers from all the overseas plants are attending the conference. Michael Chau has asked them to consider the problems outlined in the discussion document below.

Discussion document

PROBLEMS

1. Quality control

Many subsidiaries make clothing from materials supplied by several of the company's plants. Although this helps to lower costs, the materials are often of poor quality. This has resulted in cancelled orders. Recently, a German distributor refused a consignment of 50,000 blouses. The goods simply did not meet its quality standards. Cancellation of the order cost Fortune Garments half a million dollars in lost sales.

2. Responding to customer needs

Orders have also been cancelled because Fortune Garments' subsidiaries are not responding quickly to customers' needs. When customers want last-minute changes to clothing, the plants cannot meet customers' tight deadlines. For example, an Australian fashion chain cancelled an order because the US plant was not able to make minor changes to some silk jackets in time for their summer sale. The lost sale cost Fortune Garments over $US 400,000.

3. Design

When the company was smaller, it had the same low-pricing strategy, but the design of its clothing was outstanding. However, nowadays, the company seems to have lost its creative energy. Its latest collections were described by a famous fashion expert as 'boring, behind the times and with no appeal to a fashion-conscious buyer'. Other experts agreed with this opinion. The problem is that ideas are not shared between the company's designers. According to one designer, 'There's not enough contact between designers at the different production centres. The designers never meet or phone each other, and they rarely travel abroad'.

Consultant's report

Michael Chau is aware that morale is low among managers and lower-level staff. He has asked a business consultant to investigate the reason for this. Here are the consultant's main findings.

■ Management

1 Managers of subsidiaries say they are underpaid. They are demotivated and feel their contribution to the group's profits is undervalued.

2 The majority of managers say they should have a share in the profits of their subsidiary (5%–10% was the figure most commonly mentioned).

3 All managers reported that they did not have enough freedom of action. They want more autonomy and less control from head office over finance, pay, and sources of materials.

4 Managers need more advice on quality control, and would like more contact with staff from other subsidiaries.

■ Factory workers and administrative staff

1 Staff turnover is high in most factories. Industrial accidents are common, mainly because health and safety regulations are not being properly observed.

2 Factory workers complain about their wages. They are paid according to local rates, which in some countries are very low. They are often expected to work overtime without extra pay.

3 Administrative staff said their offices are overcrowded and badly ventilated (e.g. too hot in summer, too cold in winter).

4 Supervisors from head office are often of different nationality from their staff. This causes communication problems. Many factory workers said they did not always understand their supervisors' instructions.

Task

1 Form two groups, A and B.
   Group A: Discuss the problems mentioned in the *Discussion document* and decide how to deal with them.
   Group B: Discuss the problems outlined in the *Consultant's report* and decide how to deal with them.
2 Meet as one group. Present the results of your discussions to each other. Then produce an action plan to solve Fortune Garments' problems.

Writing

Write a memo, for the attention of Michael Chau, summarising the problems that you discussed. Recommend a course of action to improve the situation. Give reasons for the actions you propose.

 Writing file pages 144 and 145

Brands

> *The most distinctive skill of professional marketers is their ability to create, maintain, protect and enhance brands.*
>
> P. Kotler, American marketing guru

Starting up

A **List some of your favourite brands. Then answer these questions.**

1 Are they international or national brands?

2 What image and qualities does each one have?

3 Do the products have anything in common?
  For example, are they all high priced?

4 How loyal are you to the brands you have chosen?
  For example, when you buy jeans, do you always buy Levis?

5 If you don't buy branded goods, explain why.

B **What are the advantages of branded goods for:**
a) the manufacturer?   b) the consumer?

C **A recent survey named the brands below as the world's top ten.**
Which do you think is number one? Rank the others in order.

10. Marlboro	9. AT&T	5. Ford	4. General Electric	7. Intel
3. IBM	2. Microsoft	1. Coca-Cola	8. McDonald's	6. Disney

Check your answer on page 156. Are you surprised?

Vocabulary
Brand management

```
          — awareness
luxury —
          — image
   BRAND — stretching
          — loyalty
          — leader
classic — — manager
```

A Look at the eight word partnerships with the word *brand*. Match them to the definitions below. Use a good dictionary to help you.

1 A brand associated with expensive, high quality products
2 The person responsible for planning and managing a branded product
3 The brand with the largest market share
4 A famous brand with a long history
5 The ideas and beliefs which consumers have about a brand
6 The tendency of a customer to continue buying a particular product
7 Using a successful brand name to launch a product in a new category
8 The knowledge which consumers have of a brand

B Complete these sentences with word partnerships from the list.

1 Levis, which has been established for over a 100 years and is world-famous, is a ......classic........ .
2 The aim of the advertising campaign is to enhance .....awareness... so that consumers become more familiar with our coffee products.
3 Volvo's .....image........ is that of a well-engineered, upmarket, safe car.
4 Suchard is a .....brand......... of Swiss chocolate.

C Make four sentences of your own using the remaining word partnerships.

Listening
What is branding?

▲ Lynne Fielding

A 🎧 **2.1 Lynne Fielding, a marketing specialist, is talking about *branding*. Complete this extract from the interview with the words below. Then listen to the first part of the interview and check your answers.**

money	name	differentiate	synergy	quality	competitors'

'What is branding and why do we need brands?'

'A brand can be a ....[1], a term or a symbol. It is used to ....[2] a product from ....[3] products. The brands guarantee a certain ....[4] level. Brands should add value to products. It's a ....[5] effect whereby one plus one equals three. But customers must believe they get extra value for ....[6] .'

B 🎧 **2.2 Now listen to the second part of the interview and complete the chart.**

BRANDS

Stand-alone or ....individ.... brands	Corporate or ....family.... brands
Ariel	Heinz
Hagen Das	Virgin
Direct Line Ins.	Marks & Spencer
Marlboro Cig-s	Levis

C 🎧 **2.3 Finally, listen to the last part and complete the summary below.**

1 Customers want:
a) .....choose..... b) .....selection..... c) ....
   choice of dif prod.

2 Customers like to:
a) rely on the ....quality..... guaranteed by the company.
b) ....trust.......... products. c) ...identify..... with brands.

Reading
Fashion piracy

A Discuss these questions before you read the article.

1 Do you own a product which is an illegal copy of a well-known brand? If so, what is it? Where did you buy it? How much did it cost?

2 How can manufacturers protect their brands from piracy (illegal copying)?

B Match these words and phrases with the definitions.

1 global offensive	a) plans of a company to achieve its objectives
2 counterfeiter	b) agreements which allow a company to make and sell a registered product locally
3 copyright abuse	c) taking strong action all over the world
4 a network	d) a person who copies goods in order to trick people
5 merchandise	e) to copy someone else's work, for example their designs, without permission
6 corporate strategy	f) a large number of people or organisations working together as a system
7 logo	g) goods for sale
8 licensing rights	h) to change the way something is organised
9 to rip off	i) the symbol of a company or other organisation
10 restructure	j) to sell illegal copies of a brand as if they are the real thing

C Read the article quickly to find out:

1 which Calvin Klein products are commonly copied.
t-shirts, jeans, baseball caps
2 why the problem is getting worse.

3 how the company is dealing with it.

D Read the article again and answer these questions.

1 What was Calvin Klein's attitude to counterfeiting in the past? *relatively passive approach*
2 Why has the company changed its way of dealing with counterfeiters? *b/c it has decreased its sales and damaged brand image*
Counterfeit 3 What has the company done to change the way its business operates and to increase its size? *hired specialists to uncover copyright abuse and expanded.*

Calvin Klein is tired of piracy, says **Alice Rawsthorn**, and has started a global offensive against counterfeiters

Fashion victim fights back

Walk into a street market anywhere from Manila to Manchester, and someone will be selling T-shirts branded with the distinctive CK logo of Calvin Klein, the New York fashion designer.

If the price is very low, the T-shirts are probably fakes. Calvin Klein, like most other internationally-known fashion designers, has, for a long time, had problems with counterfeiters selling poor-quality merchandise bearing his brand name. Now he is doing something about it. 'As the Calvin Klein brand has become well-known, we've seen a big increase in counterfeit activity,' says Gabriella Forte, chief executive of Calvin Klein. 'The better-known the brand name, the more people want to rip it off.'

In the past Calvin Klein took a relatively passive approach to the counterfeit problem. The company has now got tougher by establishing a network of employees and external specialists to uncover copyright abuse.

The move began with a general change in corporate strategy whereby Calvin Klein has aggressively expanded its interests outside North America. Calvin Klein has been one of the leading fashion designers in the North American market since the mid-1970s. Now Calvin Klein is building up its fashion business in other countries. It has increased its investment in advertising, and restructured its licensing arrangements by signing long-term deals with partners for entire regions such as Europe or Asia, rather than giving licensing rights to individual countries. But as sales and brand awareness have risen, Calvin Klein has become an increasingly popular target for Asian and European counterfeiters, alongside other luxury brands such as Gucci, Chanel and Ralph Lauren.

The fake goods, mostly T-shirts, jeans and baseball caps, not only reduce the company's own sales but damage its brand image by linking it to poor quality merchandise. 'You'd be amazed at how many people pay $5 for a T-shirt without realising it's counterfeit,' said one executive.

From the *Financial Times*

FINANCIAL TIMES
World business newspaper.

Language review
Past simple and present perfect

Complete the rules with the words *past simple* or *present perfect*.
○ We use the .... to connect the present to the past. One of its main uses is to show the relevance of a past event in the present: *Calvin Klein **has been** a leading fashion designer since the mid-1970s.*
○ We use the .... to talk about a finished action at a definite time in the past: *In the past, Calvin Klein **took** a passive approach to the problem.*

➡ page 134

A Complete the memo with the past simple or present perfect forms of the verbs in brackets.

Memo

TO: Peter Schofield
FROM: Jaqueline Delacroix
DATE: 5 July

RE: Counterfeiting

I'm worried about the sales of the range of fragrances we ...launched...[1] (launch) two years ago. In the first year, sales ...ed...[2] (increase) steadily. However, since the beginning of this year, sales ...have fallen...[3] (fall) by almost 10%.

The reason for this is clear. Several firms in SE Asia ...have copied...[4] (copy) our designs and are now flooding the French market with them. This ...has become...[5] (become) a serious problem.

Last month, I ...ed...[6] (organise) a team of investigators. Up to now, they ...have found...[7] (find) many counterfeit goods, which the police ...have seized...[8] (seize) and impounded. Yesterday, I ...ed...[9] (contact) several firms who ...ed...[10] (inform) me that they ...have had...[11] (have) similar problems. They all ...lost...[12] (lose) sales because of counterfeiting.

J. D.

B Work in pairs. Role play either the fashion designer or the general manager.

Fashion Designer

You are a self-employed young fashion designer at the start of your career. A large store is selling T-shirts which look exactly the same as some of your new designs which you haven't sold yet. You meet the general manager of the store to make your complaint and ask for financial compensation.

General Manager

You are going to meet a young designer who thinks you have stolen their designs. It is quite common for the store's design team to get ideas for products from student fashion shows and art school exhibitions. Be sympathetic, but admit nothing.

Discussion
Three promotions

Read the three case studies below.
Then discuss the questions that follow each one.

Case 1 McDonald's

The famous fast food company, McDonald's, launched Campaign 55 to help it compete against rivals like Burger King and Wendy's. They had a six-week promotion costing $320 million. McDonald's offered a Big Mac (a type of hamburger) for 55 cents instead of $1.90. When customers were at the cash register, they found that they had to buy french fries and a drink at the full price to get the cheap burger.

- Why do you think this promotion was unpopular with McDonald's customers?
- How do you think McDonald's dealt with the situation?

Case 2 Pepsi

The Pepsi Cola company had the idea of offering a Harrier jump jet (see picture) as a 'joke' promotion. The advertisement was first shown in the Seattle area in the US. It showed a teenager modelling some merchandise available as part of the Pepsi Stuff promotion. At the end, a Harrier jet landed outside the school and the boy came out of the cockpit saying, 'It sure beats taking the bus to school.'

The promotion rules allowed customers to save up Pepsi Stuff points by collecting labels from Pepsi drinks or buying them directly for 10 cents each. The advert stated – jokingly – that 7 million points were needed for someone to claim the jet. A business student, John Leonard, intends to take Pepsi Cola to court regarding the promotion because he thinks they should give him the prize.

- What prize do you think John Leonard is claiming from Pepsi Cola?
- What did he do to claim the prize?
- Why do you think Pepsi Cola have described his claim as *frivolous* (not serious)?

Case 3 Irish Tourist Board

1   2   3

The Irish Tourist Board used to have the shamrock (see picture) as its symbol[1]. Recently it spent £100,000 developing a new logo to attract tourists to Ireland[2]. The logo showed two people with their arms outstretched in welcome. A tiny shamrock can be seen between the two bodies.

The new logo was part of a campaign to promote Ireland as a modern country offering good food and company. It was put on all the Tourist Board's promotional material. The television and advertising campaign included music by the well-known group The Cranberries and showed pictures of a romantic, fun-loving Ireland. It was very successful abroad. Tourism increased by 14% in four months.

Unfortunately the Irish people didn't like the new logo. The Minister of Tourism ordered the Tourist Board to get rid of the logo and bring back the shamrock – or something similar[3].

- Why do you think the Irish people disliked the logo so much?
- Was the Minister right to get rid of the logo?
- Which logo do you prefer?

Skills

Taking part in meetings

A You work for a marketing agency representing a well-known chain of book shops. Answer the questionnaire below, inventing the information you need.

Questionnaire

What is the name of your client's company?

Who are their target customers (age, social class, etc.)?

Do they specialise in any particular type of book?

Do they sell any other products?

Do they offer discounts or other special services?

What is their brand image? *Ideas & beliefs consumers have about it*

What is their share of the market?

Who is their main competitor?

Where are their shops located (city centres, suburbs, train stations and airports, etc.)?

B Recently sales have fallen. Hold a meeting to discuss the possible reasons. Make suggestions to improve your client's sales and its brand awareness amongst its target consumers. Use phrases from the Useful language box.

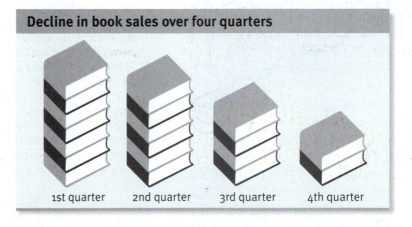

Decline in book sales over four quarters

1st quarter   2nd quarter   3rd quarter   4th quarter

Useful language

Interrupting
Hold on ...
Could I just say something?
Sorry, but ...

Asking for opinions
How do you feel about ... ?
What do you think?
What's your opinion?

Giving opinions
I think ...
In my opinion ...

Agreeing
That's true.
I agree.
I totally agree.

Disagreeing
I'm sorry, I don't agree.
I'm afraid I don't agree.
Maybe, but ...

Making suggestions
I think we should ...
How about ... ?
Why don't we ... ?

Rejecting suggestions
I don't think it's a good idea.
I'm not keen on it.

Caferoma

Background

Caferoma, a well-known brand of coffee, is owned by the Pan European Food and Drink Company (PEFD), based in Turin, Italy. It is promoted as an exclusive ground coffee for gourmets. Its image is that of an Italian-style coffee. It has a strong full-bodied flavour and a slightly bitter taste. It costs more per 100 grams than almost every other ground coffee product on the supermarket shelves.

Problems

In the last two years, Caferoma's share of the European quality ground coffee market has declined by almost 25% (see chart). There are several reasons for this:

Brand loyalty: Consumers have become less loyal to brands and are more willing to trade down to lower-priced coffee products.

Price: Supermarkets have been producing, under their own label, similar products to Caferoma at much lower prices.

'Copycat' products: Competing brands of Italian-style ground coffee at prices 30% to 40% lower than Caferoma's price have cut into Caferoma's market share.

Brand image: Consumer surveys show that the Caferoma brand no longer conveys a feeling of excitement and enthusiasm, and that it does not give the impression of being up-to-date and contemporary.

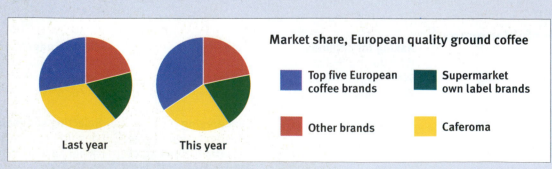

Market share, European quality ground coffee

- 🟦 Top five European coffee brands
- 🟥 Other brands
- 🟩 Supermarket own label brands
- 🟨 Caferoma

Last year   This year

Possible solutions

Repositioning the product

Change Caferoma's image to appeal to a different market segment. (Which segment, and what changes should they make to taste, quality, packaging, logo, labelling, etc?)

Pricing

Reduce the price by, say, 20% to 30% to make it more competitive.

Advertising

Devise a new advertising campaign. (The new message, kind of campaign, and any special promotions need to be considered.)

Multiple brands

Sell Caferoma, with minor product changes, under different brand names at lower prices.

Own label products

Sell Caferoma coffee for supermarkets to package and sell under their own labels (but continue to market the Caferoma brand at the same time).

A new product

Bring out an instant coffee or decaffeinated product under the Caferoma brand.

Stretching the brand

Allow selected manufacturers of coffee equipment (cafetieres, percolators, coffee machines, etc.) to use the brand on their goods – for a licensing fee, of course.

Task

You are members of PEFD's European marketing team. Hold an informal meeting to discuss Caferoma's problems. Decide what actions are necessary to halt the decline in the product's market share and to increase profits.

Writing

Write a memo for the attention of Caferoma's Managing Director, Mario Cumino. Summarise what action you agreed to take at the meeting to solve Caferoma's problems. Explain your reasons.

Writing file pages 144 and 145

Travel

' *Travellers are always discoverers, especially those who travel by air. There are no signposts in the sky that a man has passed this way before.* '

Anne Morrow Lindbergh, American writer

Starting up

A **Answer these questions individually. Then compare answers with a partner.**

1 How often do you travel by air, rail, underground, road and sea?

2 What do you enjoy about travelling? What don't you enjoy?

3 Which is the best/worst airline you have flown? Why?

B **Which of these things irritate you the most when flying? Rank them in order of *most* and *least* irritating.**

diversions	jet lag	long queues at check-in
sitting next to someone who talks non-stop	bad weather	bad food
	strikes	sitting next to children
cancellations	not enough room	no trolleys available
dirty toilets	lost or delayed luggage	overbooking

C **Which word in each pair below is American English?**

petrol – gasoline^B   truck – lorry^B   car park – parking lot^B
holiday – vacation^B   cab – taxi^B   baggage – luggage^B
return – round trip^B   tube – subway^B   flight attendant – steward/stewardess^B
motorway – freeway^B   line – queue^B   timetable – schedule

Reading
Free flight offer

A **Read the letter on the opposite page and answer these questions.**

1 What is the purpose of the letter? *to gather info. about Emirates existing customers*

2 What incentive is the company offering if you fill in the questionnaire? *free economy flight voucher*

3 What condition is attached to the offer? *Must take 1st/Bc trip w Em. b4 July.*

4 Why do companies run this type of promotion?

encourage pple. to respond -

Emirates
BE GOOD TO YOURSELF, FLY EMIRATES.

Emirates, First Floor, Gloucester Park, 95 Cromwell Road, London SW7 4DL

Mr Paul Foley
31 Church Street
ST ALBANS
Herts   SA5 3BN
                                                                    2 January

Dear Mr Foley

A free flight voucher and a chance to win a luxury Far East holiday

As someone who has flown Emirates in the past year, you will have experienced our
outstanding service to the Middle East. But were you aware that Emirates also flies to
an extensive network of major destinations all around the world?

By filling in the enclosed questionnaire, you'll be helping us with our research on your
5 views as a business traveller, as well as providing an update for our database. This will
ensure that we only send out information and offers that are relevant to you personally.

To thank you for your time and effort we will send you a free flight voucher. You can
use this to claim a free Economy ticket if you take a First or Business Class trip with
Emirates before July this year.

10   In addition we will be entering all respondees' names in a free prize draw, and the   *ok?*
winner will receive a Business Class trip for two people including seven nights' luxury
hotel accommodation in a choice of three exotic locations – Hong Kong, Singapore, or
Bangkok.

To qualify for your free voucher and enter the prize draw, please ensure your
15 completed questionnaire reaches us by 22 January.

You'll find full details in the enclosed leaflet. I do hope you find the information in it
interesting and that you take advantage of our free flight offer – and I wish you the best
of luck with our prize draw. The winner will be notified by 5 March. Most of all, I hope
we will be welcoming you once more on board an Emirates flight.

Yours sincerely

Vic Sheppard

Vic Sheppard
Sales Manager – UK & Ireland

B There are a number of countable and uncountable nouns in the letter.
Countable nouns can have a plural form; they can be used with *a* or *an* (*an
office, two offices*). Uncountable nouns do not have a plural form.

Which of these nouns from the letter are countable? Which are uncountable?

research ᵁ   questionnaire ᶜ   accommodation ᵁ
location ᶜ   network ᶜ   information ᵁ

C Correct the mistakes in the use of countable and uncountable nouns below.

Alpha Airlines flies to an extensive network of major destinations. We need
informations from you. Help us with our researches by filling in two
questionnaires and you will be entered into a prize draw for a trip for two
people including seven nights' luxury hotel accommodations in one of three
exotic locations.

Language review
will

Underline every use of *will* or *'ll* in the Emirates letter on page 23. Number them from 1 to 9.

1 What is the form of *will* in each example that you have underlined? Write each example number next to the appropriate form below.

will + the perfect .....*1*.....   *will* + the passive ....

will + the infinitive (without *to*) .....*3*.....   *will* + *be* + verb + *ing* ....

2 Which example refers to the past?

3 Which are promises or guarantees?

4 Which example refers to a document outside the text? ➡ page 135

The leaflet below was sent with the Emirates letter on page 23. Find seven places in the leaflet where *will* needs to be added.

A service designed for the business traveller

As a regular business traveller we need you to tell us about your views, requirements and habits in terms of business travel.

This information help us to shape and refine our service in the future. Your feedback also allow us to up-date our records and ensure that any special offers or information we may send about Emirates in the future be of genuine relevance to you.

So by picking up a pen and filling in the attached questionnaire, you be doing us a great favour too.

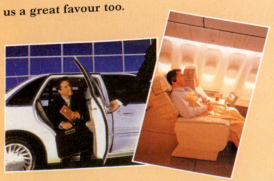

By sending off the attached questionnaire you could be jetting off to the Far East.

All completed questionnaires received by 22 January be entered in a free prize draw. The winner enjoy an Emirates Business Class trip to Singapore, Hong Kong or Bangkok for two people, including seven nights' luxury hotel accommodation.

FREE ECONOMY FLIGHT

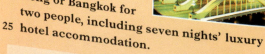

There's another excellent reason for completing our questionnaire. We thank everyone who responds by sending them a voucher entitling them to a free Economy Class ticket for every Emirates First or Business Class flight they take between February and June this year.

Skills

Making arrangements on the telephone

(A) **Study the Useful language below. Then do the exercises that follow it.**

Useful language

Making arrangements
Could we meet on Monday at 10.30?
Are you free sometime next week?
How about next Friday?
What about April 10th?
Would Wednesday at 2pm suit you?
Is 11.15 convenient?

Responding
That'll be fine.
That's OK.
No sorry, I can't make it then.
My diary's rather full that day/week.
Sorry, I've already got an appointment at that time.

Changing arrangements
I'm afraid I can't come on Friday/then.
We've got an appointment for 11.00, but I'm afraid something's come up.
Could we fix another time?

(B) 🎧 3.1, 3.2 **Philippa Knight, Sales Director at *The Fashion Group* in New York, makes two calls to Maria Bonetti, a fashion buyer in London.**
Listen and note: a) the purpose of each call b) the result.

(C) 🎧 3.1 **Listen to the first call again and complete the extract below.**

Knight   I'm calling because I'll be in London next week and *I'd like to make an appt. to see*[1] you. I want to tell you about our new collection.

Bonetti Great. What *day would suit you*[2]? I'm fairly free next week, I think.

Knight   *How about Wed*[3]? In the afternoon? Could *you make it*[4] then?

Bonetti Let me look now. Let *me check my diary*[5]. Yes, that'd be no problem at all. *What about*[6] two o'clock? Is that OK?

(D) 🎧 3.2 **Listen to the second call again and complete the extract below.**

Receptionist Thank you. I'm putting you through. Hello, I'm afraid she's engaged at the moment. *Will you hold*[1] or can I take a message?

Knight   I'll leave a message please. The thing is, I should be meeting Ms Bonetti at 2pm, *but smthgs come up*[2]. My plane was delayed, and I've got to reschedule my appointments. If possible, *I'd like to meet her*[3] tomorrow. *Preferably*[4] in the morning. *Could she call me back*[5] here at the hotel, please?

Receptionist Certainly. What's the number, please?
Knight   It's *020 7585 3814*[6].

(E) **Role play these two telephone situations.**

1 One of you is a company employee who has arranged to meet a colleague (your partner) from one of your subsidiaries. Explain that you cannot keep the appointment, and give a reason. Suggest an alternative time.

2 You are on a business trip and you want to stay an extra day. Telephone the airline office to arrange a different flight.

Reading 2
Air rage

A Answer these questions before you read the article.

1 In what ways do people behave badly when flying?

2 Have you ever seen or heard about someone misbehaving on a plane? What happened?

B Now read the article. Find two examples of passengers behaving badly.

C Which of the following reasons are given for passengers behaving badly?

1 Flights don't leave on time.

2 Passengers don't feel safe.

3 Airline staff don't put the customer first.

4 Flight attendants aren't polite.

5 Some terminals are too crowded.

6 Passengers feel worried and nervous.

7 The airline food is poor quality.

8 Some passengers get drunk.

9 Some airlines don't have no-smoking policies.

10 Passengers don't respect authority.

Passengers behaving badly

The abusive passenger is becoming a world-wide problem. Delta Air Lines crew suffer 100 verbal and
5 physical assaults a month, while cabin crews in some airlines are seeking early retirement at 50 because of their stressful work. One
10 businessman was recently less than happy when airport staff told him his luggage had been lost. Already frustrated by a
15 delayed flight, he stormed onto the runway, took out a pistol and shot out the aircraft's front tyre.

'Every time there is an
20 incident where the cabin crew feel compelled to bring someone off the flight-deck, there will be safety issues,' says Leslie
25 Berkowitz, in-flight services manager at the International Air Transport Association.

The cause of most pas-
30 senger misbehaviour is stress, according to Farrol Kahn, director of the Aviation Health Institute. Overcrowding and queuing

35 at the airport raises adrenaline levels. Normally these levels decrease through gaining control of a situation, either by standing up
40 and fighting or by running. Instead, passengers are kept in cramped conditions on an aircraft, where they have no control. 'In these

45 circumstances, they wait for one little excuse and then let rip,' says Dr Kahn. In one recent case, a septuagenarian hit a steward
50 after being told there was no more steak.

Much of the abuse is down to alcohol. Dahlberg and Associates, the avia-
55 tion consultancy, recently discovered that 202 out of 708 major incidents noted by a US carrier over a six-month period were alcohol-
60 related. Seventy-four incidents were smoking-related: more carriers are banning on-board smoking, leading the nicotine-
65 dependent into conflict as they try to have a secret cigarette.

Dahlberg also blames 'changes in society's views
70 on technology and authority' and 'stresses related to mass travel'.

From the *Financial Times*

FINANCIAL TIMES
World business newspaper.

D The words in the box are from the article above.
Which are used as countable nouns and which are used as uncountable nouns?

staff	luggage	stress	passenger	crew
steward	alcohol	travel	work	

E Write a short letter of complaint to an airline about an incident (true or invented) that occurred on a flight. Use at least four of the words above.

F Role play the situation below.

The Customer Relations Manager of Alpha Airlines has a problem. A local university uses the airline regularly to fly its sports teams to Eastern Europe to take part in inter-university matches. Unfortunately, on several return flights, team members have behaved badly. They have become very drunk and noisy, and have been rude to flight attendants and passengers. Yesterday, the basketball teams returned from Moscow. Students were throwing drinks and food at each other, and upset everyone on the plane.

After investigating the incident, the Customer Relations Manager phones the university's Sports Director to discuss the matter.

You are *either*:
the Customer Relations Manager (turn to page 152), *or*
the Sports Director (turn to page 155).

Listening
Business travellers' problems

▲ David Creith

A 3.3 **David Creith, Customer Service Teaching Manager for an international airline, is talking about the problems he has to solve for business travellers.**

1 Before you listen, predict what the problems might be.

2 Now listen to the first part of the interview and check your answers.

B 3.3 **Listen again to the first part of the interview and answer these questions.**

1 David Creith is the Customer Service Teaching manager:
   a) for which airline?   **b)** at which terminal?   **c)** at which airport?
   B.O   *4*   *Heathrow*

2 Some people want:
   a) .....*Window*.....   **b)** ...*aisle*...... .   **c)** *to sit next to their colleague.*

3 Why is it not possible to give everyone the seat they want?

4 Why do airlines have to oversell flights?

5 Who are Gold Card holders?

6 What do Gold Card holders often ask for?

C 3.4 **In the second part of the interview David Creith talks about how he deals with telephone complaints. Listen and complete the chart.**

Listen ....*very carefully*..............

|
Find ....

|
Example: ....

Not caused by ....by ....

Make sure it doesn't ....

Offer an ....if required

CASE STUDY

3

The team-building seminar

Vienna

Background

IDP is a computer software company based in Los Angeles, USA. The manager of its company travel service is making arrangements for 20 senior managers to attend a team-building seminar in or near Vienna, Austria. Most participants are American. Four European participants will be making their own travel arrangements. The seminar starts on Friday and ends on Sunday.

The seminar will include informal meetings to discuss work and to play executive games designed to encourage teamwork. Above all, the purpose of the seminar is to reward the managers for their hard work. They will expect to relax, enjoy the amenities of the hotel, explore the surrounding area, and have a really good time.

Task

You are *either*:
Manager, IDP's travel service (turn to page 151)
or
Head, Corporate Travel, Universal Airlines (turn to page 153).

You should keep these roles throughout the case study.

Arranging the seminar

Stage 1

The Manager of IDP's travel service phones the Head of Corporate Travel at Universal Airlines. The Manager asks Universal to propose two hotels in Vienna for the seminar. The Head of Corporate Travel wants more details about the seminar and its participants.

Read your information files. Then role play the telephone conversation.

Stage 2

Read the fax from the Head of Corporate Travel at Universal Airlines, and note its contents.

UNIVERSAL AIRLINES
CORPORATE TRAVEL

To   Manager (travel service), IDP
From   Head, Corporate Travel, Universal Airlines
Date   August 16
Pages 1

There are two hotels which I think would be suitable for your needs:

1) MONARCH HOTEL *****

Situated near the centre of Vienna in one of the city's oldest and most exclusive areas.

2) DORFMANN HOTEL ****

Situated 30 kilometres outside Vienna in the countryside.

The price per participant, excluding sales tax and air fares, for accommodation, facilities and meals would be:

MONARCH HOTEL   US$ 2,000 approx. per person
DORFMANN HOTEL   US$ 1,400 approx. per person

I suggest we meet to discuss the offers and to decide which hotel would suit you best. Would Wednesday 28 August be convenient for you? I'm fairly free most of the day.

Best wishes,

Stage 3

The Manager of IDP's travel service cannot meet the Head of Corporate Travel, Universal Airlines on the following Wednesday, as suggested in the fax, and must arrange an alternative time.

Read your information files. Then role play the telephone conversation.

Stage 4

The Manager of IDP's travel service meets the Head of Corporate Travel, Universal Airlines to decide on the hotel for the seminar. After discussing the two proposals, the Manager should make a choice.

Read your information files. Then role play the negotiation.

Writing

As Head of Corporate Travel at Universal Airlines, write an e-mail to the manager of the hotel chosen for the team-building seminar. Confirm the booking, giving details of the number of participants, arrival and departure times, meals, equipment and any other special requirements.

 Writing file page 143

Advertising

> *Advertising is the greatest art form of the twentieth century.*
> Marshall McLuhan (1911–1980), Canadian author

Starting up | **A** Discuss the advertisements below. Which do you like best? Why?

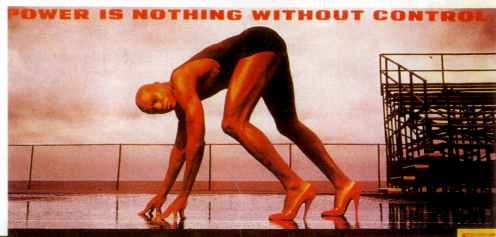

B 🎧 **4.1 Listen to five people describing their favourite advertisements.**

1 Listen and make notes. Use the following two headings:
   • Product   • Reasons for liking the advertisement
2 What is your favourite advertisement? Why do you like it?
3 What kind of advertisements do you like?

Discussion
Good and bad advertisements

A **What makes a good advertisement? Use some of the words below.**

clever	interesting	funny	inspiring	eye-catching
powerful	humorous	shocking	informative	sexy

B **Do you think that the advertising practices described below are acceptable? Are there any other types of advertisement that you find offensive?**

1 Using children in advertisements
2 Using nudity in advertisements
3 Promoting alcohol on TV
4 Comparing your products to your competitors' products
5 An image flashed onto a screen very quickly so that people are affected without noticing it (subliminal advertising)

only noted by subconscious mind.

C **Which of the following statements do you agree with?**

1 People remember advertisements not products.
2 Advertising raises prices.
3 Advertising has a bad influence on children.

Vocabulary
Advertising media and methods

A **Newspapers and TV are two advertising media. Can you think of others?**

B **Complete the table with the words in the box. Can you think of other words? Use a good dictionary to help you.**

ad. for product in a place where it is sold

directories	persuade	promote	cinema
run	mailshots	place	free samples
commercials	public transport	launch	leaflets
exhibition	billboards/hoardings	word-of-mouth	radio
point-of-sale	posters	research	sponsor
target	endorsement	slogans	television
press	jingles	sponsorship	publicise

ADVERTISING

Where? "see" *How?*

Media	Methods	Verbs
radio	jingles	persuade
directories	commercials	run
exhibition	exhibition	target
press	mailshots	promote
*mailshots	public transport	launch
public transport		place
billboards		publicise
posters	point-of-sale	research
word of mouth	endorsement	sponsor
cinema	slogans	
leaflets	sponsorship	
TV	free samples	

✱Confusing activity. Difficult to see diff. btw. categories? Maybe next time manipulate words?

Media M. V. ☐ ☐ ☐
Ss can move cards around.

Reading
Outdoor advertising

H.W.

A What do you understand by *outdoor advertising*? Give examples.

B Before you read the article below, match these words to their definitions.

1	segments	a)	a place in a television schedule
2	soaring	b)	rising quickly
3	mass market	c)	small open-fronted shop in the street for selling newspapers, etc.
4	TV slot	d)	concerned with non-luxury goods that sell in large quantities
5	kiosks	e)	parts of a larger market or category of customers

C Complete this statement with four of the words above.

The cost of a prime-time ....TV Slot........¹ is ....soaring........² . However,
advertising on ....kiosks........³ is cheap. Outdoor advertising is one of the
fastest growing ....segments........⁴ in the market.

D Read the article. Then answer the questions on the opposite page.

Outdoor advertising – A breath of fresh air

The world of outdoor advertising billboards, transport and 'street furniture' (things like bus shelters and public toilets) – is worth about $18 billion a year, just 6%
5 of all the world's spending on advertising. But it is one of the fastest-growing segments, having doubled its market share in recent years.

Outdoor advertising's appeal is
10 growing as TV and print are losing theirs. The soaring costs of TV are prompting clients to consider alternatives. Dennis Sullivan, boss of Portland Group, a media buyer, calls outdoor advertising the last
15 true mass-market medium. It is also cheap. In Britain, a 30-second prime-time TV slot costs over £60,000 ($100,000); placing an ad on a bus shelter for two weeks works out at about £90.
20 Adding to its attractions has been a revolution in the quality of outdoor displays. Famous architects such as Britain's Sir Norman Foster are designing arty bus shelters and kiosks with backlit
25 displays. Backlighting, introduced in Europe by Decaux and More, and plastic poster skins have vastly improved colour and contrast.

Movement is possible too. Smirnoff
30 used new multi-image printing to make a spider, seen through a vodka bottle, appear to crawl up a man's back. And Disney advertised its '101 Dalmatians' video on bus shelters with the sound of
35 puppies barking.

This sort of innovation has attracted a new class of advertiser. Recent data from Concord, a poster buyer, shows that in Britain, alcohol and tobacco have been
40 replaced by entertainment, clothing and financial services as the big outdoor advertisers, like car makers, are using it in new ways. BMW ran a 'teasers' campaign in Britain exclusively on bus shelters.
45 Particularly attractive to the new advertisers is street furniture, the fastest growing segment of the outdoor market. It accounts for some 20% in Europe and about 5% in America.

From The Economist

1 Complete the table using information from the first paragraph of the article.

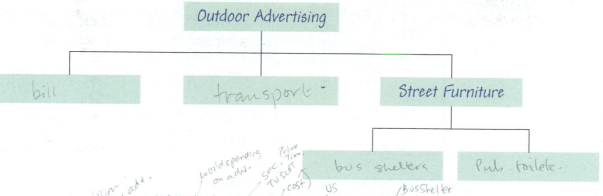

Outdoor Advertising

bill   transport   *Street Furniture*

bus shelters   Pub. toilets

[handwritten notes: world spending on adv. / Prime Time / Sec. Time / TV Slot / cost / US / Bus Shelter 2 wks]

[handwritten left margin: 18 billion outdoor adv.]

2 What do these numbers in the article refer to?
18   6%   30   60,000   100,000   90   20   5

3 Why has outdoor advertising become more popular? List the reasons.

4 Which industries are becoming more involved in outdoor advertising?

E **Discuss these questions.**

1 Outdoor advertising is increasing in many countries. Is this a good thing?

2 What products do you think are suitable for outdoor advertising?

[handwritten: H.W. go out and find some (5) examples]

F **Choose one of the advertising media below.**
Make a short presentation on its advantages and disadvantages.

television   billboards   newspapers   street furniture

Listening

Successful advertising campaigns

[handwritten: cheese / Jams / coffee / jams]

A Andrew Pound, a marketing manager for Kraft Jacobs Suchard, talks about successful advertising. Before you listen, answer these questions. *[handwritten: Frank Coopers marmalade / cost effective – very little ant. / competition]*

1 What kind of products do you think Kraft Jacobs Suchard make?

2 Andrew mentions two successful advertising campaigns.
What reasons do you think he will give for their success?

[handwritten: Radio Classical Music Breaky Program Retail Outlets]

B 4.2 Now listen to the first part of the interview. Check your answers. *[handwritten: targeted morn. / breakfast program]*

C 4.2 Listen again to the first part of the interview. Answer these questions. *[handwritten: Kraft Cheese Spread children]*

1 Who was the target consumer in each campaign? *[handwritten: Marmalade – Older ppl.]*

2 What advertising media did Andrew use in each campaign? *[handwritten: radio & TV / radio/radio classical/older ppl. Tv.]*

D **In the second part of the interview Andrew explains why advertising is not a waste of money. What reason do you think he will give?** *[handwritten: promotional techniques. No Time today so advert. helps. One way to persuade customers]*

▲ Andrew Pound

E 4.3 Now listen to the second part of the interview. Check your answer.
Do you agree with Andrew? *[handwritten: "Front of Mind"]*

F **Match words from each box to form word partnerships.**
Then make a sentence for each word partnership.

advertising	techniques
marketing	promotions
public	outlets
retail	campaign
price	relations
promotional	mix

[handwritten: Glossary back of book! p.168]

[handwritten: Marketing Mix = 4 P's. product place price promotion]

Language review
Articles

the	We use *the* when we think our listener will know what we are talking about: ***The** report's on **the** desk.*
a/an	We use *a* or *an* before singular countable nouns when we don't know which one, or it doesn't matter which one we are talking about: *Would you like **a** coffee?*
	We often use *a* or *an* to refer to people's jobs: *He's **an** accountant.*
a	We use *a* before consonants: ***a** billboard*
an	We use *an* before vowel sounds: ***an** advertising campaign*

→ page 135

A The text below is about an unusual advertising campaign for a car. It uses a famous actor who died nearly 20 years before the advertisement was made. There are no articles in the text. Write in the articles *a*, *an*, or *the* where appropriate.

AN ADVERTISEMENT FOR THE NEW FORD PUMA

More than 6,000 famous advertising people from around *the* world gathered in Cannes at end of last month for 44th International Advertising Festival.

5   Many of those looking through 4000-plus commercials were searching for multinational advertiser ideal: simple idea that crosses borders and appeals to people on same level in different markets. Unfortunately most of awards were for
10 ads created specifically for local markets.

   New Ford Puma campaign was created too late for this year's festival, but expect to see it shine at 45th. Designed to launch Ford's new sporty coupé across Europe, it contains that
15 instantly recognisable idea that those multinational agencies' clients seek.

   Essentially, late, great Steve McQueen drives Ford Puma through <u>streets</u> of San Francisco in manner in which he drove 20 1960s Ford Mustang in his classic movie *Bullitt*.

   Footage from <u>film</u>, supplied by Warner Brothers, is combined through use of extraordinary computer technology with footage of Ford Puma. <u>Car</u> follows one of <u>routes</u> <u>Mustang</u> 25 took in film.

   As McQueen 'drives' around <u>city</u>, <u>car</u> receives admiring glances from passers-by ranging from traffic cop to attractive woman out walking. Finally he pulls into his garage where 30 he parks <u>Puma</u> alongside original <u>Mustang</u>.

B Put *a* or *an* before the words in the box.

advert	commercial	concept	USP (Unique Selling Point)	university
VIP	hour	European	exhibition MBA	employee endorsement

C Look at the underlined words in the text. Then answer the questions below.

1 In paragraph 4 which *streets* are we talking about?
2 In paragraph 5 which: **a)** *film* **b)** *car* **c)** *route* **d)** *Mustang* are we talking about?
3 In paragraph 6 which: **a)** *city* **b)** *car* **c)** *Puma* **d)** *Mustang* are we talking about?

D Why do we use *the* to answer the questions in Exercise C?

E Why do we use *a* or *an* instead of *the* before these words?

1 a Ford Puma (paragraph 4) 3 a traffic cop (paragraph 6)

2 a 1960s Ford Mustang (paragraph 4) 4 an attractive woman (paragraph 6)

Skills
Starting presentations

A Decide whether each sentence in the Useful language box is *formal* or *informal*. Write *F* (formal) or *I* (informal).

Useful language

Introducing yourself

F • On behalf of myself and *Focus Advertising*, I'd like to welcome you. My name's Sven Larsen.

I • Hi, I'm Dominique Lagrange. Good to see you all.

Introducing the topic

F • This morning, I'd like to outline the campaign concept we've developed for you.

I • I'm going to tell you about the ideas we've come up with for the ad campaign.

Giving background information

I • I'll give you the background and talk you through the results of the market study.

F • I've divided my presentation into three parts.

Inviting questions

F • If you have any questions, please don't hesitate to interrupt me.

I • If you're not clear about anything, go ahead and ask any questions you want.

B 🎧 4.4 Listen to the openings of one formal presentation and one informal presentation. Check your answers to Exercise A.

C Presenters can use different techniques to get their audience's attention at the start of a presentation. Match the techniques below to the examples.

a) tell a personal story **c)** ask a question

b) offer an amazing fact **d)** state a problem

c 1 I wonder if any of you here know the answer to this question: What's the most popular holiday destination in Europe for people under the age of 25?

a 2 When I was on holiday a few years ago in Greece, the owner of a taverna told me that in 20 years' time, the little village where he lived would be a popular tourist resort.

b 3 Let me give you a statistic: 92% of Americans do not own a passport. Consider the opportunity this presents to the travel industry.

d 4 We're facing a crisis with our market share. What are we going to do about it?

D Choose one of the presentation situations below. Prepare four different openings using the techniques above. Practise the openings with a partner.

1 Your company is developing a small car aimed at women. Audience: a group of car dealers.

2 Your bank wishes to encourage young people to save money. Audience: a group of students.

3 Your firm has produced a new lamp which has unique features. Audience: a group of buyers at a trade fair.

Focus Advertising

Background

Focus, a large advertising agency based in Paris, has a reputation for creating imaginative and effective campaigns. Recently however, Focus's reputation was damaged when two major clients changed to rival agencies. Focus now needs to convince potential clients that it still has plenty of creative ideas to offer.

At present, Focus is competing against some well-known agencies for several contracts. It has been asked to present ideas for advertising campaigns to the managements of the companies concerned. Concepts are required for the following advertising campaigns:

- **A sports car** A high-priced, hand-finished model with a classic design. The car was popular in the 1950s and 60s. An American firm now wants to re-launch it. (Target consumers will be high-income executives with a sense of fun and style.)
  Aim: An international campaign, with advertising adapted to local markets.

- **A perfume** A unisex perfume, with bio-degradable packaging. Produced by a well-known up-market manufacturer. The company now wishes to enter the lower end of the market.
  Aim: Launch the perfume in an English-speaking country.

- **A chain of eight London restaurants** The restaurants (specialising in your national cuisine) are in prime positions and offer extensive menus. They are reasonably priced, but are not attracting enough customers.
  Aim: A creative campaign to improve sales.

- **A major bank** The bank (in an English-speaking country) wants to advertise the following new services:
  1 Competitive low-interest mortgages
  2 Direct telephone banking
  3 A foreign travel service
  It has also asked your agency to suggest others.
  Aim: Develop loyalty among existing customers and attract new ones.

Task

You are members of an advertising team at Focus. Prepare an advertising campaign for one of the products or services. Use the *Key questions* below to help you. Then present your campaign to the management of the company concerned. (At this stage, you have not been asked to prepare a budget.)

When you are not presenting your campaign, play the role of the company's management. Listen and ask questions. Use the *Assessment sheet* below to choose:

a) the best campaign concept
b) the most effective presentation.

KEY QUESTIONS (ADVERTISING TEAM)

- What is the campaign's key message?
- What special features does the product or service have?
- What are its USPs (Unique Selling Points)?
- Who is your target audience?
- What media will you use? Several, or just one or two?
  If you use:
  an advertisement   – write the text and do rough art work.
  a TV commercial   – use a story board to illustrate your idea.
  a radio spot   – write the script, including sound effects and music.
  other media   – indicate what pictures, text, slogans, etc. will be used.
- What special promotions will you use at the start of the campaign?

ASSESSMENT SHEET (MANAGERS)
Give a score of 1–5 for each category: 5 = outstanding 1 = poor

Campaign concept		Presentation	
1 Will it get the target audience's attention?		1 Was it interesting? Did it impress you?	
2 Will it capture their imagination?		2 Was it clear?	
3 Does it have a clear, effective message?		3 Was there enough eye contact?	
4 Will it differentiate the product or service?		4 Was the pace too quick, too slow, or just right?	
5 Will it persuade the target audience to buy the product or service?		5 Was the language fluent, accurate and appropriate?	
6 Will the target audience remember the campaign?		6 Was the voice clear enough? Was it varied in pitch or monotonous?	
TOTAL: 30		**TOTAL: 30**	

Writing

As leader of one of Focus's advertising teams, prepare a summary of your concept for your Managing Director. The summary will be used as a discussion document at a forthcoming board meeting.

Employment

❝ *It is all one to me if a man comes from Sing Sing* or Harvard.*
We hire a man, not his history. ❞ *(a famous US prison)

Henry Ford (1863–1947), American car manufacturer

Starting up

A In your opinion, which factors below are important for getting a job?
Choose the seven most important. Is there anything missing from the list?

> age   sex   appearance   astrological sign   contacts and connections
> experience   family background   handwriting   hobbies   intelligence
> marital status   personality   qualifications   references
> sickness record   blood group

B Think about jobs you've had and interviews you've attended.
Ask each other about your worst:

1) boss   **2)** job   **3)** colleague   **4)** interview

Reading
Choosing the right candidate

A Discuss this question: Do people change during their working lives? If so, how?

B Now read the article. What does it say about the question above? Find the answer as quickly as you can.

How to select the best candidates – and avoid the worst

By Adrian Furnham

THESE ATTACKS OF SHYNESS YOU KEEP HAVING..?

INTERVIEW PANEL

CV

Investing thousands of pounds in the recruitment and training of each new graduate recruit may be just the beginning. Choosing the wrong candidate may leave an organisation paying for years to come.

Few companies will have escaped all of the following failures: people who panic at the first sign of stress; those with long, impressive qualifications who seem incapable of learning; hypochondriacs whose absentee record becomes astonishing; and the unstable person later discovered to be a thief or worse.

Less dramatic, but just as much a problem, is the person who simply does not come up to expectations, who does not quite deliver; who never becomes a high-flyer or even a steady performer; the employee with a fine future behind them.

The first point to bear in mind at the recruitment stage is that people don't change. Intelligence levels decline modestly, but change little over their working life. The same is true of abilities, such as learning languages and handling numbers.

Most people like to think that personality can change, particularly the more negative features such as anxiety, low esteem, impulsiveness or a lack of emotional warmth. But data collected over 50 years gives a clear message: still stable after all these years. Extroverts become slightly less extroverted; the acutely shy appear a little less so, but the fundamentals remain much the same. Personal crises can affect the way we cope with things: we might take up or drop drink, drugs, religion or relaxation techniques, which can have pretty dramatic effects. Skills can be improved, and new ones introduced, but at rather different rates. People can be groomed for a job. Just as politicians are carefully repackaged through dress, hairstyle and speech specialists, so people can be sent on training courses, diplomas or experimental weekends. But there is a cost to all this which may be more than the price of the course. Better to select for what you actually see rather than attempt to change it.

From the *Financial Times*

FINANCIAL TIMES
World business newspaper.

C Read the article again and answer these questions.

1 What types of failures do companies experience, according to the article?

2 What does a *fine future behind them* (line 31) mean?

3 What advice does the article give to managers?

D In another part of the article (not included here), the writer suggests that selectors should look for three qualities:
a) intelligence and ability b) emotional stability c) conscientiousness.

1 Do you agree? Explain your opinion.

2 Complete the table with the adjectives below. What other words can you add?

mischievous clever & judicious shrewd crafty

| astute | ~~bright~~ | ~~calm~~ | clever | easy-going | hard-working | moody |
| neurotic | punctual | quick-tempered | ~~reliable~~ | responsible | sharp | slow |

irrational or depressive thought due to behaviour.

Intelligence and ability	Emotional stability	Conscientiousness
bright	calm	reliable
clever	neurotic quick-tempered	punctual
sharp	easy-going	hard-working
slow	moody	responsible
astute		

Listening
Recruitment interviewing

▲ Alan Lawson

A 🎧 **5.1 Alan Lawson, National Sales Manager with a Japanese electronics company, is talking about interviewing.**
Listen to the first part of the interview and answer these questions.

1 According to Alan, which of the following is the most important when trying to impress an interviewer:
   Find out about job
   a) qualifications b) character c) appearance d) preparation e) enthusiasm?

2 What mistake did Alan make?

B 🎧 **5.1 Listen again to the first part of the interview.**
Complete the 'advice sheet' for candidates below.

Find out about the job	At the interview
Ring up the Press Officer.	*Congratulate* Compliment the interviewer on a recent success.
or marketing dept.	
press releases	
annual reports	*FIND OUT ABOUT THAT COMPANY*
	SHOW ENTHUSIASM & interest
Visit the company	**CV**
Talk to the receptionists.	Make sure it's easy to read.
- go a few days b4	*well-written*
- find out what the	*concise - don't ramble.*
dress code	
- get a company	
newspaper	
dress code	

cv/personality

what do they like most? about [present job, travelling, meeting new people] least? working weekends

What are your weaknesses? ... Strengths?

C 🎧 **5.2 Now listen to the second part of the interview.**

1 What four questions does Alan usually ask candidates?
2 What examples does he give of candidates' likes and dislikes?

D Complete these word partnerships from the listening.

1 press   ......*officer*......
2 marketing   ......*department*......
3 press   ......*release*......
4 ......*annual*...... report
5 company   ......*newspaper*......
6 ......*dress*...... code

Discussion
Personal appearance at work

A Read the two case studies on the opposite page and answer these questions.

1 What job did the men do?
2 Why were their employers upset?
3 Who apologised? Who accepted the change?
4 Who intends to sue his employer? Why?

CASE 1

JOHN HUMPHRIES, aged 62, is a lorry driver who is proud of being well-dressed for work. However, his employer told him that he must not come to work in a collar and tie to drive his 17-tonne lorry. If he did so, he faced the sack. When working, Mr Humphries, an ex-Royal Airforce man, wore dark blue trousers, a light blue shirt, and a red and grey striped tie. He felt he looked smart and impressed the customers. 'If you present yourself properly, you look good and get respect,' he said.

Mr Humphries' employers were not impressed when he refused to give up his collar and tie. They wanted him to conform to the company's new image of casual clothing such as T-shirts or sweat shirts. They even threatened to dismiss him if he didn't accept their new dress code. Union officials advised him to accept the change and follow the company's policy. He agreed.

CASE 2

Yoshiaki Nishiura, a 25-year-old lorry driver from western Japan, was sacked because he dyed his hair brown. (This is a popular fashion with a growing number of young Japanese.) Although he apologised and dyed it black again, he was still fired. His employer, Mr Yamago, believed that behaviour like Mr Nishiura's undermined company discipline and corrupted morale. He blamed it on American influence. 'We need drivers to maintain a professional appearance to make a good impression,' he said. A Japanese journalist said, 'Japanese firms expect all employees to look the same and think the same. When you enter a company, you sign away your human rights.'

Mr Nishiura is going to sue his employer for unfair dismissal.

B Discuss these questions.

1 What do you think of:
   a) the employers' decisions?   **b)** the employees' reactions?
2 How important is your personal appearance at work?
   Think about formal clothing, uniforms, men with earrings, and tattoos, etc.

C Match the adjectives in column A to the nouns in column B.
Make six word partnerships.

A	B
growing	dismissal
human	appearance
company	number
professional	rights
good	discipline
unfair	impression

D Now complete these sentences with word partnerships from the list.

1 It is important to make a ......*good*...... ......*impression*...... at an interview by dressing appropriately.
2 In a case of ......*unfair*...... ......*dismissal*......, an employee may sue a company to get their job back or to receive financial compensation.
3 A ...*growing*...... ...*number*...... of firms realise that their employees' appearance is important. Therefore, many companies are introducing dress codes for their staff.
4 If a management allows staff to be absent from work without reason, this will affect ......*company*...... *discipline*......
5 When dealing with customers directly, it is important to have a ......*prof*...... ......*appearance*......
6 Some people say that being able to go on strike and having a minimum wage are basic ......*human*...... ......*rights*...... .

Language review
Questions

Read ✗

Match the rules 1–4 with the examples a–d.

1 If *who/what/which* is the subject of the sentence, we do not use *do/does/did*.

2 Direct questions are usually made by putting an auxiliary verb before the subject.

3 We often use indirect questions to ask for information or to be polite. The word order is different from a direct question. We often begin indirect questions with expressions like *Do you know …* or *Could I ask you …* .

4 When a verb phrase has no auxiliary verb, the question is made with the auxiliary *do*: **Do** *you live in Paris? (I live in Paris.)*

2 **a)** *When can you come to the interview?*

4 **b)** *Do you work in sales?*

1 **c)** *Who got the job?*

3 **d)** *Do you mind if I ask you what your weaknesses are?*

 page 136

ed *formal – simple past* *informal – only spoken simple present*

(A) **Present and past simple *wh-* questions do not always use *do* or *did*. Study these examples.**

Mark applied for the job.	Annie interviewed him.	He got the job.
• *Who applied for the job?*	• *Who did Annie interview?*	• *Who got the job?*
• *What job did he apply for?*	• *Who interviewed Mark?*	• *What job did he get?*

✗ **Work with a partner. Write five *wh-* questions about the situation described in the sentence below. For example, *Who did Mr Yamago sack?***

Mr Yamago sacked Mr Nishiura because Mr Nishiura dyed his hair brown.

(B) **For each direct question below, tick the correct indirect question.**

1 What are your strengths?

   a) Could you tell me what your strengths are? ✓

   b) Could you tell me what are your strengths?

2 What would your colleagues say about you?

   a) I'd like to know what would your colleagues say about you.

   b) I'd like to know what your colleagues would say about you. ✓

3 How have you changed in the last five years?

   a) Could you tell me how you have changed in the last five years? ✓

   b) Could you tell me how have you changed in the last five years?

(C) **You are interviewing someone for a job. How would you find out *politely* the following information?**

   1 Their age   **3** The reasons for leaving their last job

   2 Their current salary   **4** Their weaknesses

(D) **Role play this job interview situation.**

Interviewees
Choose a position in your company (or in another company) which you would like to have. Tell your partner what the position is.

Interviewers
Possible areas to cover include:
• personal qualities • skills
• weaknesses   • strengths
• qualifications   • experience
• achievements   • interests

Skills
Managing meetings

Useful language

Starting
OK, let's get down to business.
✓ Right, can we start please?

Asking for reactions
✓ How do you feel about ...?
What do you think?

Dealing with interruptions
— Could you let her finish please?
Could you just hang on a moment please?

Keeping to the point
✓ I'm not sure that's relevant.
Perhaps we could get back to the point.
Let's leave that aside for the moment.

Speeding up
✓ I think we should move on now.
Can we come back to that?

Slowing down
Hold on, we need to look at this in more detail.
✓ I think we should discuss this a bit more.

Summarising
✓ OK, let's go over what we've agreed.
Right, to sum up then ...

A 🎧 5.3 **A group of managers are discussing whether to offer an employee a full-time contract. Listen and tick the expressions in the Useful language box that you hear.**

B **You are managers of a retail fashion chain called *Space*, which has clothes stores in most major European cities. You are holding your regular management meeting. Use the Managing Director's notes below as an agenda for your discussions. A different person should chair each item.**

1 DRESS CODE
Following complaints from customers, we need to discuss a dress code for all employees, and guidelines on personal appearance.

2 POLICY FOR SMOKERS
Non-smoking staff complain that staff who smoke take frequent 'cigarette breaks' outside the store. Should smokers work extra time to make up for the time lost?

3 CUSTOMER SERVICE
Should sales staff meet informally after work once a month to consider how to improve customer service? (Attendance will help their chances of promotion.)

4 COMMISSION PAYMENTS
At present, commission is based on quarterly sales at each store and is divided equally between all staff. Now, our Sales Director wants each person to receive commission according to their individual sales.

5 END-OF-YEAR BONUS
Staff receive sales vouchers as an end-of-year bonus. The vouchers give discounts on a range of goods at major department stores. Some management are proposing to issue no sales vouchers this year. Instead, staff will be invited to an end-of-year party.

6 STAFF TURNOVER
Because staff tend to be young, employee turnover is high. As a result, training costs have increased dramatically. What can be done to keep staff longer?

Read thru all.
Choose one you want to chair.

Slim Gyms

Background

SLIM GYMS owns and operates six health and fitness clubs in Manhattan, New York. The clubs aim to appeal to people of all ages and income groups.

All the clubs have a large gymnasium, with the latest equipment, an aerobics studio, a solarium, a swimming pool, sun decks, a cafe, bar and clubroom. There are always several fitness instructors on hand to advise people and provide them with personalised fitness programmes. A wide range of aerobic and relaxation classes run throughout the day and during the evening. The clubs try to create a friendly atmosphere, organising numerous social activities to bring members together. Three of the clubs are located in areas where large numbers of Spanish, Chinese and Italians live.

Slim Gyms recently advertised for a General Manager.

SLIM GYMS

General Manager

Required for our chain of Health and Leisure Clubs

- Salary negotiable
- Excellent benefits package

Apply to:

88 Harvey Place 11 – C
New York
NY 10003 – 1324

THE JOB

- Developing a customer-oriented culture in the organisation in the clubs
- Increasing the revenue and profits of the six clubs in Manhattan
- Exploiting new business opportunities
- Liaising with and motivating our team of managers and their staff
- Contributing to marketing plans and strategies

THE PERSON

- Dynamic, enthusiastic, flexible
- A strong interest in health and fitness
- A good track record in previous jobs
- The ability to work with people from different cultural backgrounds
- Outstanding communication skills
- A flair for new ideas and sound organisational skills

Task

You are directors of Slim Gyms. Study the file cards on the four short-listed candidates on the opposite page. Hold a meeting to discuss the strengths and weaknesses of each person. Try to agree on who seems to be the best candidate for the job.

Then listen to the interview extracts with each of the candidates and come to a final decision on who should get the job: ∩ 5.4 Isabella Rosetti, ∩ 5.5 Michael Bolen, ∩ 5.6 Bob Wills, ∩ 5.7 Stephanie Grant.

Writing

Design a promotional leaflet to increase membership of the six Slim Gyms clubs. It will be sent to various sports goods stores in New York. It will also be included in specialist health and fitness magazines.

Name: Isabella Rosetti
Age: 35

Marital Status: Single:

Education: Princeton University – Master's degree in Business Administration (MBA)

N EG H

Experience: Advertising agency for the last eight years. Important position liaising with clients and managing a team of 10 people. Previously worked as Sales Manager in a department store (Chinatown area).

Outstanding achievement: Got a contract with a major advertiser.

Skills: Fluent Italian, judo expert, paints.

Personality/appearance: Well dressed and self-confident. Says she is usually successful when she wants to be. Thinks women are better managers than men: 'They listen more and use their intuition to solve problems.'

Comments: Positive reference, but employer suggested she sometimes took days off work with no good reason. Several good ideas for increasing revenue, e.g. by setting up beauty centres in our clubs. Didn't mention the cost of doing this! Above average score on our aptitude test.

Handwriting sample:

I am currently working for…

Name: Michael Bolen   **Age**: 36

Marital Status: Married, with three children

Education: Columbia University – Master's degree in Business Administration (MBA)

P H

Experience: Four years with international sports goods manufacturer – Marketing Director. Previous experience with a variety of firms (sales, administration). Wants to work for a smaller organisation.

Outstanding achievement: Successful product launch in previous job.

Skills: Numerate and good with computers. Only a few words of Spanish.

Personality/appearance: Forceful, determined, with strong views. Likes to 'keep his distance' from people until he knows them well. According to the letter of reference, 'Some women find him too assertive and cold.'

Comments: Unhappy in present position. He has often changed jobs. Aptitude test – average score.

Handwriting sample:

I am looking for a new challenge…

Name: Bob Wills   **Age**: 40

Marital Status: Single

Education: Park High School

M K K

Experience: Twenty years in US army – Physical Fitness Instructor. Travelled all over the world. Left army three years ago. Has taken courses in marketing, management and computing. Over the last two years has run a fitness centre in Lower Manhattan very successfully.

Outstanding achievement: Two decorations for bravery.

Skills: Speaks Spanish fluently (his girlfriend is Puerto Rican). Is a successful disc jockey in a downtown club.

Personality/appearance: Correctly dressed in a dark suit, but has tattoos. Sociable, with a lot of friends. Enjoys parties and dancing.

Comments: Believes you should always stick to the rules. Values honesty and reliability. Can be quick-tempered if people are not doing their best. Very enthusiastic with many good ideas. High score on aptitude test.

Handwriting sample:

I am writing to apply for the post of '…

Name: Stephanie Grant
Age: 30

Marital Status: married, no children

Education: New York University – BSc in Business Administration

M I H

Experience: Former swimming champion. Competed at Olympic Games. For last six years, highly successful presenter (children and sports programmes).

Outstanding achievement: Voted Top Sports Personality on a cable TV channel four years ago.

Skills: Exceptional sportswoman.

Personality/appearance: Beautiful, clever and successful. Good sense of humour. On television, handles people well. Presents an image of a caring, sympathetic person.

Comments: 'She'll do anything to get what she wants,' wrote one journalist. At 24, she gave up competitive swimming, following rumours of drug-taking. Aptitude test – above average.

Handwriting sample:

I would love the opportunity to contribute to your…

UNIT 6

Trade

‘Every time we buy a foreign car we put someone else out of work.’
Woodrow Wyatt (1918–1998), British politician and writer

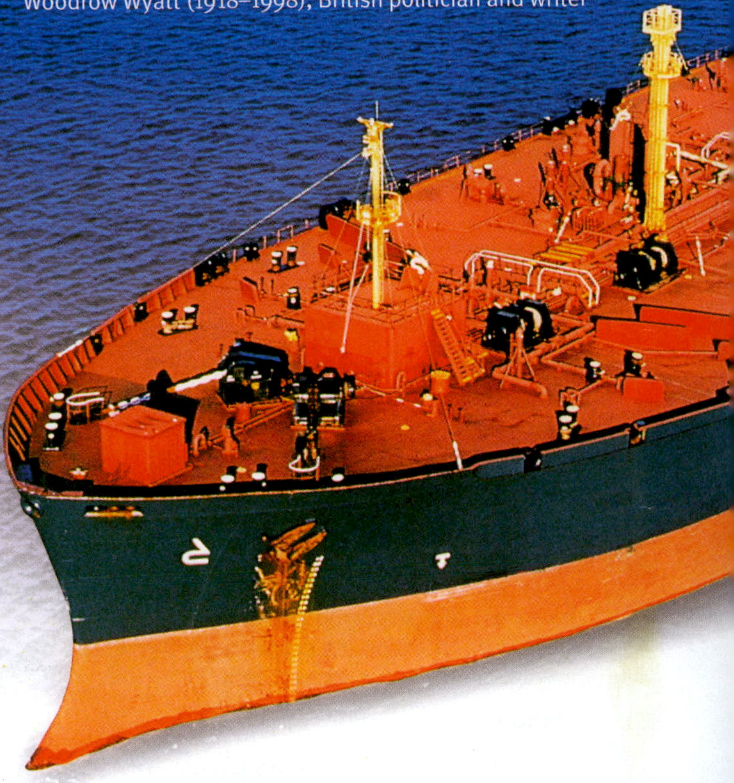

OVERVIEW

Starting up

A **Think of some of the things you own (for example, shoes, TV, car). Which are imported? Where were they made?**

B **What are your country’s major imports and exports? Do you think products made in your country are better than products made in other countries?**

C **Place these countries on the chart below. Then compare your chart with a partner.**

Brazil France Germany Greece Italy Japan
Russia Singapore UK USA your country

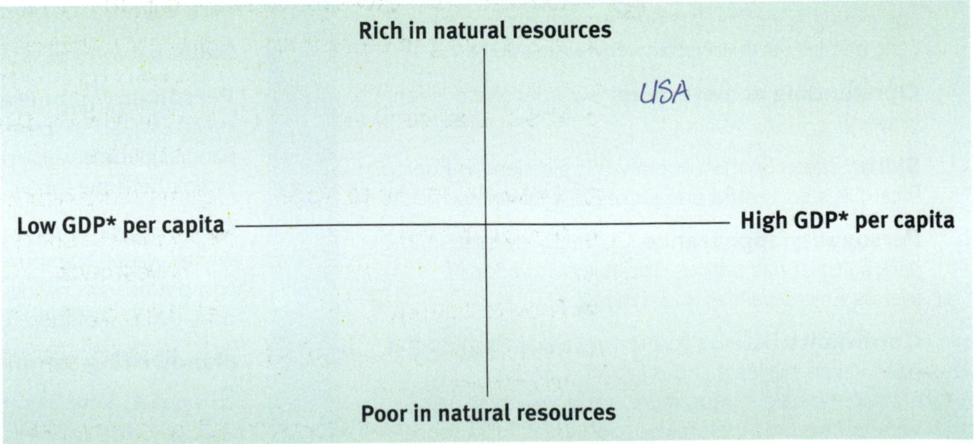

Rich in natural resources
USA
Low GDP* per capita
High GDP* per capita
Poor in natural resources

(**GDP* or *Gross Domestic Product:* the total annual value of a country’s goods and services)

D **Why are some of the countries on the chart richer than others?**

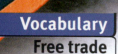

Vocabulary
Free trade

A Use the words in the box to complete the table. Use a good dictionary to help you.

> ~~barriers~~   dumping   protectionism   quotas   ~~open borders~~   tariffs
> laisser-faire   deregulation   free port   strategic industries   liberalise
> subsidise   infant industries   restrictions   customs

in favour of free trade*	against free trade*
open borders	barriers

(*Free trade: trade without restrictions on the movement of goods across borders)

B Discuss these questions.

1 Is free trade always a good thing?

2 Do you think it leads to the creation of jobs, or to unemployment?

3 Should certain industries be protected. If so, which?

C Match the first halves of the sentences to the second halves.

1 We're trying to break into

2 You should carry out

3 If you would like to place

4 If you can't meet

5 They've quoted

6 Let us know if you want us to arrange

7 It's essential to comply with

a) all regulations if you want the delivery to go through without problems.

b) the delivery date, let us know as soon as possible.

c) insurance cover for the shipment.

d) a market survey before you make a major investment.

e) the Japanese market.

f) an order, dial *one* now.

g) us a very good price for the consignment.

D Find verb + noun partnerships in the sentences above. For example, *to break into a market*. Which of them is normally done by the:

1 exporter?   2 importer?   3 exporter and importer?

Reading
Letters of credit

A Read the letter on the opposite page and complete the application form below.

NATIONAL BANK ⊙ OF COMMERCE

Exporter *Julian Montero* ....   Goods ....

Importer ....   Quantity ....

Value ....

Method of payment ....

Documents required ....

....

Contract restriction ....

B Answer these questions.

1 When will the seller receive payment for the goods?

2 What information must be included in the letter of credit?

3 Who will pay for the cost of transporting the cases of wine?

4 What does Vivian Eastwood want Denise Morgan to send her?

C You own a wine business in Slovenia. You decide to write to Connoisseur because you want to become a distributor for them in your country.

Match the halves of the sentences below. Then use them to write the letter. Describe the benefits your company can offer, and give references.

1 Our company is a	a) distributing high quality wines.
2 We specialise in	b) we could discuss the rate of commission and your terms of payment later.
3 We have contacts	c) is one of the biggest in the country.
4 Our sales network	d) well-known and reputable firm with many years' experience.
5 We have four warehouses	e) we could be appointed your sole distributor.
6 We would be willing to	f) from a bank and our local Chamber of Commerce.
7 We would appreciate it if	g) accept our offer and we look forward to hearing from you soon.
8 If you are interested in our offer	h) share the costs of an advertising campaign to promote your wines.
9 We can supply references	i) with major retail outlets throughout the country.
10 We hope you will	j) located in Slovenia's major cities.

Our ref: JM5/02

Connoisseur

IMPORTER OF FINE WINES

18 Park Avenue
Los Angeles, CA 90008
Tel: (213) 555 9765
Fax: (213) 555 8521
e-mail: wincon@aol.com

Ms. Denise Morgan
Documentary Credits
National Bank of Commerce
35 Main Street
Los Angeles, CA 90005

July 31

Dear Ms. Morgan:

Application for letter of credit* in favor of Julian Montero srl

We have contacted Julian Montero, the Argentine supplier of the wine we are importing. We will be importing 500 cases of white and red wine and the total value of the contract is US $50,000.

Please open a letter of credit to cover the shipment. Details are as follows:

1. Beneficiary: Julian Montero srl, San Nicolas 1746, Buenos Aires, Argentina.
2. Sr. Montero's bank: Bank of Argentina, Buenos Aires.
3. Irrevocable Letter of Credit 30 days. To be confirmed by your correspondent bank in Argentina.
4. The letter of credit must cover the enclosed list of wines which specifies the brands and quantities we have ordered.
5. Four clean copies of the Bills of Lading.
6. No part shipment permitted.
7. Shipping terms: CIF*

We look forward to receiving a copy of your letter to your correspondent bank in Argentina as soon as possible. Please let me know if there is any further information you require.
Yours sincerely,

Vivian Eastwood

Vivian Eastwood
Manager

(*Letter of credit: A letter from one bank to another which enables a seller to obtain money. The most common way of financing international trade.)

(*CIF: All costs, insurance, and freight charges are to be paid by the exporter, Julian Montero)

Language review
Conditions

A common structure used in negotiating is:
If + present simple, *will* + infinitive (without *to*).
We use the structure to link a concession we are prepared to make, with our *condition* for making it.

Concession	Condition
If we *order* 1000 cases,	*will* you *give* us a 10% discount?
We *'ll give* you a 10% discount	*if* you *pay* within 30 days.

As long as and *provided that* can be used in the same way as *if* in the structures above.

→ page 136

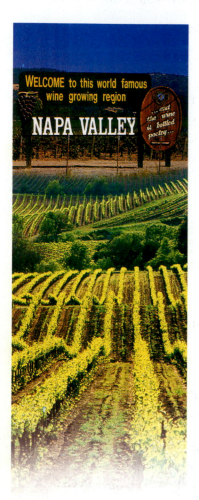

WELCOME to this world famous wine growing region
NAPA VALLEY
...and the wine is bottled poetry...

A ⌒ 6.1 **Bella Ford, a buyer for Empire Wines, is negotiating with Pierre Hemard, Sales Director for Marques Vineyards, Napa Valley, California. Listen and fill in the missing words.**

Bella   If ....[1] more than 500 cases of the Reserve, what discount can you offer us?

Pierre   On 500, nothing. But if ....[2] 1000 cases, we'll offer 15%.

Bella   Let me think about that. Now, if ....[3] an order for 1000, will you be able to despatch immediately?

Pierre   I don't know about immediately, but certainly this month.

Bella   Well, if ....[4] to us before the Christmas rush, it'll be OK. I take it your prices include insurance?

Pierre   Actually, no. You'd be responsible for that. If ....[5] your order, then we'd be willing to cover insurance as well.

Bella   I'll need to do some calculations ...

Pierre   Let's look at methods of payment. Since we've not dealt with you before, we'd like to be paid by banker's draft.

Bella   Well, this is a large order. We've done business with many well-known wine producers and we've always paid by letter of credit.

Pierre   OK. If ....[6] to you paying by letter of credit, then you'll have to pay us within 30 days.

Bella   That should be fine.

B **Bella and Pierre then negotiate the terms for another wine, the Santa Rita. Use the notes below to write the conversation. Then practise reading your conversations to each other.**

Pierre   Now let's talk about your order for the Santa Rita.
Bella   OK, I hope you'll offer me good terms ...

Pierre   • *Order 2000 cases /10% discount /deliver before Christmas rush / cover insurance*
Bella   • *Less demand for Santa Rita /10% discount OK*
          • *want only 1500 cases*
Pierre   • *Cannot agree*
Bella   • *Order 2000 /want another 3% discount*
Pierre   • *1% only and 30 cases of champagne /fair offer!*
Bella   • *A deal!*

C **Role play this negotiation. A wine importer telephones Julian Montero to order 100 cases of the Montero Chardonnay wine. The list price is US$150 a case. Julian Montero offers a 3% discount, delivery in six weeks by sea freight, and asks for payment by banker's draft. The importer tries to negotiate a better price, discount, delivery and payment.**

Listening
Negotiating techniques

▲ Kevin Warren

A 🎧 **6.2** Kevin Warren, an Executive Vice President at Coca-Cola (UK), is talking about negotiating. Listen to the first part of the interview. What do the letters L-I-M stand for?

L ...ike............. I ...ntend............. M .....ust...............

ike to win that day

B In the negotiation that Kevin describes, what was his L-I-M? *— done enough to keep dialogue open.*

must leave group thinking consistent, professional

C In the second part of the interview, Kevin gives three negotiating tips. *able to meet their needs.* What do you think the tips will be?

— make sure you know who you're talking to. —

D 🎧 **6.3** Listen to the second part of the interview. Were your guesses correct?

E Kevin uses the words below. Choose the correct definition for each.

1 classic errors
   a) typical mistakes
   b) old mistakes

2 go straight to the point
   a) move towards the end
   b) state your purpose directly without delay

3 long-term relationship
   a) a business contact over a long period
   b) a friendship over a long period

4 hassle free
   a) without extra payment
   b) causing no difficulty or trouble

5 switch
   a) change
   b) turn on

6 royalty
   a) kings and queens
   b) a payment for a service

7 to tailor
   a) to make more suitable for a particular purpose
   b) to make clothes

Skills
Negotiating

A Work in pairs. Try to sell something you have on you (watch, bracelet, etc.), or a household object, to your partner.

B Discuss these questions.

1 Were you pleased with the outcome of the negotiation in Exercise A above?

2 What strategy or tactics did your partner use to achieve their objective?

C In his book *The Art of Winning*, Harry Mills says that most negotiations have seven stages. These are listed below, but are in the wrong order.
Put the stages in order. What word do the initial letters of the stages spell?

R-E-S-P-E-C-T.

#4 • **Probe with proposals**
Make suggestions and find areas of agreement.

#6 • **Close the deal**
Bring the negotiation to a clear and satisfactory end.

#3 • **Signal for movement**
Signal that you are prepared to move from your original position.
Respond to signals from the other side.

#5 • **Exchange concessions**
Give the other side something in return for something you need or want.

#7 • **Tie up loose ends**
Confirm what has been agreed. Summarise the details on paper.

#2 • **Explore each other's needs**
Build rapport. State your opening position. Learn the other side's position.

#1 • **Ready yourself**
Prepare your objectives, concessions and strategy.
Gather information about the other side.

D In his book *The Pocket Negotiator*, Gavin Kennedy describes two extreme styles of negotiator: *Red stylists* and *Blue stylists*.

Read the summary of the two styles. Then decide if you are:

1 A Red stylist

2 A Blue stylist

3 Somewhere between the two styles

Red stylists

- Want something for nothing.
- Try to win by showing they are stronger than the other person.
- See negotiation as a short-term activity.
- Use tricks and pressure to get what they want.

Blue stylists

- Want to trade something for something.
- Try to succeed by cooperating with the other person.
- See negotiation as a long-term activity.
- Do not use tricks. They think about each other's interests.

E Study the Useful language box below. Then role play this situation.

> **One of you is a company employee. The other is the employee's boss.**
>
> **Employee:** You think you should have a 10% salary increase.
>
> **Boss:** You think the company can only afford a 2% increase.
>
> **Negotiate with each other and try to get a good outcome.**

F Write an X on the line below to indicate your partner's negotiating style.

RED .... | .... BLUE

Useful language

Starting
Could we begin now please?
OK, let's get started, shall we?

Exploring positions
What do you have in mind?
How would you feel about a bigger discount?

Making offers and concessions
If you order now, we'll give you a discount.
We'd be prepared to offer you a better price if you increased your order.

Checking understanding
When you say there are delivery problems, what do you mean?
Have I got this right? You said a discount on an order of 1000.
If I understand you correctly ...

Refusing an offer
I'm sorry, we can't accept that.
I'm not sure about that.

Accepting an offer
I think we can agree to that.
That sounds reasonable.

Playing for time
I'd like to think about it.
I'm sorry, but I'll have to consult my colleagues about that.

Closing the deal
That's it, then. I think we've covered everything.
Great! We've got a deal.

6 Ashbury Guitars

Background

The Kim Guitar Company (KGC) in Seoul, South Korea, makes electric guitars for Japanese manufacturers and distributors in Europe and the US. It creates its own branded products but also makes guitars to distributors' specifications.

A major US distributor, Ashbury Guitars, has contacted KGC about marketing a range of guitars under its own brand name for the Californian market. Ashbury Guitars is a well-established company with an up-market image. It has had no previous dealings with KGC. Ashbury's owner, Richard Grant, plans to put three models on the market: the Ashbury SG1000 (the most expensive model), the SG500 and the SG200. The body of the guitars will have an experimental shape as well as advanced technical features. Ashbury's guitars will appeal to any musician who wants an instrument with a distinctive sound and exotic appearance.

It is now early January. KGC has agreed to manufacture the guitars for Ashbury, even though it is a very busy time of the year for them. The two companies have had some initial correspondence by fax and now a face-to-face meeting is required.

Several points of the contract need to be negotiated. KGC's owner, David Kim has flown to San Francisco to meet Richard Grant. At the meeting, the Marketing Director of each company will be present. The purpose of the meeting is to make a deal acceptable to both sides, and which could be the basis for a long-term relationship.

Task

You are negotiating as either:
- The KGC team: David Kim and Marketing Director turn to page 156.
- The Ashbury team: Richard Grant and Marketing Director turn to page 154.

Read your information files. Identify your priorities and work out your strategy and tactics. Then negotiate so that you get the best deal for your company.

Writing

As the owner of either Ashbury Guitars or KGC, write a fax summarising the points agreed during the negotiation. Indicate any terms of the contract requiring discussion or clarification.

 Writing file pages 143 and 145

Innovation

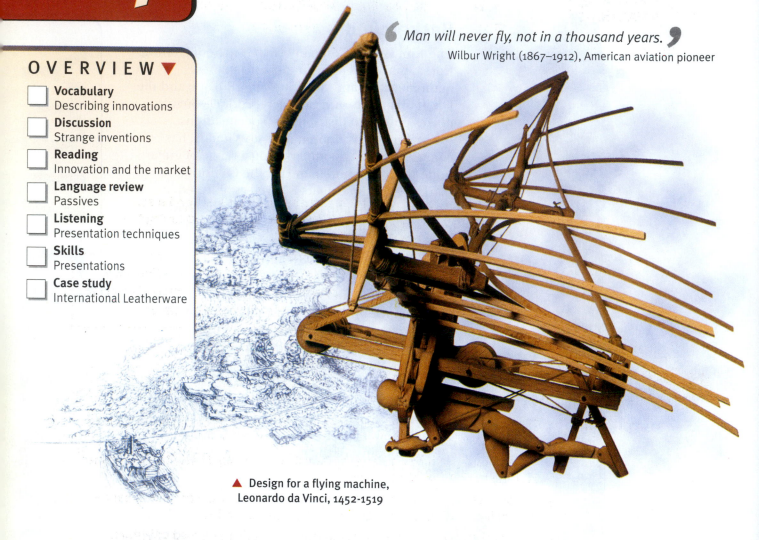

Man will never fly, not in a thousand years.
Wilbur Wright (1867–1912), American aviation pioneer

▲ Design for a flying machine,
Leonardo da Vinci, 1452-1519

Starting up

A **What inventions or innovations do you associate with these names?**

| Biro | Dunlop | Edison | Gillette | Kellogg |
| Benz | Singer | Hoover | Pilkington | Otis |

B **What are the most important inventions or innovations for you:**
a) at work?   b) at home?

C **The words below are often used when talking about innovation.**
What do they mean?

| R & D | brainwave | blueprint | prototype |
| | setback | breakthrough | patent |

D **Work in groups. One person thinks of an invention. The others ask questions to guess what the invention is. You can only ask *yes/no* questions. For example:**

- Was it invented in the 19th century?   Yes.
- Is it made of metal?   Partly.
- Does it work with electricity?   Yes.
- Do you find it in the home?   Yes.
- Is it used for communication?   Yes.
- Is it the telephone?   Yes, it is.

Vocabulary
Describing innovations

A Complete the table with appropriate forms of the words.

VERB	NOUN (thing)	NOUN (person)	ADJECTIVE
develop		developer	
	design		–
		inventor	
	innovation		
			productive
create			
	–	pioneer	
patent			

B The words below can be used to describe inventions or new ideas. Which have a positive meaning? Which have a negative meaning? Write + or – next to each one.

> \+ efficient brilliant beneficial useless revolutionary
> – pointless ridiculous uneconomical marketable ground-breaking
> feasible viable impractical ingenious clever

Discussion
Strange inventions

Read about the real inventions and innovations below.
What is your opinion of each one? Give your reasons.

1 The laser shaver, by Frenchman Eugene Politzer, gets rid of stubble by burning rather than cutting.

2 The self-extinguishing cigarette, by Danish inventor Kaj Jensen, has a container of water buried near the filter tip.

3 The petless leash, invented by two scientists from Illinois, can mew or bark — depending on whether you want a non-existent cat or dog.

4 Glow-in-the-dark toothpaste was invented in America as a road safety aid.

5 Ice cubes that crackle louder according to the strength of your drink have been developed in Japan.

6 Economy Class passengers could be carried in pressurised containers in the holds of jets, says a Washington design firm.

7 Chocolate shock absorbers can reduce the effects of a vehicle travelling over bumpy surfaces because the chocolate becomes a gel when electrified, say Michigan scientists.

8 A collapsible coffin which can be carried on the bus has been designed by an inventor in Zimbabwe.

Adapted from the *Daily Mail*

Reading
Innovation and the market

A **Discuss these questions. Then read the article.**

  1 Do you think it is better to innovate or imitate products and services?

  2 Can you name any companies which were a) innovators? b) imitators?

Why the last shall be first

IT HAS POTENTIAL BUT UNFORTUNATELY MASS PRODUCTION AND MARKETING HAVEN'T BEEN INVENTED YET

BEALE

By John Kay

Have you heard of Berkey or Ampex? Gablinger or Chux? Perhaps you should have, because each occu-
5 pies an important place in the history of product innovation. Berkey pro-duced the first hand-held electronic calculators,
10 Ampex the first video recorders. Gablinger devel-oped low-alcohol lager and Chux sold the first dispos-able nappies.
15 Or perhaps you should not, because none of these companies made a commer-cial success of their innova-tions. Today the calculators
20 we use are probably made by Casio, our video recorder comes from Matsushita, our low-alcohol beer is Miller Lite, our nappies are
25 made by Proctor & Gamble. In each of these markets the innovator was swept away.
Xerox looks like an
30 exception to this sorry cat-alogue. The company was first into the photocopier market and, even if its dominance was ultimately
35 challenged by Canon, it remains a large and suc-cessful company today. But Xerox was also a pioneer in fax machines and personal
40 computers. Each of these eventually proved to be a success — but not for Xerox Corporation.
As we all know, it was
45 Apple that developed the personal computer market. But Apple's leadership quickly disappeared when IBM came on the scene.
50 Apple then jumped ahead by introducing the graphi-cal user interface. Its win-dows and mice brought personal computing within
55 the reach of everyone. But it is Microsoft that does this now.
The business world is not kind to pioneers. Even if
60 you know how a market will develop, timing is a matter of luck — or of quite exceptional skill.
There are two closely
65 related lessons. One is that being first is not often very important. The other is that innovation is rarely a source of competitive
70 advantage on its own. Individuals and small com-panies can make a great deal of money out of good new ideas. The success of
75 large established corpora-tions — Matsushita, Philip Morris, IBM or General Electric is generally based on other things: their
80 depth of technical exper-tise, their marketing skills. And time and again these characteristics enable them to develop the innov-
85 ative concept far more effectively than the innova-tors themselves.
This is not to say that there is no role in business
90 for the great innovator. After all, General Electric was built on the extraordi-nary creativity of Thomas Edison's mind, the Ford
95 motor company on the abil-ities of its eponymous founder. The imagination of Walt Disney created a company that is still with-
100 out parallel or rival. Perhaps Akio Morita of Sony occupies a similar place in the annals of mod-ern business.

From the *Financial Times*

FINANCIAL TIMES
World business newspaper.

B **Make notes about the first four paragraphs of the article.**
Use the following headings:

Innovator	Developer	Product
Berkey	Casio	hand-held calculator

C **Answer these questions about the article.**

  1 What is the main point made by the writer?

  2 Several well-known companies are mentioned.
  What reasons are given for their success?

  3 What is the connection between Disney, Ford, General Electric and Sony?

  4 Look at the cartoon. What innovation does the word *it* refer to?

D **Use words from each box to make word partnerships from the article.**
For example, *personal computers*.

commercial	competitive	technical		skills	expertise	success
~~personal~~	established	marketing		advantage	~~computers~~	corporation

Language review
Passives

- We make passive verb forms with the verb *to be* + past participle:
  *In each of these markets the innovator **was swept away***.
- We often choose a passive structure when we are not interested in who performs an action or it is not necessary to know:
  *Low-alcohol lager **was developed** as an alternative to traditional soft drinks.*
- If we want to mention who performs the action, we can use *by*:
  *Low-alcohol lager was developed **by** Gablinger.*
- We often use a passive structure to be impersonal or formal (for example, in notices, announcements, reports):
  *It **has been agreed** that a report **should be commissioned**.* page 137

A Look at these sentences from the article. Which use passive structures?

1 Unfortunately mass production and marketing haven't been invented yet.
2 Chux sold the first disposable nappies.
3 Today the calculators we use are probably made by Casio.
4 Our nappies are made by Proctor & Gamble.
5 In each of these markets the innovator was swept away.
6 The company was first into the photocopier market.
7 Its dominance was ultimately challenged by Canon.
8 It was Apple that developed the personal computer market.

Find two more passive structures in the last two paragraphs of the article.

B The sentences below describe stages in the launch of a new drug. Use the verbs in the box to complete the sentences. Then put them in a logical order.

develop	~~test~~	test	publish	apply for
approve by	carry out	train	grant	

a The drug ...*was tested*... on animals.
b The drug .... in the labs.
c Market research ....
d The drug .... on humans.
e The trials .... the Ethics committee.
f A licence ....
g The results of the trials ....
h Approval .... by the authorities.
i The drug representatives ....

C Use the notes below to describe stages in the launch of a new car. Include passive and active structures. Use words like *first*, *next*, *then* and *finally*.

1 designer – choose
2 design – produce
3 model – build
4 modifications – make – R & D / engineers
5 design – modify
6 prototype – build
7 new engine – use – or existing engine – develop – can be very costly
8 new model – test – special tracks or roads
9 deal with problems – costly if problems serious
10 journalists – invite – test-drive model
11 reviews – write – by journalists – major newspapers and car magazines
12 model – display – famous motor exhibition – Geneva or Earls Court Motor Show

Listening
Presentation techniques

▲ Pamela Pickford

7.1 Pamela Pickford trains business people to make presentations. Which of the points below does she make? Listen and mark each one either *T* (true) or *F* (false).

1 When preparing a presentation, try to find out what your audience already knows.
2 Everyone in your audience should be at the same language level.
3 Visit the room in which you are presenting before you actually make the presentation.
4 The first stage of your presentation is when you should get the full attention of your audience.
5 If you memorise the introduction, you will be more confident when making a presentation.
6 The whole text of your presentation should be written on postcards.
7 If you use an overhead projector, you should remember to turn it off when you don't need it.
8 Remember that the content of the presentation is much more important than your presenting style.

Skills
Presentations

A Comment on the following statements. In your opinion are they:
a) essential b) helpful c) unhelpful for a successful presentation?

1 Tell a joke at the beginning.
2 Speak more slowly than you normally do.
3 Smile a lot.
4 Involve the audience.
5 Invite questions during the presentation.
6 Always keep to your plan.
7 Move around during your presentation.
8 Use a lot of gestures to emphasise important points.
9 Read out your presentation from a script.
10 Stand up when giving your presentation.

B 7.2 Listen to a presentation to a company's sales team about the launch of their new chocolate bar. Tick the expressions in the Useful language box on page 59 that you hear.

Useful language

Introducing yourself
Good morning everyone.
Let me introduce myself. My name is ...
I'm a specialist in ...

Structuring the presentation
I'm going to divide my talk into four parts.
First I'll give you ...; after that ...; finally ...

Inviting questions
If you have any questions, don't hesitate to ask.
I'll be glad to answer any questions (at the end of my talk).

Giving background information
I'll give you some background information.
Let's start with the background.

Referring to the audience's knowledge
As you know ...
As you are aware ...

Changing the topic
Right, let's now move on to ...
OK, I'll now look at ...

Concluding
To sum up ...
So to summarise ...

Referring to visuals
If you look at the graph ...
Could I draw your attention to the chart?
If you take a look at the first year, you'll see ...

Ending
Thanks very much. Any questions?
Well, that's all I have to say. Thank you for listening.

C Choose one of the situations below.
Prepare a short presentation of three to five minutes.
Include phrases from the Useful language box.

Topic	Audience	Suggestions	
A country you have visited on holiday or done business in	A group of people who will shortly be working there	• way of life • transport • accommodation • food and drink • standard of living	• customs and traditions • weather • language • people • entertainment
Your company's main competitors	The board of directors of your company	• who they are • their strengths and weaknesses • how powerful they are in the market relative to you	
Your job	A group of high school students at a careers evening	• responsibilities and tasks • the future • perks and special advantages, e.g. foreign travel • qualifications • career structure	

D Now make your presentations in groups. After each presentation, discuss these questions.

1 Was the presentation interesting? Was it lively? Was it clear?

2 Did the beginning have impact? Did you want to hear more?

3 Did the presentation have a logical structure – a beginning, middle and end?

4 Was it divided into sections? Did you know when the presenter was moving from one part of the talk to another?

5 Was there a summary or a conclusion?

International Leatherware

Background

The International Leatherware Association (ILA) represents leather goods manufacturers and retailers. One of its main functions is to promote the use of leather for new products. Each year the Association awards prizes to companies with outstanding new ideas. Companies send a detailed product description and a marketing plan, and the four best proposals are selected. These companies then present their product concepts to a panel of judges. The presentations and awards are televised and the event is broadcast worldwide.

Task

Your company is competing for the ILA's top prize. You believe that you have an outstanding idea for a new leather product. Read the Case study documents. Then, prepare your product presentation and present it to the rest of the group. Answer any questions they may have. When you are not making a presentation, you are a member of the judging panel. Decide who should get top prize. (You may not vote for your own product concept.)

ILA guidelines to competitors

1 The purpose of the competition is to encourage innovation in the leather goods industry. The competition aims to raise the profile of leather as a material for producing goods.

2 Any product made with leather may be entered in the competition.

3 Product concepts should be very creative and have excellent sales potential.

4 It will be an advantage if a company can offer a product showing a new use for leather.

5 Guidelines for the presentation are available upon request.

Innovative designs at ILA awards

There was huge excitement and tension before Solange Marchand, President of the International Leather Association, announced the winner and runner-up. Could it be Hungary's turn with Stephen Nalti's 'Mobile Office', a state-of-the-art briefcase, with compartments for a PC and mobile phone? Would Sweden's Nadia Lindstrom win the top prize with her firm's leather computer covers? Perhaps Anna Petrov, a Moscow designer, would win with her exciting range of leather furniture?

When the result was announced, cheers and applause greeted the popular winner. Anna Petrov had won first prize. Smiling, almost in tears, the happy winner accepted the cheque. After congratulating the other competitors, she said that she hoped many people all over the world would enjoy the products she had created.

▲ Newsline magazine article on last year's competition

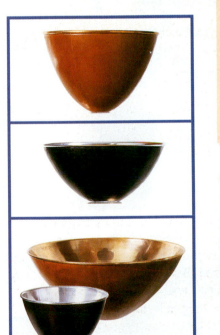

STOP PRESS Leatherware competition

The annual competition, sponsored by the International Leather Association, takes place on 29 June, at the Chambre de Commerce, Geneva, Switzerland. The judges will be chaired by Solange Marchand. The winning company will receive a prize of US$100,000. Runners-up will each receive $US25,000. The event will be televised by Channel 8 Television.

Guidelines for presenters

1 Introduce your team. Outline the structure of your presentation.
2 Describe the product design, features and consumer benefits.
3 Describe the product's target market.
4 Mention other competing products.
5 Present your strategy for the new product. For example:
   • branding, packaging, other product features (guarantee, etc.)
   • pricing strategy
   • distribution (What sales outlets will be used?)
   • promotion (What advertising, product launch and sales promotion?)
6 Describe any ideas for television or radio commercials.

Writing

The editor of your company's in-house magazine has asked you to write a short article about the leatherware competition. Include information about some of the products presented at the event and mention who received the top prize. Say whether you think the judges made a good choice.

61

UNIT 8 Organisation

> *How many people work in your office?*
> *About half.*
>
> Anonymous

OVERVIEW ▼

☐ **Vocabulary**
Company structure

☐ **Reading**
New ways of working

☐ **Language review**
Noun combinations

☐ **Listening**
A new office complex

☐ **Skills**
Introductions,
socialising and
leaving-talking

☐ **Case study**
Faredeal Travel Agency

Starting up

A Would you like to work in the office in the photo above. Explain why or why not.

B How important is each of the following for showing a person's status in an organisation? Give each one a score from 1 (not important) to 5 (very important).

- a reserved parking space
- an office with a window
- a uniform
- a personal business card
- your own office
- a company car
- your name on your door

- having a secretary
- taking holidays when you like
- the size of your desk
- having more than one seat in your office
- flying business class
- a company credit card
- having to clock in when you arrive

Vocabulary
Company structure

A Read the three descriptions of company structures. Then answer the questions. Use a good dictionary to help you.

Sole trader

One person sets up and runs the company. The person provides all the capital and has unlimited liability for business debts, even if this means selling personal assets.

Limited company

In a limited company (*AmE* corporation), the capital is divided into shares, which are held by shareholders. Shareholders have limited liability, but they can vote at the Annual General Meeting to elect the Board of Directors. There are two types of limited company:
1) In a **private limited company**, all shareholders must agree before any shares can be bought or sold.
2) In a **public limited company**, shares are bought and sold freely, for example on the stock exchange.

Partnership

A group of people provide the capital, set up the company and manage it together. There are two types of partnership:
1) Partners in an **unlimited partnership** are like sole traders – if the business fails they are fully liable for all debts, and may even have to sell personal assets.
2) In a **limited partnership** there can be sleeping partners who do not participate in the management of the company. Sleeping partners have limited liability – in the event of bankruptcy, they only lose their investment, not their personal assets.

1 What are most people's main personal assets?
2 How can a sole trader get the capital to set up a business? Think of five methods.
3 If a limited company has 5000 shares and each share is worth £2.50, what is the capital of the company?
4 What are the advantages and disadvantages of being a sleeping partner?
5 What is the difference between a sleeping partner and a shareholder?
6 If a private limited company goes bankrupt, do the shareholders lose their personal assets? Why?
7 What must you do to sell your shares in a private limited company?
8 What are the advantages of a public limited company? Think of three.

B Make ten common business expressions with the words below. For example, *sleeping partner, annual general meeting*. Use some words more than once.

annual	company	exchange	meeting	private	stock
assets	unlimited	general	of	public	trader
board	debts	liability	partner	sleeping	
business	directors	limited	personal	sole	

C Discuss these questions.

1 Which of the words below can describe:
   a) good qualities of an organisation? **b)** bad qualities of an organisation?

professional	impersonal	cold	caring	disciplined
democratic	decentralised	paternal	hierarchical	welcoming
centralised	slow-to-respond	flat	market-driven	bureaucratic

2 Which words could you use to describe your own organisation or an organisation you know well?

Reading
New ways of working

A Here are some ideas for creating a good working environment. Which do you consider a) crazy? b) good for motivating staff?

- singing at meetings
- dressing in strange clothes at meetings
- having no individual offices
- having no dress code
- unisex toilets
- organising company holidays

- encouraging managers to invite staff home for dinner
- buying birthday presents for staff
- keeping small animals and birds at head office
- supplying flowers regularly for all offices

B Read the article. Which of the ideas above are used by the Finnish company, SOL?

Pioneer preaches flexibility while her firm cleans up

A Finnish innovator finds new ways to work that earn big returns in a tough sector. **Alan Tillier** *reports*

Smart in yellow uniforms, staff hurry about in Finland's $60 million-a-year SOL cleaning
5 company carrying laptops and the latest Nokia mobile phones, as well as heavy-duty vacuum cleaners.

This is a company in which
10 people work when they like, and flexibility is being strongly tested. It is one that Dr Joseph Juran, the management guru based in New York, considers to
15 be the future.

SOL's owner, Liisa Joronen, a slim, charismatic brunette of 50, back from a 90-mile keep-fit cross-country ski run in Lapland,
20 says that she has thrown out traditional management styles and hierarchies in favour of people motivation and the strict auditing of targets.

25 She has brought fun to the workplace in a nation noted for its engineering innovation, but also for its people's shyness and introversion. This most extrovert
30 of Scandinavian business leaders sometimes dresses as a sunflower and sings at sales meetings if it will help. The company's name is from the Spanish for sun, and
35 its sun logo has a curved line turning it into a smile.

The key words around SOL are freedom, trust, goals, responsibility, creativity, joy of
40 working and lifelong learning, Ms Joronen says. People's creativeness is restricted by routine and traditional office hours. As work becomes more
45 competitive, so we need more flexible, creative and independent people.

To help staff towards independence of mind, Liisa has
50 abolished territorial space, such as individual offices and desks, and organised a communal area similar to a social club. It has a colourful playground, with trees,
55 caged birds and small animals, a nursery, a billiard table, sofas, modern art and kitchen corners.

Staff sit anywhere. There is not a secretary in sight. The boss
60 makes the tea if everyone is on the phone to the field teams. Headquarters can be empty in the day and busy in the evenings and weekends. One headquarters
65 worker, keen to go to midweek tango classes, was switching tasks with a colleague. The person supervising the cleaning of Helsinki's metro was working
70 from home.

Flying the country Economy Class, Liisa tells 3,500 staff at 25 branches to kill routine before it kills you. At SOL Days, Japanese-
75 style motivation sessions, she has the whole hall dancing, and urges staff: The better you think you are, the better you will become.

Half the country sees Liisa as
80 a revolutionary boss, and several television programmes have been devoted to her. The other half thinks she is crazy.

From The Times

C Work in two groups. Group A completes the information file on Liisa Joronen. Group B completes the information file on her company, SOL. When you have finished, check each other's files.

SOL cleaning company

Location: _____

Number of staff: _____

Number of branches: _____

Logo: _____

Working conditions/practices:

_____

_____

_____

_____

Liisa Joronen

Age: _____

Position: _____

Physical appearance:

_____

Personality: _____

Leadership ideas/style:

_____

_____

Public image: _____

_____

D Which of these adjectives describe the type of worker SOL likes to employ?

> fun-loving   competitive   ambitious   responsible   animal-loving
> shy   punctual   independent   flexible   creative

E Read these extracts from the article.
Which word is similar in meaning to the underlined word in each extract?

1 <u>Smart</u> in yellow uniforms, staff rush about in Finland's $60 million-a-year SOL cleaning company.
   a) intelligent   **b)** colourful   **c)** well-dressed

2 SOL's owner, Liisa Joronen, a slim, <u>charismatic</u> brunette of 50 ...
   a) powerful   **b)** charming   **c)** inspiring

3 This most <u>extrovert</u> of Scandinavian business leaders sometimes dresses as a sunflower ...
   a) lively   **b)** quiet   **c)** creative

4 People's creativeness is <u>restricted</u> by routine and traditional office hours.
   a) developed   **b)** destroyed   **c)** limited

5 Liisa has <u>abolished</u> territorial space, such as individual offices and desks.
   a) increased   **b)** stopped   **c)** reduced

6 One headquarters worker, keen to go to midweek tango classes, was <u>switching</u> tasks with a colleague.
   a) changing   **b)** planning   **c)** sharing

F Discuss these questions.

1 Would you like to work in a company like SOL?

2 Which of Liisa Joronen's ideas would you like to introduce into your own company or organisation? Which would you not like to introduce? Why?

Language review
Noun combinations

Two or more nouns can be combined in several ways.

1 's possessive

3 phrases with *of*

2 one noun used as adjective

4 compound nouns forming one word

Match these examples from the SOL article on page 64 with the categories above.

a) *workplace*

c) *independence of mind*

b) *SOL's owner*

d) *office hours*

 page 137

A Find noun combinations in the SOL article on page 64.
Write them under the following four headings:
- **'s possessive**
- **one noun used as adjective**
- **phrases with *of***
- **compound nouns forming one word**

B Nouns used as numerical adjectives are singular.
For example, *60 million <u>dollar-a-year</u> SOL cleaning company* ...

1 Find another example in paragraph three of the article.

2 Now change the following phrases into noun combinations.
For example, a hotel with five stars: *a five-star hotel*
   a) a job with a salary of a hundred thousand pounds
   b) a research project costing five million dollars
   c) a takeover bid worth two million pounds
   d) a meeting which lasts 45 minutes

C Underline the best noun combination.

1 a) the boss of Mr Smith
   b) Mr Smith boss
   c) <u>Mr Smith's boss</u>

2 a) the workforce
   b) the work force
   c) the work's force

3 a) a research project
   b) a researches project
   c) a project of research

4 a) a resignations letter
   b) a letter of resignation
   c) a resignation's letter

Listening
A new office complex

A Look at the photograph of British Airways' new office complex, Waterside. What is your impression of the building?

B 8.1 Listen to the first part of an interview with the British Airways Project Manager for the complex, and make notes. Then answer these questions.

1 What were Chris Byron's three main objectives concerning Waterside?

2 What three special features of Waterside does he mention?

C 8.2 Now listen to the second part of the interview.

1 What does Chris Byron mean by the term *flexible working*? Give examples.

2 Which of the facilities below are provided at Waterside for employees?

- open-learning education
- a supermarket in the building
- electronic shopping
- excellent meals
- free videos
- company cars

3 Why were there so few problems when staff moved to Waterside?

D Discuss these questions.

1 How will Waterside help to improve efficiency and profitability?

2 What other facilities could Waterside provide for BA employees?

3 Would you like to work at Waterside? Give your reasons.

Skills
Introductions, socialising and leave-taking

Useful language

Introductions
Yves, this is Jim.
Bernie, do you know Patrice?
Anne, have you met Maria?
Can I introduce you to Mark Barnard our Finance Director?
I'd like you to meet …
Are you Ms Valdez by any chance?
You must be Larry Koplan.

Responding
Nice to meet you.
It's a pleasure.
Pleased to meet you too.

Mentioning common interests
I think you | both know Iwona.
| both like skiing.
| are both interested in the new project
I know you have both | been to Brazil.
| worked in R&D.

Leaving
Well, I really must be going.
Anyway, I'll see you soon.
Hope to see you again soon.
It was nice meeting you.
It was good to see you again.

A Match the beginnings of these sentences with the endings. Then make similar sentences about yourself.

1 I work in the   a) a lot of overseas travel.
2 I'm a   b) design department.
3 I'm responsible for   c) work abroad.
4 My job involves   d) research chemist.
5 I spend a lot of time   e) credit control.
6 In the future, I hope to f) visiting suppliers.

B Fill in the missing letters. *(vowels)*

1 We	pr o v i d e s e ll pr o d u c e s u pply d i str i b u t e	car parts.	2 We have	br a nch e s p a rtn e rs c o nt a cts a g e nts f a ct o r i e s	in Asia.

C Match the beginnings of the sentences with the endings. Then make similar sentences about your company.

1 The company was founded   a) in three divisions.
2 There are   b) multinational food companies.
3 It's organised   c) in 1992.
4 Our main competitors are d) 200 people working here.

D Work in groups of three. Two of you work for the same company. One if you is a visitor. Practise making introductions. Ask about each other and each other's company. Then finish the conversation.
Use phrases from the Useful language box above.

CASE STUDY

Faredeal Travel Agency

Background

Faredeal Travel Agency was founded by its owners, Claudia and Manuel Ortega. It is now one of the largest travel agencies in the City, the financial centre of London. In a few months' time it plans to open branch offices in Birmingham and Edinburgh. Almost 60% of profits come from its corporate business accounts. Its goals and philosophy are set out in its mission statement:

> Our objective is to provide an outstanding travel service to the City of London.
>
> Our strategy is to rapidly expand our corporate business and to steadily develop our Travel Shop.
>
> Our main asset is our employees. We aim to provide them with secure, interesting and well-paid work, in a pleasant working environment.

'Although the firm is doing well, the Ortegas know that it could be more profitable if it was better organised. A consultant has done a study of the agency and recommends reorganisation in three areas: 1) management structure 2) office layout 3) working conditions.

1 Management structure

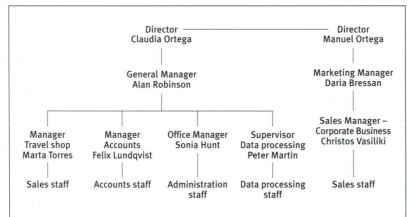

CONFIDENTIAL

1. Alan Robinson has too much responsibility and feels very stressed. He complains also of having no contact with Manuel Ortega.
2. Christos Vasiliki wants better communication with Manuel Ortega. Manuel is often away on business trips, so Christos is not able to get his approval for important decisions like discounts for important customers.
3. Daria Bressan reports to Manuel Ortega. However, most of her work is with Claudia Ortega, whose speciality is marketing.
4. The Accounts Department want more cooperation with the Data Processing Department. On the other hand, Sonia Hunt says that Peter Martin is always 'interfering' in their office.

2 Office layout

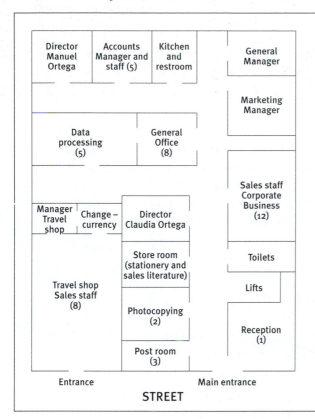

The office space is not used efficiently and needs a complete reorganisation. (For example, Accounts and General Office staff have to walk too far to the photocopying room, etc.)

Also the following facilities are not available to staff at the moment:
a) A canteen in the building. (There are no restaurants nearby.)
b) A room for smokers. (People smoke outside the main door.)
c) Crèche facilities for staff with young children.
d) Facilities for disabled staff. (There are two disabled staff.)

3 Working conditions

Working conditions: staff survey

1. 72% want better facilities and more opportunity to express their opinions to the Ortegas.

2. 65% find their work 'interesting' and 'enjoyable'. 35% say their work 'lacks variety', mostly in Accounts, General Office and Data Processing. Absenteeism in these departments is high.

3. 58% would prefer flexitime so that they can avoid travelling to and from work during the rush hour.

4. 62% think their pay is adequate. 38% (mostly in Accounts, the Travel Shop and the General Office) think they are underpaid by at least 10%. They want more perks, for example, discounts on travel and more company social events.

5. Sales staff say they do too much unpaid overtime to complete their paperwork. There are too many complicated forms.

6. Sales staff in the Travel Shop complain that people in the Corporate Business section earn 30% to 40% more than them, and have a better office. They also receive end-of-year bonuses.

Task

Faredeal's directors have created work groups to consider the reorganisation.

Stage one
Work in pairs. Discuss what action to recommend for one of the three problem areas:
either **1)** Management structure
or **2)** Office layout
or **3)** Working conditions

Stage two
Form groups of three. Your group should include someone from each of the pairs in stage one. Discuss your recommendations for all three problem areas and decide how to reorganise the company. Then compare the decisions made in each group.

Writing

The General Manager has invited members of staff to send him a short, informal report on how to reorganise the company. As a member of staff, write the report.

 Writing file page 146

Money

> *Money talks they say. All it ever said to me was "Goodbye."*
> Cary Grant (1904–1986), American film star

Starting up **A** Do the quiz individually. Then compare answers with a partner.

QUIZ

1 How much cash do you have with you at the moment? Do you:
  a) know exactly?
  b) know approximately?
  c) not know at all?

2 Do you normally check:
  a) your change?
  b) your bank statements and credit card bills?
  c) restaurant bills?
  d) your receipts when shopping?
  e) prices in several shops before you buy something?

3 Do you:
  a) give money to beggars?
  b) give money to charities?
  c) give away used items, such as clothing?

4 If you go for a meal with someone you don't know well, do you:
  a) offer to pay the whole bill?
  b) suggest dividing the bill into equal parts?
  c) offer to pay the whole bill but expect them to pay next time?
  d) try to avoid paying anything?

5 What do you think about people who do not pay the correct amount of tax? Is this:
  a) a serious crime?
  b) morally wrong but not a crime?
  c) excellent business practice?

6 If you lend a colleague a small amount of money and they forget to pay it back, do you:
  a) say nothing?
  b) remind them that they owe you money?
  c) arrange to go for a drink with them and say you've forgotten your wallet or purse?

7. Do you know how much money you have in your bank account right now?

B Write one more question to add to the quiz above. Ask a partner to answer it.

C Discuss your answers to the quiz. What do they say about your attitude to money? What do they say about your culture?

Skills
Dealing with figures

Useful language

Saying numbers

Years

1984	*nineteen eighty four*
2001	*two thousand and one*

Currencies

£3.15	*three pounds fifteen*
$7.80	*seven dollars eighty*
€250	*two hundred and fifty euros*

Decimals

16.5	*sixteen point five*
17.38%	*seventeen point three eight percent*
0.185	*(nought /zero) point one eight five*

Bigger numbers

3560   *three thousand five hundred* | ***and** sixty (BrE)*
sixty (AmE)

598, 347   *five hundred* | ***and** ninety-eight thousand, three hundred **and** forty-seven (BrE)*
ninety-eight thousand, three hundred forty-seven (AmE)

1,300,402   *one million three hundred thousand, four hundred* | ***and** two (BrE)*
two (AmE)

1m	*one /a million (1,000,000)*
3bn	*three billion (3000,000,000)*
$7.5bn	*seven point five billion dollars*

£478m   *four hundred* | ***and** seventy eight million pounds (BrE)*
seventy eight million pounds (AmE)

A Read the article below. Then write all the numbers and symbols in full, according to the way they are pronounced. For example, 1999: *nineteen ninety-nine*; £3.1 m: *three point one million pounds.*

B 🎧 9.1 Listen and check your answers.

BUSINESS IN BRIEF

EuroDisney runs new project
The French Government yesterday approved a Ff4.6bn urban development project east of Paris, coordinated by EuroDisney, and designed to create 22,000 jobs by 2015.

Yule Catto takeover bid
Yule Catto, the chemicals group, launched a £240m bid for Holliday Chemical. Yule shares fell 32p (about 10%) to 274 in response to the news. Holliday's shares dropped 8p to end at 225p.

Prince invests in media and technology
The worldwide fall in stock markets last month encouraged Prince Alwaleed bin Talal to invest in media and technology companies. The Saudi prince spent $400m on a 5% stake in News Corporation, $300m on 1% in Motorola and $150m on 5% of Netscape Communications.

Monet market
A beach scene painted in 1870 by French impressionist Claude Monet when he was desperately short of money made £3.8m at Christie's Auction House in London.

FT sales record
Sales of the *Financial Times* hit an all-time record in November. Worldwide sales were 12.4% up on November, last year.

New car registrations in Europe
New car registrations in Western Europe in November rose 10.4% to 991,800 from 898,400 a year ago, said the European Auto Manufacturers Association.

Language review
Trends

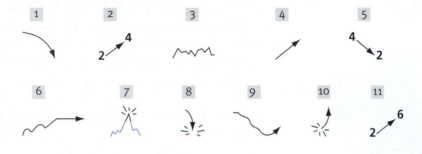

We can describe trends in English in different ways. For example:

1 **Verbs of change**   *Profits are **falling**.*
*Unemployment is **rising** in many areas.*

2 **Prepositions**   *Our business grew **by** 10% last year.*
*Sales grew **to** $5.8 million.*

3 **Different tenses**   *In recent months our profits **have risen** dramatically.*
*In January we **were making** a loss.*
*We've **been going through** a difficult period.*

➡ page 138

A What kind of movement do the verbs below describe? Match them to the symbols. Then compare your answers with a partner. (Use some symbols more than once.)

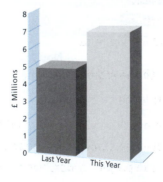

decline (7)	gain (4)	drop (1)	increase (4)	rocket (10)	plummet (5) (8) .
double (2)	fall (1)	halve (5)	level off (6)	triple (11)	recover . (9) .
decrease (1)	fluctuate (3)	improve (4)	peak (7)	rise (4)	

B Which of the above verbs also have noun forms? What are they?
For example, *to increase – an increase*.

C Complete these sentences about the graphs below with appropriate prepositions.

1 Sales have increased .....*from*..... £5m .....*to*..... £7m.

2 Sales have increased .....*by*..... £2m.

3 There has been an increase .....*of*..... £2m in our sales.

4 Sales now stand .....*at*..... £7 million.

5 Sales reached a peak .....*of /at*..... £7 million in July.

6 Sales reached a low point .....*of /at*..... £1 million in April.

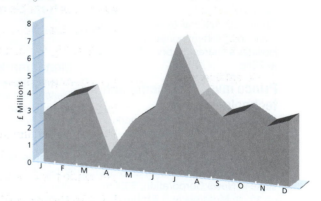

D Write two more sentences about each of the graphs above.

E **Peter Bingham, President of a clothing company, is in a meeting with his Sales Director John Amidon, and his Financial Director, Kate Simmons. Complete their conversation with appropriate forms of the verbs in brackets. Sometimes more than one tense is possible.**

Peter   I'm glad you managed to make it today. I'd like to start by taking a look at the year's sales and profit figures. First of all John, could you summarise the sales figures?

John   Well, we had a good January – 5.2 million. January's a difficult month because sales always ....drop........[1] (drop) after Christmas. In February we launched the new children's line and it went very well. Total sales ....rose........[2] (rise) to almost 8 million, which was nice. Unfortunately they then ..plummeted...[3] (plummet) after the fire in the main factory. But by the end of April we ..had recovered.[4] (recover) – 10.2 million was the figure – and since then sales .have gone up..[5] (go up) steadily month by month. The December figures aren't in yet, but it looks like we 'll probably......[6] (probably reach) 15 million this month.

Peter   Good. I've got a couple of questions, but I'll save them for later. Kate, sales have increased, but has that meant higher profits?

Kate   Yes, it has. We're waiting for the final figures, but we already know that overall, in the first three quarters of the year, profits .have risen....[7] (rise) by 15% compared to last year, from 960,000 to 1.1 million. In fact since April, profits .have increased[8] (increase) every single month and they are still going..[9] (still go up).

Peter   What about next year?

Kate   Well, as you know, next year we're going to centralise distribution, so costs ..will decrease..[10] (decrease). Even if sales .level off......[11] (level off), profits ..will improve...[12] (improve).

F 🎧 **9.2** **Now listen and check your answers.**

Listening
Making loans

A **Gerard Gardner, an executive director of EFG Private Bank Ltd, lends money to businesses. In this interview he describes three important factors to consider when deciding whether to make a loan.**
What do you think these factors will be?

B 🎧 **9.3** **Listen to the first part of the interview and check your predictions.**

C 🎧 **9.3** **Listen again and make notes about the three factors.**

D 🎧 **9.4** **Listen to the second part of the interview. Gerard mentions two examples from his experience.**

1 What does he say about them?

2 What big opportunity did Gerard miss?

▲ Gerard Gardner

E **Complete this summary with the words below.**

intuitively   clear   confidence   logically

The business plan needs to be ....[1] and presented ....[2] . The presenter should speak with ....[3] to persuade the investor that the project is worthwhile. However, at the end of the day, the investor may feel ....[4] that the project is not worth investing in.

assets

A In your opinion, which of the following give the best return on your money? Which are very risky? Which are less risky?

- gold
- precious stones
- stocks and shares
- currencies
- property
- land/real estate
- a high-interest deposit account
- antiques and paintings
- a new business venture

B Choose the best answer.

If someone *speculates*:

a) they take a risk to make a quick profit.

b) they make a safe investment for long-term security.

C Work in three groups. Each group reads *a different text: either* **The South Sea Bubble** *or* **Tulipomania** *or* **The Wall Street Crash. Make notes on the key points.**

The South Sea Bubble

Lisa Anja Mo

The South Sea Bubble is the name given to a speculation in 1720, and associated with the South Sea Company in London. People bought shares in the 5 company expecting to make a huge profit, but the boom in shares collapsed and many investors lost all their money.

The South Sea Company was founded in 1711 to trade with Spanish America. The 10 company's stock offered a guaranteed interest of 6% and it sold well. Unfortunately, however, Spain allowed the company to send only one ship a year to trade in the area.

The first voyage in 1717 was a success. Then 15 King George I became governor of the company in 1719. This created confidence in the business, and soon it was paying 100% interest.

In 1720, there was a boom in the South Sea Company's shares because it agreed to take over the 20 country's national debt. It expected to get back its money by increased trade and a rise in the value of its shares.

The shares did, in fact, rise dramatically. The stock of the company, which had been around £128 25 in January 1720, reached £1,000 in August. However, by September the market had collapsed, and the price fell back to £124. Eventually, with the support of the Government, the shares levelled off at around £140.

The South Sea Bubble had burst and it led to 30 an economic depression in the country.

Tulipomania

Benson Howie

The first modern stock market appeared in Amsterdam at the beginning of the 17th century. In Holland in the 1630s, there was one of the first and most extraordinary speculative explosions in history. It was not in stocks and shares, in real estate or in fine paintings, as you might expect, but in tulip 5 bulbs. It has become known by the name Tulipomania.

People from all classes invested in the bulbs. Many sold their property so that they could pay for the bulbs they had bought in the tulip market. Foreigners joined in the rush to buy the flowers and money poured into Holland from other countries. 10

In 1637, the boom in the market ended. No one knows why, but people began to sell. Others followed suit. Soon there was a panic among investors and the tulip market collapsed. Many people who had offered their property as security for credit went bankrupt. People who had agreed to 15 buy tulips at inflated prices were unable to pay their debts. When sellers took legal action to recover their money, the courts were not helpful because they saw such investment as a kind of gambling.

It is not surprising that the collapse in prices led to a severe 20 economic recession in Holland.

The Wall Street Crash

The stock market crash in the United States in 1929 was huge and it led to a severe and lasting economic crisis in the world. Many bankers and industrialists lost their money and reputations.
5 Some went to prison and others committed suicide.

Share prices on the New York stock exchange had begun rising in 1924, and in 1928 and 1929 they rocketed to unbelievable levels. In spring
10 1929 there was a break in the rising prices when the Federal Reserve Bank said it might raise interest rates to slow down the boom. However, a major bank, the National City Bank, assured investors that it would continue to lend money to
15 them at affordable rates.

Soon the market took off again. People could buy stock for 10% of its value and borrow the remaining 90%. The lending rate varied from 7% to 12%. Almost everyone was optimistic. One
20 economist, at the peak of the boom, said that people generally agreed 'stocks are not at present overvalued'.

It all ended on 21 October, 1929. The market opened badly and there was heavy selling.
25 Confidence in the market disappeared. There was a rumour that the big bankers were getting out of the market. Share prices fell dramatically and kept on falling. The boom was over. But its consequences would last for years to come.

D Form new groups of three people, each of whom has read a different text. Exchange information and complete the chart below.

	South Sea Bubble	Tulipomania	Wall Street Crash
Where did it happen?			
When did it happen?			
Who was involved?			
What happened?			
Why did it happen?			
What were the consequences?			

E Discuss these questions.

1 What are the similarities and differences in the three speculations?

2 What do you think people will speculate in during the next 20 years?

F Work in groups. Find words or phrases in the texts which are similar in meaning to the definitions below. The first group to finish is the winner.

South Sea Bubble
1 a very large amount of money
2 set up
3 sudden increase in buying and selling
4 to accept responsibility for
5 go up very fast
6 in the end
7 remained stable

Tulipomania
1 great increase in buying and selling, usually of shares
2 land and buildings
3 flowed quickly
4 copied
5 ended suddenly
6 offered to a lender when you borrow money
7 unable to pay their debts

Wall Street Crash
1 a powerful business person controlling large companies
2 went up very fast
3 a change for a short period
4 became very active
5 highest point
6 sold at too high a price
7 selling all of their shares

CASE STUDY

Angel Investments

Background

Angel Investments plc (AI), is based in Warsaw, Poland. It provides finance for start-up or young companies which need capital to develop their businesses. AI is run by a group of extremely rich people of various nationalities who made their fortunes in the computer and financial services industries. They enjoy the excitement of working with start-ups and small companies, and believe that Central and Eastern Europe offers outstanding opportunities for investment. They are willing to take risks and back projects which seem unusual or extraordinary. However they also expect to make money, usually by taking a stake in the business or a share of the profits.

A team of AI investors is currently considering several proposals. After hearing presentations from individuals and companies, AI will decide which projects it will invest in, and how much money it will give to each one. They have £5.5 million to invest in the projects.

Key points for product presentations

1. The Business
A description of the business – What does it do? Who is it for? Brief details about the team (age, education, experience, etc.).

2. The Product or Service
A brief description – including artwork, if possible.
What are the advantages of the product or service? What need does it fill?
What are its unique features?

3. Marketing
Who are the existing or target customers?
Who are the competitors or possible future competitors?
What are the competing products, if any?
What about pricing policy?
How will the product or service be launched and promoted?
What are the selling and distribution methods?

4. Finance
How much finance is required and for what purposes?

Task

You are *either*:
a) an AI investor; *or*
b) an entrepreneur who needs finance for a new project.

- AI investors turn to page 152.
- Entrepreneurs turn to page 157.

This is difficult if small class. Organisation takes more

Make sure entrepreneurs take on diff. proposals.

Proposals

New magazine You need to finance the first edition and launch of a new magazine. Amount required: £2.5 million, to finance production, editorial, office administration, distribution costs and promotion.

Flotation tank centres At these centres, stressed business people can float in tanks and forget about their problems. Other services will include advice about diet and skin care, a solarium, and sunbeds, etc.
Amount required: £2 million, to finance premises, equipment, staff and promotion.

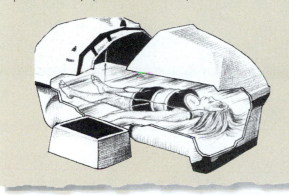

High-tech products Your company is developing two products. The PX15 prevents people from using mobile phones in enclosed spaces, for example in restaurants or trains. Sweep-Safe is a device for clearing mines. It can also find other objects buried underground.
Amount required: £3.5 million, to finance research and development, production and marketing.

New sport league You have a background in sport and public relations. You want to set up a league for a sport which at present is not well-known, but could become very popular.
Amount required: £2.5 million to finance administration and promotion, endorsements of the league by famous sports people, travel and legal costs.

Your own idea for a product or service You have an idea for a product or service. You have not yet written a business plan, but the AI team are willing to listen to your presentation.
Amount required: At least £3 million, to finance development, production, personnel, launch and marketing costs.

Airships Your company wants to manufacture airships to advertise companies' products and to entertain potential customers, etc.
Amount required: £5 million, to finance research and development costs, production, and marketing.

Writing

You are head of the AI team. Write a report to the Chairman of AI, Jacek Piotrowski. Describe the successful proposals and explain why AI should invest in them. Indicate how much money each will receive, and on what terms.

 Writing file page 146

UNIT 10 Ethics

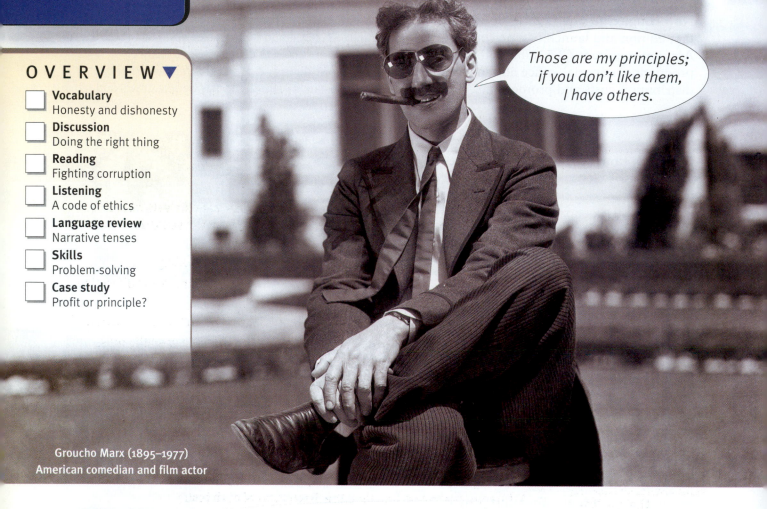

Those are my principles; if you don't like them, I have others.

Groucho Marx (1895–1977)
American comedian and film actor

Starting up

A **Discuss these questions.**

1 What is the purpose of a business, in your opinion? Is it just to make money?

2 What do you understand by these phrases?

   a) business ethics   **b)** a code of good practice   **c)** a mission statement

3 Should mission statements include statements about ethics?

4 Rank the professions below according to how ethical you think they are.

accountant	civil servant	lawyer	police officer
banker	estate agent	nurse	teacher
car sales executive	journalist	dentist	taxi driver

B **Discuss this list of unethical activities. In your opinion, which are the worst? Are any common in your country?**

1 Avoiding paying tax

2 Claiming extra expenses

3 Using work facilities for private purposes (for example, personal phone calls)

4 Accepting praise for someone else's ideas or work

5 Selling a defective product (for example, a second-hand car)

6 Using your influence to get jobs for relatives (nepotism)

7 Ringing in sick when you are not ill

8 Taking extended lunch breaks

9 Giving good references to people you want to get rid of

10 Employing people illegally

Vocabulary
Honesty and dishonesty

— for presentations .

A The sets of words and phrases below are related either to *honesty* or to *dishonesty*. Which word is different from the others in each set? Use a good dictionary to help you.

1 trustworthy	law-abiding	crooked
2 a slush fund	a sweetener	compensation
3 insider trading	industrial espionage	disclosure
4 a whistleblower	a swindler	a conman
5 a bribe	a bonus	a commission
6 fraud	deceit	integrity

Bribe=
kickback
sweetener
backhander
baksheesh
greasing of palms .
= Formal = (court room)
illicit payments .

LOOK IN /
BACK .

B Complete these sentences with words and phrases from the sets above. Choose from the first set to complete sentence 1, from the second set to complete sentence 2, and so on.

1 Our company does nothing illegal. We are very ..*law-abiding*... .
2 We've got ..*a slush fund*.. which is used in countries where it is difficult to do business without offering bribes.
3 Their car looked so much like our new model. We suspect *industrial espionage*
4 They fired him because he was ..*a whistleblower*.. He informed the press that the company was using under-age workers in the factory.
5 He denied accepting ..*a bribe*..... when he gave the contract to the most expensive supplier.
6 I admire our chairman. He's a man of his word and is greatly respected for his ...*integrity*... .

Discussion
Doing the right thing

A Work in groups. Discuss the ethical questions below. A different person should lead the discussion of each issue.

1 You have a shortlist of people for the post of Sales Manager. One of the female candidates is clearly the best qualified person for the job. However, you know that some of your best customers would prefer a man. If you appoint a woman you will probably lose some sales. What should you do?

2 Your company, a large multinational, has a new advertising campaign which stresses its honesty, fairness and ethical business behaviour. It has factories in several countries where wages are very low. At present it is paying workers the local market rate. Should you increase their wages?

3 A colleague in a company which tests medical equipment has been making bad mistakes recently at work. This is because she has a serious illness. You are her friend and the only person at work who knows this. She has asked you to keep it a secret. What should you do?

4 You are directors of a potato snack manufacturing company. Research has shown that any price increase causes an immediate dip in sales (although sales recover within six months). It has been suggested that you could maximise your profits by simply reducing the weight of the product in the packets and maintaining the current price. What should you do?

B Do you agree with this statement? Give your reasons.

'If we face a recession we should not lay off employees. The company should sacrifice a profit. It's management's risk and management's responsibility. Employees are not guilty; why should they suffer?'

Akio Morita (1921–1999), co-founder of Sony

Reading
Fighting
corruption

A Discuss these questions.

1 Which is worse, in your opinion: to offer or to accept a bribe? Why?

2 Which do you think are the most corrupt countries in the world? Which do you think are the least corrupt? Give your reasons.

B The chart in the article below is from a survey of 52 countries. Guess where the countries in the box are placed in the chart. Do not read the article yet.

New Zealand	Colombia	Pakistan	Germany	Nigeria
Finland	Bolivia	Sweden	Denmark	Russia	Britain

C Compare charts with a partner. Explain your choices.

D Now read the article. Did you complete the chart correctly?

Britain Moves Higher In Bribery League

From **Roger Boyes** in Bonn

Britain is seen as more corrupt than seven other European countries, including Germany, according to an authoritative annual league table
5 released yesterday by the Berlin-based Transparency International group. Transparency International is a private group, set up in 1993 to fight corruption, and bases its information
10 on seven international surveys of business people, political analysts and the public.

The cleanest countries this year were Denmark, Finland and Sweden,
15 which moved New Zealand from the top position. Britain came relatively low, in 14th position, its image apparently damaged by stories of sleaze. It was overtaken by Germany, although
20 the Germans still tolerate companies which hand out bribes to foreign contractors.

Germany has been under pressure, especially from the United States, to
25 plug legal loopholes which allow German businessmen to write off bribes abroad against tax. Yet both Britain, and even the United States, which has strict legal barriers against
30 international bribery, are behind the Germans. In part, this is probably because of the nature of the survey, which does not track such areas as company-to-company bribery.
35 The most corrupt countries this year are regarded as Nigeria, followed by Bolivia, Colombia and Russia. Pakistan has improved its position, earning only one out of ten

BEST AND WORST COUNTRIES FOR CORRUPTION			
LEAST CORRUPT (Marks out of ten)		MOST CORRUPT	
1	9.94	1	1.76
2	9.48	2	2.05
3	9.35	3	2.23
4	9.23	4	2.27
5 Canada	9.10	5	2.53
6 The Netherlands	9.03	6 Mexico	2.66
7 Norway	8.92	7 Indonesia	2.72
8 Australia	8.86	8 India	2.75
9 Singapore	8.66	9 Venezuala	2.77
10 Luxembourg	8.61	10 Vietnam	2.79
11 Switzerland	8.61	11 Argentina	2.81
12 Ireland	8.23	12 China	2.88
13	8.23	13 Philippines	3.05
14	8.22	14 Thailand	3.06

Source: *Transparency International*

for honesty last year but 2.53 this
40 year. The chairman of Transparency International, Peter Eigen, issued a warning against focusing on Third World corruption.

'Corruption is perceived to be
45 greatest there, but I urge the public to recognise that a large share of the corruption is the product of multinational corporations, headquartered in
50 leading industrialised countries, using massive bribery and kickbacks to buy contracts in the developing world and the countries in transition.' The Third World, in other words, would be less
55 corrupt if developed states stopped offering bribes.

Indeed, the most revealing standings are buried deep in the table.

Belgium, for example, is now regard-
60 ed as more corrupt than Mediterranean nations such as Portugal, Spain and Greece.

'Every day that the poor scores in the Corruption Perception Index are
65 not being dealt with means more impoverishment, less education and less healthcare,' said Dr Eigen. Money was diverted from development into over-priced contracts.
70 A study by Harvard associate professor Shang-Jin Wei found that a rise in corruption levels had the same effect on foreign investments as raising the marginal tax rate by more than 20 per-
75 cent. 'Awareness is a first step to fighting or reducing corruption,' he said.

From *The Times*

E Answer these questions about the article.

1 Does Peter Eigen think the Third World is more corrupt than the developed countries? What reasons does he give for his opinion?

2 According to the article, what are the results of corruption?

3 Where does Transparency International get its information from?

4 According to Peter Eigen, what information is missing from the survey?

F Match these phrasal verbs from the article to a verb with a similar meaning.

write off   solve
hand out   establish
deal with   offer
set up   cancel

G Make word partnerships with the verbs in Exercise F and the nouns in the box. For example, *to hand out a bribe*.

a bribe	a company	a debt	corruption
a loss	a problem	a bonus	an organisation

H Discuss these questions.

1 There is a proverb, 'When in Rome, do as the Romans do.'
What does the proverb mean? Do you agree with this advice?

2 Would you continue to do business with someone if you disapproved of their private life? Explain why or why not.

3 Give examples of behaviour which would cause you to stop doing business with someone.

Listening
A code of ethics

A Discuss the following questions.

1 Is it important for companies to have a written code of ethics?

2 Is it more important for some industries than others to have a code of ethics?

B 🎧 10.1 Claire Bebbington is External Affairs Manager for a division of BP (British Petroleum). Listen to the first part of the interview. Decide whether these statements are true or false, according to Claire.

1 The issue of ethics is simple.

2 If a company puts its code of ethics in writing, it is more likely to act on it.

3 Following up a code of ethics is difficult.

C 🎧 10.1 Listen again to the first part of the interview. Complete the two extracts below.

1 'Firstly, it makes a .... to certain good .... and so it's a way of communicating the importance of ....
.... to all of its employees and partners.'

2 'If you express these things in ...., especially, then you can be held .... for them.'

D 🎧 10.2 Now listen to the second part of the interview. Complete the question that Claire asks. What examples does she give to illustrate the question?
'When does a facilitation .... become a .... ?'

Language review
Narrative tenses

A 🎧 10.3 **The sentences below describe stages in an unsuccessful product launch. Put them in a logical order. Then listen to the conversation and check your answers.**

a) The newspapers asked questions. e) The product was tested.
b) The product was recalled. f) The number of complaints doubled.
c) The company lost a lot of money. g) People started to complain.
d) The product was launched. h) The product sold well.

B **Answer these questions about the product launch.**

1 What was the product? 2 What was the problem?

> **We can use different tenses to narrate a story.**
>
> Past simple   *The newspapers **heard** about it.*
> Past continuous *It **was going** really well.*
> Past perfect   *We'**d tested** it for over six months, and there'**d been** no bad reaction to it.*
> Present perfect *Since then, we'**ve kept** away from skin care products.*
>
> **Which tense is normally used for:**
>
> 1 Setting the scene and providing background information?
> 2 Events which happen before the story begins?
> 3 Events in the story?
> 4 Saying what the present results of the story are?   ➡ page 138

C 🎧 10.3 **Listen again to the conversation. Note down examples of each of these tenses: a) past simple b) past continuous c) past perfect d) present perfect.**

D **Complete the story below with the correct tenses of the verbs in brackets.**

That reminds me of the problem we ....*had*.......¹ (have) with our new milk carton. We ....² (introduce) it a few months earlier and it ....³ (become) popular with customers. People ....⁴ (buy) it, ...⁵ (talk) about it and ....⁶ (recommend) it to their friends, and so on. Then we ....⁷ (change) to a new supplier who ....⁸ (be) cheaper and we ....⁹ (start) to get lots of complaints. People ....¹⁰ (can not) open the cartons any more. We were surprised about the problem because we ....¹¹ (test) it on some of our workers. They ....¹² (say) it was fine.

In the end, we ....¹³ (decide) to go back to our original supplier. We ....¹⁴ (look) really stupid. In the meantime, we ....¹⁵ (lose) a lot of customers. We ....¹⁶ (be) very careful about choosing suppliers for packaging ever since.

E **Tell a story about any of these ideas.**

1 A significant news event you remember well.

2 An ethical problem you know about.

3 A memorable event in your life (good or bad).

4 An unusual or memorable experience while you were travelling abroad.

5 Your first or last day in a job or organisation.

Skills
Problem-solving

Useful language

Stating options
We have a number of options.
There are several ways we could deal
   with this.

Balancing arguments
Let's look at the pros and cons ...
Let's discuss the advantages and
   disadvantages.
On the one hand ... On the other
   hand ...

Changing your approach
Let's look at this another way.
Let's look at this from a different angle.

Considering less obvious options
We could try ...
It might be worth ...

Discussing possible effects
Let's think about the consequences of ...
If we do this then ...

Making a decision
The solution then is to ...
The best way forward is to ...

Stating future action
What we've got to do now is ...
So the next thing to do is ...

A 🎧 10.4 **Listen to two company directors discussing a problem concerning one of their managers. Tick the expressions in the Useful language box that you hear.**

B **Role play this situation.**

> You are senior managers at a hi-fi manufacturer. Your company is losing market share. You strongly suspect your main rival is using unfair methods to promote its products.
>
> For example, you are almost sure that your rival has been:
> a) making cash payments to main dealers;
> b) offering expensive gifts to important customers.
>
> Hold a meeting to consider how to solve the problem.

CASE STUDY

Background

Nikos Takakis is the CEO of Livewire, an Australian manufacturer of electrical appliances. During the last three years, his General Manager Carl Thomson, has turned Livewire round from being a loss-making company into a profitable organisation with an exciting range of new products. Both men want the company to grow as fast as possible.

Problems

- Valerie Harper is Personal Assistant to Carl Thomson. Valerie joined Livewire just over a year ago. In the beginning she was considered to be an outstanding employee. However, more recently she has been having difficulties working with Carl. They have been seen shouting at each other, and often Valerie appears upset when leaving his office. Nikos has received the following memo.

MEMORANDUM
PERSONAL AND CONFIDENTIAL

To	Nikos Takakis
From	Valerie Harper
Date	2 July
Subject	Complaint about Carl Thomson

I would like to make a formal complaint about Carl Thomson's unprofessional behaviour.

1   Mr Thomson has been putting pressure on me to have a personal relationship. When I showed no interest he became aggressive and unpleasant. He gave me too much work, set impossible deadlines, and criticised me in front of the other staff.

2   Mr Thomson gives orders to me rather than polite instructions. He never encourages or praises me. I think he would like to hire a new Personal Assistant who would be more 'friendly' to him.

3   He has frequent long lunches with female staff. He returns to the office late in the afternoon, then expects me to work overtime (unpaid) in the evening.

I feel that unless the situation improves, I shall be unable to continue working for the company.

- After receiving the memo, Nikos Takakis decided to consult Carl Thomson's personal file.

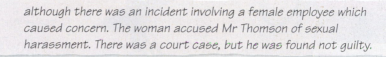

although there was an incident involving a female employee which caused concern. The woman accused Mr Thomson of sexual harassment. There was a court case, but he was found not guilty.

- The same day, Nikos Takakis had lunch in the staff canteen.

  🎧 **10.5** First he spoke to a senior manager, Bob Dexter. Listen to their conversation and note down what they say.

  🎧 **10.6** Next he overheard a conversation between two female employees. Listen to their conversation and note down what they say.

- That evening, Nikos Takakis found out that Carl had advised a friend to buy shares in Livewire just before it announced excellent annual results. The share price rose sharply and the friend made a quick profit.

- The next day Joan Knight, Livewire's Marketing Director, sent Nikos a message about an electrically operated can opener, code-named DC01, which Livewire is about to launch.

Subject: DC01
From: Joan Knight
To: Nikos Takakis

I read a report in Business Weekly about new products. Rochester Electronics have put a new can opener on the market. It's electronically operated and looks just like our DC01. Yesterday, I took a look at it in our local stores. It's very similar to ours, with just a few modifications to make it look different. This will cost us money. Do you think someone is leaking information to our rival? Or have we just been unlucky? What action do you think we should take?

Task

You are members of Livewire's board of directors. Hold a meeting to discuss these questions.
1 What is the best way to deal with the bad relations between Valerie Harper and Carl Thomson?
2 What action should you take concerning Carl's behaviour?
3 What action should you take concerning the possible leak of information?

Writing

Choose one of the tasks below. You are Nikos Takakis.

1 Write a letter to Carl Thomson informing him of any action you are taking concerning him, together with your reasons.
2 Write a letter to Valerie Harper telling her how you intend to solve her problem.

 *Writing file* page 142

There is nothing permanent except change.
Heraclitus of Ephesus (535–475 BC), Greek philosopher

OVERVIEW ▼

☐ **Reading**
Managing change

☐ **Listening**
Resistance to change

☐ **Language review**
Reporting

☐ **Skills**
Meetings

☐ **Case study**
Acquiring Metrot

Starting up

Ⓐ Which of these situations would you find the most stressful?

1 Divorce
2 Going on holiday
3 Moving house
4 Moving to another country
5 Losing your job
6 A personality clash with your boss
7 An annual health check-up
8 Being the victim of a robbery

Ⓑ What has been the most significant change in your life?

Ⓒ Which of these business situations would worry you most? Why?

1 You read in the paper that your company will probably be merging with another company.
2 You keep your job after a merger, but you are in a less powerful position.
3 Your company has to relocate to the other side of the city.
4 You are asked to relocate to an exotic foreign country.
5 You are promoted but are now in charge of a hostile workforce.
6 You have to decide who to make redundant in your new department after a merger.

Reading
Managing change

A Jack Welch successfully led General Electric through a period of great change. Do you think he sees change as a danger, an opportunity or a challenge?

B Read the quotations quickly. What is Welch's general attitude to change?

1 'We want to be a company that is constantly renewing itself, leaving the past behind, adapting to change. Managements that hang on to weakness for whatever reason – tradition, sentiment, or their own management weakness – won't be around in the future.'

4 'Gradual change doesn't work very well in the type of transformation General Electric has gone through. If your change isn't big enough, the bureaucracy can beat you. Look at Winston Churchill and Franklin Roosevelt. They said, "This is what it's going to be." And then they did it. Big bold changes.'

2 'How do you bring people into the change process? Start with reality. Get all of the facts out. Give people the rationale for change, laying it out in the clearest, most dramatic terms. When everybody gets the same facts, they'll generally come to the same conclusion.'

5 '(GE leaders always) have enormous energy and the ability to energise and invigorate others, to stimulate and relish change and not be frightened or paralysed by it, and to see change as an opportunity, not a threat.'

3 'The difference between winning and losing will be how the men and women of our company view change. If they see it as a threat, we lose. But if they are provided with the educational tools and are encouraged to use them – to the point where they see change as an opportunity, then every door we must pass through to win big around the world will swing open to us.'

6 'Most bureaucracies unfortunately still think in incremental terms rather than in terms of fundamental change. Changing the culture means constantly asking now how fast am I going, how well am I doing versus how well I did a year or two years before? How fast and how well am I doing compared with the world outside? Are we moving faster, and are we doing better against that external standard?'

Adapted extracts from *Jack Welch Speaks*, by Janet Lowe

C Which quotation:
1 refers to how people react to change?
2 refers to the qualities and abilities that a leader of General Electric should have?
3 gives examples of a famous British and American political leader?
4 suggests that giving people full and clear information is important?
5 suggests that companies that do not change will not survive?

D Write sentences about how companies should or shouldn't react to change, according to Jack Welch.
For example, *Companies should adapt to change; they shouldn't hang on to weaknesses*.

E Underline words and phrases in each quotation which suggest the idea of change. Then compare your list with a partner.

F Find words or phrases in the quotations which mean:
1 the reasons for an action (quotation 2)
2 potential danger (quotation 3)
3 courageous (quotation 4)
4 to enjoy (quotation 5)

Listening
Resistance to change

▲ Jeremy Keeley

A Why do people sometimes resist change? Make a list of reasons.

B 🎧 11.1 Listen to the first part of an interview with Jeremy Keeley, an independent management consultant.
Why do people resist change, in his opinion? List the points he mentions.

C 🎧 11.2 Now listen to the second part of the interview. Jeremy talks about a situation in which change was handled well.
Make notes under the headings below. Then compare notes with a partner.
• Situation   • Chief Executive   • Communication   • Difficult decisions

D Complete these sentences from the interview. Use the words in the box. The words in brackets will help you.

volume	margins	significantly
lead	vision	segment

1 The client had to .... (*considerably*) reduce its costs.
2 It was trying to compete with its major competitor on a basis of .... (*production of large quantities*).
3 The major competitor has a major .... (*a position ahead of all others*).
4 Every single person in the organisation knew this chap's .... (*idea of how the future will be*).
5 They were going to .... the market (*divide the market into parts*).
6 The company was going to go for much larger .... (*difference between a product's price and costs*) and for much more 'value added'.

E Work in small groups. Describe a business or personal situation that involved change. Was the situation handled well or badly?

Language review
Reporting

There are a number of ways to report what people say.
1 If the reporting verb is in the present, there is no tense change.
  'I **hate** change.'   He says he **hates** change.
2 When the reporting verb uses a past tense, we usually move the verb in the other clause one tense back.
  'I'm **leaving** the company.'   He said he **was leaving** the company.
3 We use *would* to report statements about the future with *will*.
  'The meeting **will** start at 2pm.' She said the meeting **would** start at 2pm.
4 When reporting *yes/no* questions, we use *if* or *whether*. Change the tense if necessary.
  'Are you happy in your job?'   She asked me **if** I **was** happy in my job.
5 If a question begins with a question word, we report the question using a different word order.
  'Why **don't you like** your boss?'   He asked me why **I didn't like** my boss.

 page 139

A A management consultant is helping to introduce changes at a large engineering company. He has prepared a summary for the Chairman about a recent management meeting.
Change the words in italics into what the people actually said.
For example, *'I'm looking forward to the changes'*. (Head of Finance)

The Head of Finance said (1) *he was looking forward to the changes* and (2) *wanted to know when the report would be published*. The publication date will be decided by the end of the week.

The Head of Research and Development was very unhappy and complained that (3) *nobody ever told her anything*. I think that the most resistance to change will come from her department.

The Head of Personnel was worried about the impact on staff morale brought about by job losses. She said that (4) *many staff had taken time off work*. I would add that this is the standard symptom of resistance to change and you often see increased levels of sickness and absenteeism at the beginning of a change process, along with unco-operative attitudes.

As you predicted, the Sales and Marketing Departments were both in favour of change. The Head of Sales wondered (5) *whether we could bring forward the next round of changes*.

The Head of Marketing said that (6) *we needed to recognise that resistance to change was natural*. The Head of Production pointed out that (7) *the changes did not affect the shop floor workers, but they should know what was going on*.

B The engineering company in Exercise A held a meeting for staff to discuss the changes. Report the comments below. Use reporting verbs such as *say, ask, wonder, complain, emphasise,* and *add*.
For example, *Klaus said that he didn't understand why it was happening.*

Klaus   I don't understand why this is happening.

Joel   I'm very worried about the future.

Lisa   I feel out of control of the situation.

Maria   What's going to happen to me?

Diego   The new system will bring many benefits. It's good for all the staff.

Lydia   Nobody asked me what I thought.

Rosa   Will we have any training on the new computers?

Claudia   I don't trust the decision makers.

Ludmilla I welcome the changes. They'll improve the company a lot.

John   They introduced the changes too soon. Everybody was surprised.

C Work as one group. Note down some changes you would like to make in a company or organisation that you know.

Then form smaller groups. Discuss the advantages and disadvantages of the proposed changes. Take notes about points being made.

Finally form pairs or small groups consisting of members from each meeting. Report what was said in your meeting.

Skills
Meetings

TAX

~AFTER YOU...

'There are three things you can predict in life: tax, death and more meetings.'

Mike Moore,
Sydney Morning Herald

A Ask each other about the meetings you attend. Use these question words: *What kind? Where? When? Why? How often? Who?*

B Why are meetings sometimes either a) successful, or b) unsuccessful? Discuss the reasons and note your ideas. For example:

Good meetings	Bad meetings
Clear objectives	*Chairperson talks too much*

C Match the words in the box to the definitions below.

> agenda   chair   propose   attend
> to send your apologies   item   vote   any other business (AOB)
> participants   second   minutes   action points

1 the person in charge of a meeting
2 the people at a meeting
3 to go to a meeting
4 a list of topics to be discussed
5 one topic on the list
6 the last topic on the list

7 to make a suggestion formally
8 to support a formal suggestion
9 a method of making a decision
10 an official record of what was said and/or decided
11 to say that you cannot go to a meeting
12 what needs to be done after the meeting, and by whom

D 11.3 Read the agenda below. Then listen to the meeting. Tick the expressions in the Useful language box on page 91 that you hear.

AGENDA
Senior Managers' Meeting

Subject: *Changes in working practices*

DATE 1 July
TIME 11.00am – 12.30pm
VENUE Main Board Room, Head Office

1. Bonus scheme

2. Security

3. Open plan office

4. Hot-desking

E The expressions below are also used in the meeting. Put them under appropriate headings in the Useful language box.

Yes, that's true I suppose.   *I'm just not happy about this proposal.*
You've got a point there.   *How do you feel about this, Nancy?*

Useful language

Stating aims
Our main purpose will be to explore your views.
The aim of this meeting is ...

Disagreeing
I don't agree.
Point taken, but surely ... is an important factor?
I really can't agree with you there.

Asking for opinions
Stefan, what do you think?
Stefan?

Agreeing
I agree with Max.
I think so too.

Dealing with interruptions
Can I finish the point?
Let Stefan finish please, Max.

Giving opinions
I really think we need a report.
Shouldn't we have more information?
We feel ... is the best way to ...

Requesting action
Can you arrange a meeting?
Would you prepare a short report please?

Asking for clarification
Can you explain it a bit more clearly?
What exactly do you mean?
Can I get this clear?

F Read the information below and study the company organisation chart. Then role play the meeting. Your teacher will tell you which role to take.

For over 50 years, Stirling Cars has been making a classic English sports car. The car is mostly handmade, in the company's factory in northern England.

Stirling Cars produces approximately 500 cars a year. If you want to buy a Stirling car, you must wait four to five years before it is delivered. In spite of this, demand for the car is strong. However, production costs are rising each year and the company needs to increase its profits.

The top managers disagree about how to increase profitability. At the next management meeting, they will consider the four options below.

1 Automate production of the car to make about 4,000 cars a year.

2 Subcontract the manufacture of the engine to another firm, to increase production by 10% to 20%.

3 Use more mechanised tools to make the body and increase production by around 10%.

4 Raise the price of the car by around 40% and move to a bigger factory so that production can be increased.

J. Stirling, Managing Director
(turn to page 152)

L. Dickinson, Sales Director
(turn to page 150)

B. Reilly, Production Manager
(turn to page 155)

C. Bristol, Finance Director
(turn to page 157)

F. Densham, Sales Manager
(turn to page 154)

S. Dubois, Production Controller
(turn to page 156)

Background

Last June, readers of the business magazine, *Investor International*, were given some information about the Cornerstone Group.

COMPANY PROFILE

Company:	**Cornerstone Group**
Workforce:	**35,000**
Turnover:	**$4.1bn**
Located:	**Dallas, US**
Net profit:	**11% of turnover (approx.)**

Main Activities

Providing services and products for the oil, gas and electricity industries.

Recent developments

Cornerstone have recently bought the French white goods company, Jean Metrot, cie. Metrot are well known for producing cookers and refrigerators, as well as a range of household appliances. They have their headquarters to the east of Paris, and two other factories in northern France.

Reasons for Cornerstone's acquisition

1. Cornerstone will expand sales of Metrot products in Europe.
2. It will use Metrot as a base for launching its own products in Europe.
3. Metrot's biggest asset is its valuable land. Cornerstone could use this to grow the company or may sell off some of the land to finance the acquisition.

Comment

Metrot is an excellent acquisition. There may be problems when US style management is introduced. Metrot has always been family-owned, and Chief Executive, Jean Metrot, takes a personal interest in his employees.

The new Chief Executive will be Hugh Whitman. In his early 30s, trained at Harvard University, Whitman was formerly Executive Vice President of the Cornerstone Group.

Jean Metrot will remain on the board as an adviser.

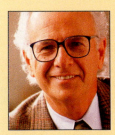

Jean Metrot   **Hugh Whitman**

🎧 **11.4** The new Chief Executive of Metrot gave a television interview for *European Business News*. He was asked about Cornerstone's plans for Metrot. Listen and note what he says.

Problems

It is now nine months later. The change of ownership and new management style at Metrot have caused many problems. The memo below illustrates some of the difficulties.

MEMO ───────────────────────────

To: **Dan Johnson, Personnel Director**

From: **Jacques Lafont, Union Organiser**

Subject: **Staff morale**   Date: **March 18**

Staff are very unhappy with the present changes.
As a result, productivity has fallen and staff turnover is high. Let me summarise some of the reasons for the staff's low morale.

1. **Factory inspections**   American managers are always checking up on us and taking notes. No one knows why they are doing this or what they are up to.

2. **Redundancies**   Since June, about 60 employees from the Development Department have lost their jobs. They were given no reasons. The staff think that this is unprofessional.

3. **Further changes**   People are looking for new jobs elsewhere. They want to move before they are pushed. People are afraid that the new management will relocate both of the factories.

4. **Management style**   Staff constantly complain about the silly changes the new management are making. I enclose a list of comments made to me by our members.
   - 'They're trying to do everything too fast – A new computer system, learning English, and maybe other languages, new product ranges, new customers.'
   - 'There was a family atmosphere before. The management really cared about us. Everything was more informal.'
   - 'We don't know where the company is going now. We've no idea what our strategy is, what our objectives are.'
   - 'We get e-mail messages from Dallas telling us what to do. Surely they can trust the management over here to make the policies and decisions?'

Task

A meeting of senior managers has been called to resolve the problems. One team, led by the new Chief Executive, Hugh Whitman, consists of American executives. The other is made up of senior executives of Metrot who have kept their jobs under the new management.
Divide into two groups: Cornerstone executives and executives of Metrot. Each group prepares separately for the meeting. Then hold the meeting as one group.
The Agenda is as follows:

1 Reasons for the resistance to change.
2 Suggestions for managing the change more effectively.
3 Action plan to raise staff morale and resolve the present problems.

Writing

Write the action minutes for the above meeting.

 Writing file page 145

Strategy

> *Strategies are okayed in boardrooms that even a child would say are bound to fail. The problem is, there is never a child in the boardroom.*
>
> Victor Palmieri, Italian turnaround expert

Starting up

A **What is strategy? Which of these definitions do you prefer? Why?**

1 Strategy is making predictions based on analysis.

2 Strategy is having a clear plan, then putting it into action.

3 Strategy is continually adapting to change.

B **Which groups below should be involved in deciding strategy? Why?**

shareholders	middle and junior managers	suppliers
boards of directors	government representatives	other employees
senior managers	trade union representatives	customers

Vocabulary
Different strategies

A **Match the terms below with the definitions. Then use three of the terms to complete the newspaper extract on the opposite page.**

d 1 a takeover   **a)** combining two or more companies

b 2 a joint venture   **b)** when two or more companies agree to work on a project

a 3 a merger   **c)** an agreement between companies to cooperate in certain business activities

c 4 an alliance   **d)** buying enough shares in a company to get control of it

BUSINESS IN BRIEF

Glaxo buys 80% stake in Polish drug group

Glaxo Wellcome, one of the world's leading pharmaceutical companies, is paying $220m (£131.7m) to take an 80% stake in Polfa Poznan, Poland's second largest drugs group. The ....[1] is the biggest made by a western pharmaceuticals producer in east Europe.

Canal Plus and Pathe in film distribution link

Canal Plus and Pathe, two of France's largest media and entertainment groups, are joining forces to form a pan-European network of film distribution companies. Their new ....[2] will negotiate the acquisition of cinema, television and video rights for pictures across Europe, both with the Hollywood studios and other European film producers.

Elf pays $528m to take 5% stake in Russian group

Elf Aquitaine, the French company, is to form a strategic ....[3] with Yuksi of Russia, paying $528m (£316m) for a 5% stake in the country's largest oil company.

B Discuss the meaning of these strategies. Use a good dictionary to help you.

cost cutting   a demerger   rationalisation

a sell off   a disposal   an economy drive   acquisition

1 Which of the above strategies can be used by companies to
   a) get bigger?   **b)** get smaller?   **c)** become more efficient?

2 Which are likely to result in people losing their jobs?

C The verbs and nouns below are often combined when talking about strategy. Make word partnerships. Then use them to write five sentences. For example, *The company has achieved its target of a 20% market share.*

Verb			Noun		
achieve	review	develop	goal	objective	target
implement	set	employ	plan	strategy	tactics

Discussion

Mission statements

A Some companies state their strategy publicly in *mission statements*. What are the advantages and disadvantages of doing this?

B Read these mission statements. What is each company trying to achieve?

1 The business of Newcastle United is football – our aim is to play attractive football, to win trophies, to satisfy our supporters and shareholders and to continually improve our position as a top European club.

(Newcastle United plc)

2 Glaxo Wellcome is a research-based company whose people are committed to fighting disease by bringing innovative medicines and services to patients throughout the world and to the healthcare providers who serve them.

(Glaxo Wellcome)

3 Pret creates handmade, natural food, avoiding the obscure chemicals, additives and preservatives common to so much of the 'prepared' and 'fast' food on the market today.

(Pret a Manger)

C Discuss these statements. Do you agree with them? Give your reasons.

1 'Small is beautiful' is a better strategy in business than 'big is best'.

2 Big companies should aim to gain market share rather than make profits.

3 Companies should focus on what they do best rather than diversify.

A Discuss these questions.

1 Why do firms merge?

2 What problems can arise before and after a merger takes place?

B In the interview below a Chief Executive describes how he and his board decided whether to merge with a larger company in the same industry. Read the interview and note down the arguments for and against the merger.

An Interview with **John T. Chambers**, Chief Executive, Cisco Systems

A merger of equals had a lot of appeal. If you combine the Number 1 and Number 2 players in an industry, by
5 definition you're Number 1 in terms of size. And when you are growing that fast, you have a number of key management openings you have to fill. By combining two companies with good management teams, you automatically build up
10 the strength of your management and you do it quickly. You can also widen your customer base and have more distribution channels.

In addition, the merger automatically makes your remaining competition second level. As a
15 result, your competition must rethink its strategy. In the end, you force a period of mergers and acquisitions on your competition. They have no choice but to respond to the changes you initiated.
20 When we looked more closely, our concerns were raised. For example, 50 percent of large-scale mergers fail. Mergers can fail on a number of levels. They can fail in terms of their benefit to the shareholders, customers, employees and
25 business partners. A decision has to be right with each of those groups, or we would not go forward with it.

If you merge two companies that are growing at 80 percent rates, you stand a very
30 good chance of stopping both of them. That's a fact. For a period of time, no matter how smoothly they operate, you lose momentum.

Our industry is not like the banking industry, where you are acquiring branch banks and
35 customers. In our industry, you are acquiring people. And if you don't keep those people, you have made a terrible, terrible investment. We pay between $500,000 and $2 million per person in an acquisition. So you can
40 understand that if you don't keep the people, you've done a tremendous disservice to your shareholders. So we focus first on the people and how we incorporate them into our company, and then we focus on how to drive the business.

From *Thought leaders*, Joel Kurtzman

C Choose the best answer.
When Cisco Systems buys another company it pays special attention to:
a) the money it has spent   b) the staff it acquires
c) the opinions of its shareholders

D What is the most interesting point that Chambers makes, in your opinion? Explain why.

When you learn a new verb it is important to know which prepositions can follow it.

- Some verbs are regularly followed by one preposition:
  *You can depend **on** that.*
- Other verbs may be followed by a number of prepositions:
  *agree **with**, agree **on**, agree **to**, agree **about**.*

A good dictionary, such as the *Longman Dictionary of Contemporary English*, will help you by listing the most common dependent prepositions after each verb.

 page 139

A Match the verbs below to the correct prepositions.
Then check your answers in the John Chambers interview on page 96.

1	build	**a)** to	**b)** up	**c)** of	(paragraph 1)
2	respond	**a)** to	**b)** on	**c)** at	(paragraph 2)
3	focus	**a)** to	**b)** with	**c)** on	(paragraph 5)
4	incorporate	**a)** to	**b)** into	**c)** at	(paragraph 5)

B Complete these sentences with a verb and a preposition from each box.

agree	apologise
think	hear refer

	for	about
about	with	to

1 The CEO thinks a joint venture is the best way to break into the Russian market, but I don't .... him.

2 Did you .... the alliance between Lufthansa and SIA?

3 If you .... the annual report it clearly sets out the facts.

4 What do you .... the latest news on the proposed merger?

5 The Chairman had to .... misleading the shareholders at the AGM.

C Write endings to complete the sentences below.

1 The Sales Director apologised ...

2 The R&D department succeeded ...

3 We all agree ...

4 The safety inspector insists ...

5 You can never rely ...

6 The Board's job is to focus ...

7 We are looking forward ...

8 Several managers don't approve ...

D Complete this letter to shareholders. Use appropriate forms of these verbs.

rely on	combine with	consist of	advise on	succeed in
budget for	spend on	account for	compete with	invest in

Dear Shareholder,

    I write to inform you that the Board has received information of a takeover bid for your company. This ....[1] an attempt by Thor Engineering to acquire a controlling interest by offering to purchase shares at a price of 650 pence. We have brought in a team of consultants to ....[2] the tactics we should use to resist the bid.

    Although the offer seems attractive, it does not reflect the true value of the company or take into account our future prospects. We have ....[3] a major programme of expansion. During the next two years we plan to ....[4] new plant and equipment. We have also allocated funds to ....[5] a new computerised stock control system which will allow us to ....[6] our much larger rivals. Furthermore, we plan to ....[7] a machine tool company in a joint venture in China. We are confident this will allow the company to ....[8] opening up new markets in Asia.

    Policies like these ....[9] our success to date and contribute to our vision of the future. Therefore, we strongly advise you not to accept Thor Engineering's offer. You can ....[10] the Board to keep you fully informed of any future developments, but for the present we advise you to take no action in relation to the offer.

Yours faithfully

Derek Hammond

Derek Hammond
Chairman

Listening
Developing a strategy

▲ Marjorie Scardino

A You will hear an interview with Marjorie Scardino, Chief Executive of the media group Pearson plc. Before you listen, choose the best definition for each of the underlined words below.

1 The assets of a company are
   a) the customers they have.
   b) the things they own.
   c) the markets they are in.

2 If a company improves its cash generation
   a) it increases its sales revenue.
   b) it has cash available at all times.
   c) it invests more in its business.

3 If a company disposes of an asset, it
   a) values it.   b) keeps it.   c) sells it.

4 If companies have an authoritarian way of management
   a) the management give responsibility to workers at lower levels.
   b) the management keep tight control over everyone and everything.
   c) the management have many ways of communicating with employees.

5 If you stitch two materials together, you
   a) separate them.   b) cut them.   c) join them.

B 🎧 12.1 Listen to the first part of the interview and make notes. Then complete the summary of what she says.

Developing a strategy

First, the management thought about five things:

1 The assets of the company.
2 What's unique about those assets.
3 *markets*
4 *markets growing*
Which 5 *best use of assets*
markets

They considered all these things, then they developed a strategy.

Their strategy consisted of three simple steps:

The first step
operate better, ↑ profits cash generation value to shareholder

The second step
locate assets which ones keep which dispose of

The third step
stitch together businesses to use assets

C 🎧 12.2 Now listen to the second part of the interview. Which of the trends below are mentioned?

1 Companies are becoming more international. ✓ *globalism*
2 Employees are becoming more valued by management. ✓ *Assets*
3 People are working more in teams. ✓
4 Management are having more control over staff.
5 Management are changing their style. ✓ *collegiality*

D Answer these questions.

1 What strategies impress Marjorie Scardino? *clear define unique goal.*
2 What three points does she make about Coca-Cola's strategy?
   integration distribution

E Discuss these questions.

1 Is the trend towards globalism that she mentions a good or bad thing?
2 Do you think Coca-Cola will have to change its strategy in the future? How?

Skills
Decision-making

A **Discuss these questions.**

1 Is decision-making only about sensible, rational choices?
Should emotion play a part? What about when choosing the following?

a wife or husband	a present for someone	a new company logo
a holiday destination	a new product to develop	someone for a job

2 Think of an important decision that you have made. How did you decide?

3 Do men and women have different ways of making decisions?

4 Who makes the big decisions in your household? Why?

B **Which ideas below do you agree with? Which do you disagree with? Why?**

1 Before making a decision:
  a) write down the pros and cons.   d) have a sleep or a rest.
  b) try to reduce stress.   e) consult a horoscope.
  c) take a long time.   f) ask as many people as possible.

2 If a choice has cost you a lot of time and money, stick to it.

3 Rely on the past to help you make a decision.

4 Reduce all decisions to a question of money.

5 Be totally democratic in group decision-making.

C 12.3 **Listen to the management of a retail group discussing problems at their store in Paris. Tick the expressions in the Useful language box that you hear.**

Useful language

Asking for the facts
Can you bring us up to date?
Can you give us the background?
Where do we stand with ... ?

Making a suggestion
We should sell out as soon as
   possible.
Why don't we sell out?

Disagreeing
I don't agree with that at all.
I totally disagree.

Identifying needs
We've got to get more information.
We need more information about
   where we're going wrong.

Agreeing
You're absolutely right.
I totally agree with you.

Expressing doubt
I am worried about the store's
   location.
I'm not sure about it.

Making a decision
The solution, then, is to keep the
   store going.
I think on balance we feel we
   should keep the store going.

Stating future action
So, the next thing to do is ...
What we've got to do now is ...

D **Marion Haynes, a well-known writer on decision-making, recommends eight steps for making decisions. Use her approach to do the role play below.**

1 Discuss and analyse the situation.   5 Think of alternatives.
2 Define the problem.   6 Decide how to evaluate them.
3 Set an objective.   7 Evaluate alternatives.
4 State what is essential and desirable. 8 Choose among alternatives.

> **You are board members in a manufacturing firm which employs 500 people. As your company is making a loss, you must cut costs. Hold a meeting to choose *one* of the following options. State what action you intend to take.**
>
> • Cut factory workers' wages by 10%   • Make 50 employees redundant
> • Reduce everyone's salary by 8%   • Pay no end-of-year bonuses

CASE STUDY

TEXAN CHICKEN

Background

Texan Chicken was founded by Eva and Ramon Martinez. They had had no previous experience in the restaurant industry. They opened their first restaurant in West London, and within five years had built up a chain of 40 outlets, using a franchising system.

The reason for their success was the quality of their product. Their delicious fried chicken was based on a recipe that Ramon had discovered when travelling in Texas. It was served with a sauce which varied from mild to very hot, depending on the customer's taste. All the restaurants offered a take-out service, which was popular with customers.

When Texan Chicken went public the share price rose by 120% within a week. There seemed to be no limit to Texan Chicken's profits and expansion.

Present situation

Unfortunately the company's share price has fallen recently by over 80%. There has also been strong pressure on Eva and Ramon Martinez to resign as co-chairmen of the business. At present, they own 40% of the shares. The other major shareholder is a South African businessman, Martin Webb, who owns 12%. Eva and Ramon Martinez have called in a team of management consultants to advise them on their future strategy.

🎧 12.4 Listen to this interview on Business News, a daily radio programme in which experts comment on topical business items. Note down four problems facing the business.

Texan Chicken recently did a survey to find out what its customers thought about its restaurants. Here are the results.

CONSUMER SURVEY (summary)

Customers

Age:
18–30	58%
30–40	32%
40+	10%

Sex:
Male	54%
Female	46%

Status:
Single	65%
Married, no children	23%
Married, with children	12%

How often customers visit the restaurants

First visit	8%
More than once a week	5%
Once a week to once a fortnight	29%

Food products bought most often

1 Quarter chicken, salad and rice
2 Chicken breast burger

Customers' opinions (%)

	good	OK	poor
Quality/freshness of food	40	50	10
Value for money	10	30	60
Service	8	38	54
Cleanliness	6	14	80
Friendliness of staff	24	48	28
Decor	1	34	65

Task

You are members of the management consultant team called in by Eva and Ramon Martinez to advise them on their future strategy. Discuss the options below. Consider any other ideas for improving profitability. Work out a plan of action which will turn the company round.

Options

The following options will be discussed by the management consultants at their next meeting.

1 Persuade Eva and Ramon Martinez to resign. Appoint a new Chief Executive with extensive experience of franchising in the food industry.

2 Seek opportunities to merge with a large fast food company which could offer management expertise and financial resources.

3 Improve profits by expanding in Europe through joint ventures. A German supermarket chain has already shown interest in such a venture.

4 Make major changes in the business. For example:
  a) Have more company-owned outlets. This would give greater control over the restaurants.
  b) Offer special promotions (e.g. huge discounts on certain meals).
  c) Launch a major advertising campaign.

Writing

Prepare a press release for distribution to the national press. Give information about Texan Chicken's strategy to improve the company's performance. Its purpose is to reassure investors that Texan Chicken has excellent future prospects.

Cultures

'The limits of my language mean the limits of my world.'

Ludwig Wittgenstein(1889–1951), Austrian philosopher

Starting up

A What is culture? Choose the four factors below which you think are the most important in creating a culture.

climate	language	social customs and traditions
institutions	arts	historical events
ideas and beliefs	religion	ceremonies and festivals
cuisine	geography	

B What do you miss most about your country or culture when you go abroad?

C Why is cultural awareness important for business people? Give examples.

D Do you think cultures are becoming more alike? Is this a good or bad thing? For example, think about:

- improved communications
- cheap foreign travel
- global business
- trading groups (EU, ASEAN, etc.)

E How important are the following things when doing business in your country? Are they: a) important b) not important, or c) best avoided?

and in Canada?

- exchanging business cards
- shaking hands
- kissing
- socialising with contacts
- small talk before meetings
- accepting interruption
- using first names
- formality (how you dress, how you talk to colleagues, what names you use, etc.)
- punctuality
- humour
- giving presents
- being direct (saying exactly what you think)

Listening

Cultural awareness

A 🎧 **13.1 Listen to the first part of an interview with Claire Bebbington, External Affairs Manager for a division of BP (British Petroleum). Tick the correct row for each of the four countries in the chart.**

	Turkey	Malaysia	Papua New Guinea	Colombia
	✓			✓
This country wanted to show a modern and developed image.		✓		
This country is sensitive to how it presents itself to the outside world.	✓			✓
In this country the culture in the capital is very different from the provinces.				✓
In this country people in the mountains are different from those by the coast.			✓	

B 🎧 **13.2 Now listen to the second part of the interview. Answer these questions.**

1 Claire talks about the ways that culture affects business. What examples does she give? *attitudes towards work – working in teams*
   – be open minded
   – solving probs

2 What is emphasised in Anglo-American culture? *action, doing, achieving.*

3 What mistake is it easy for people to make?
   Shouldn't dismiss it as ...
   – consensus – not time wasting.

Reading
Business across cultures

A The chief executives of two British-based companies have produced a ten-point guide on how to export successfully to Japan.
Before you read the article, predict what advice they will give.
Make suggestions under the headings *Do* and *Don't*.

B Read the *first sentence only* of each paragraph in the article.
Were any of your guesses correct?

C Now read the whole article. Then, summarise the information.
Use the headings below.

- language
- personal contact
- patience
- middlemen
- currency
- dialect, climate, culture
- country of origin
- meals
- customer visits
- gifts

Liverpool to Tokyo

Ian Hamilton Fazey examines a ten-point guide to doing export business in Japan.

Boodle & Dunthorne is a jewellery designer and retailer. Joloda makes equipment for loading goods on trucks. Both are based in Liverpool, UK. The chief executives are Martin Wainwright (Boodle & Dunthorne) and Wojtek Kordel (Joloda).

1. Be prepared for important cultural and language difficulties. This may seem obvious but some people try to get by in Japan without hiring a good interpreter who can also explain Japanese traditions and customs.

2. Trade on personal contact at a senior level. This is more important than trading on price. Physical presence matters. Only now, after 10 years of selling to Japan, is Joloda introducing a new salesperson. Wainwright says regular exhibitions at national trade shows in Japan is critical to building a profile in the sector you sell to.

3. Patience pays dividends. It may take several visits before an order comes through. Boodle & Dunthorne took about 16 months to get going and Wainwright spent £40,000 before getting an order. He had gone back to the UK from a trade show ready to call it a day when his sales manager, who was due to follow him the next day, got a call to see the Mitsui Corporation three days later. Boodle & Dunthorne was suddenly in.

4. Avoid middlemen so as to speed delivery. Joloda uses an agent in Japan but was able to give faster service by minimising the length of its distribution chain. Boodle & Dunthorne employs Rebecca Hawkins, a leading designer, and manufactures its own jewellery, so providing a fast, direct service with original designs.

5. Quote in local currency. Your bank should be able to help you; if it cannot, change banks.

6. There are wide variations in dialect, climate and culture. You may need a different distributor in Osaka from Tokyo, for example — and a different interpreter — because your Tokyo man may well not have the right network of contacts.

7. Emphasise your product's country of origin. Britain, say Kordel and Wainwright, is seen as quaint, old fashioned, but full of history. Whether you sell jewellery or engineering products, stress any hand crafting of your goods and the heritage of the city where you are based.

8. Develop your intuition. Wainwright and Kordel say a culture of politeness prevents the Japanese from expressing dislike and disagreement. If they visit you in the UK, Wainwright says to remember they do not usually eat big meals or too much meat. Fish restaurants are safer.

9. Some of Joloda's customers from the regions are unfamiliar with western culture. Kordel advises that UK visits by them should be well-supervised from arrival to departure, with an interpreter provided at all times.

10. Offer gifts. 'The Japanese enjoy giving and receiving beautifully presented gifts,' Kordel says. 'Status is critical, so a prestigious brand is appreciated best. However, it is not the value of the gift, but the fact it is a present from you that counts,' says Wainwright.

From the Financial Times

FINANCIAL TIMES
World business newspaper.

D Prepare a list of *dos* and *don'ts* for business people visiting your country (or one you know well). Give business tips or more general cultural ones.

E Present your ideas to your colleagues. Answer any questions they have.

Language review
Modal verbs

There are nine modal verbs in English. Fill in the missing letters.

1 ca _   **2** co _ _ _   **3** sha _ _   **4** sho _ _ _   **5** wi _ _

6 wo _ _ _   **7** ma _   **8** mi _ _ _   **9** mu _ _

- Modal verbs can express ability, obligation, permission, possibility, probability, and requests.
- Modals are always the first word in a verb group.
  For example, *We **must call** them tomorrow.*
- Modals have only one form. There is no 's' form for the third person singular of the present tense. There are no *-ing* or *-ed* forms.
- Modals are not followed by an infinitive with *to*. page 140

A These sentences are from the article on page 104 and the interview on page 103. Decide if each example is expressing ability, obligation, permission, possibility, probability, or a request.

1 This *may* seem obvious but some people try to get by in Japan without hiring a good interpreter.

2 It *may* take several visits before an order comes through.

3 If it *cannot* (help you), change banks.

4 You *may* need a different distributor in Osaka from Tokyo.

5 *Can* you tell me any problem you've had?

6 *Can* you think of any other examples?

7 It's very important to be as open-minded as you possibly *can*.

8 *Could* you tell me about yourself, please?

9 You *should* be aware of a number of things.

B Match the first part of each statement to the second part.
Find as many correct sentences as possible.

1 I will		**a)** as I'm giving a presentation.
2 I can		**b)** because I promised Susan.
3 I may		**c)** as it's part of my job description.
4 I might		**d)** because I'm free, but I don't really want to.
5 I should	go to the meeting	**e)** since I'm free all day.
6 I would	tomorrow ...	**f)** as I've just decided it's important.
7 I shall		**g)** if I had the time, but I'm too busy.
8 I could		**h)** if I get back from the sales trip in time.
9 I must		**i)** but I'm not sure.

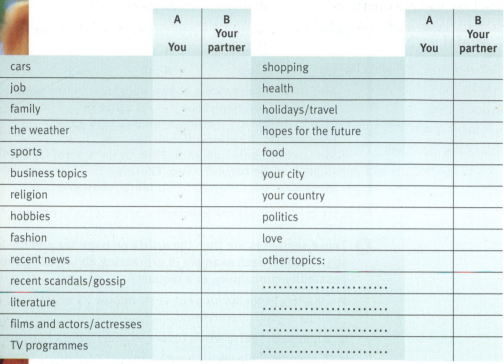

Skills

Social English

A **What do you like to talk about when you meet business people for the first time?**

1 Tick the things that you like to talk about in column A. Put a cross next to the things you don't like. Add more topics to the list.

2 Find out what the person next to you likes to talk about. Fill in column B.

	A You	B Your partner		A You	B Your partner
cars	✓		shopping		
job	✓		health		
family	✓		holidays/travel		
the weather	✓		hopes for the future		
sports	✗		food		
business topics	✓		your city		
religion	✗		your country		
hobbies	✓		politics		
fashion			love		
recent news			other topics:		
recent scandals/gossip			....		
literature			....		
films and actors/actresses			....		
TV programmes			....		

B **Have a conversation with your partner about topics you both like talking about. Show interest in what they say and try to keep the conversation going. Find out what things you have in common.**

C **In what business situations would you use the words and expressions below? Discuss your ideas with a partner.**

Congratulations!	I don't mind.	I'm afraid ...
Cheers!	Excuse me.	Please ...
Make yourself at home.	Sorry.	Could you ... ?
Help yourself.	It's on me.	That sounds good.

D **What would you say in the following situations?**

1 You don't hear someone's name when you are introduced to them.
2 You have to refuse an invitation to dinner with a supplier.
3 You are offered food which you hate.
4 You want to end a conversation in a diplomatic way.
5 You have to greet a visitor.
6 You have to introduce two people to each other at work.
7 You have to introduce two people to each other at a party.
8 You have to propose a toast.
9 Your colleague's been made redundant.
10 You arrive half an hour late for a business lunch.

E **Match the questions on the left with the answers on the right.**

1 Is this your first visit to the Far East?
2 Oh really. What do you do?
3 Where are you based?
4 How long have you been there?
5 Have you been to Hong Kong before?
6 Business or pleasure?
7 How long have you been here?
8 How long are you staying?
9 Where are you staying?
10 Is it comfortable?
11 What's the food like?
12 So, what do you think of Hong Kong?

a) In the UK, in Oxford.
b) Nearly ten years.
c) No, I come here quite often.
d) No. Actually this is my first trip.
e) I'm the Marketing Director for a small import–export company.
f) Business I'm afraid.
g) Till tomorrow night.
h) A week.
i) I really like it. There's a lot to do.
j) It's good, but eating in the Peninsular can be quite expensive.
k) Very! And it has a great view over the harbour.
l) At the Peninsular Hotel.

F **How important are the following for a successful conversation?**

Listen carefully.   Be polite.   Stay silent.
Give only *yes* or   Interrupt a lot.   Keep eye contact.
  no answers.   Ask questions.   Be friendly.

G **You are attending an international conference on 'cultural awareness'.**

1 Invent a new identity for yourself. Then fill in the form with the details.
2 The night before the conference you attend a dinner for all the delegates. Find out as much as possible about the person next to you and tell them about yourself. Show interest and try to keep the conversation going.

Name:	Languages spoken:
Age:	Time with company:
Nationality:	Why you are at the conference:
Family:	Foreign countries lived in or visited:
University:	How you travelled to the conference:
Subjects studied:	Future plans:
Company:	Hobbies or interests:
Company activity:	Other information:
Position:	One interesting thing you did or that happened to you recently:
Responsibilities:	

• **Turn to pages 148 and 149 to play The social-cultural game.**

CASE STUDY

Visitors from China

Background

Toyworld is a profitable toy retailer based in Seattle, US, with subsidiaries in over 30 countries. Toyworld buys its products from suppliers all over the world.

Mr Lee Chung, head of a toy manufacturing firm based in Guandong, China, is going to visit the Toyworld subsidiary in your country. He will be accompanied by his Export Manager, John Wong. The purpose of his visit is to get to know Toyworld's management better and to learn more about the company. He may set up a joint venture with Toyworld if he has confidence in them and considers them to be a suitable partner. This is Mr Chung and Mr Wong's first visit to your company, and to your country.

Task

You are members of the planning committee for Mr Chung's visit. Read the documents. Then, plan a draft programme in small groups. After that, compare your ideas with the rest of the class and produce the final programme.

Toyworld Senior Managers

CHIEF EXECUTIVE
|
Managing Director

Finance Director — Marketing Director — Warehouse Manager

Personnel Manager — Chief Accountant — Sales Manager — Public Relations Manager — Advertising Manager — Transport and Distribution Manager

Chief Buyer — **Administrative staff: 82; Warehouse workers: 20**

MEMO

From: Chief Executive
To: Manager, Public Relations   Date: 2 June

Subject: Mr Lee Chung's visit

Mr Lee Chung and Mr John Wong will arrive at 9.10am on Monday 20 June and leave on Thursday, 23 June.

When you prepare the draft programme, please schedule a meeting (morning or afternoon) during which we can discuss our business plans with Mr Chung and Mr Wong. Also, make sure that our visitors have opportunities to meet our staff and gain a complete understanding of our business.

Above all, we do not want to make any cultural mistakes during the visit. We want Mr Chung and Mr Wong to leave with an excellent impression of our company and the way we treat foreign visitors.

To help you plan the visit, I enclose some comments from our manager in Hong Kong, Kenneth Eng. He knows both our visitors well, and he is an expert on Chinese business culture.

1. Chinese relationships are built on personal trust and respect. Everything you do during the visit must show that you consider Mr Chung and Mr Wong to be important people.
2. Relationship building activities and a successful social programme will be more important than the business meeting.
3. Mr Chung communicates fairly well in English, but has some problems understanding difficult expressions. Mr Wong has a much higher level of English.
4. Both men are rather fussy about food. For example, Mr Chung was unhappy when he had to attend a wine and cheese party last year – he hates cheese! They both enjoy high quality alcoholic drinks.
5. Your visitors will expect to have some basic information about Toyworld, and to be offered activities which give them a better understanding of the company.
6. Mr Chung and Mr Wong will be particularly interested in your warehousing facility and in your sales network.
7. Be careful about topics for discussion at social events. Do not embarrass your visitors by introducing 'difficult' topics.
8. They will be eager to learn about life in your country and about its culture.
9. Punctuality is very important to Mr Chung. He gets angry if people arrive late for a meeting – he thinks it shows a lack of respect.
10. 'Sincerity' is a word which Mr Chung and Mr Wong use frequently. They value it a lot.

Good luck with the visit!

Kenneth Eng

Best wishes,
Kenneth Eng

Key questions for the planning committee

1 Where will the visitors stay?
2 Who will meet them? What transport will be used?
3 What arrangements should be made for meals?
4 When will the business meeting take place?
5 What topics would be suitable for discussion at meals?
6 How will the visitors be entertained? Trips? Special events?
7 What gifts would be suitable? When and how should they be given?
8 Should there be local press and television coverage?
9 Is it necessary to provide an interpreter?
10 Any other arrangements to encourage 'relationship building'?

Writing

As Marketing Director at Toyworld, send a fax to Mr Chung with details of the programme for his visit. The tone of the fax should be friendly and show that you and your colleagues are looking forward to meeting him soon.

 Writing file page 143

Leadership

" We all work together as a team. And that means you do everything I say. "

Michael Caine, British film actor (in the film *The Italian Job*)

Starting up

Ⓐ Discuss these questions.

1 What do you know about the leaders pictured above?
Compare your answers with the information on page 150.

2 Which modern or historical leaders do you most admire?
Which do you admire least? Why?

3 What makes a great leader? Write down a list of characteristics.
Compare your list with other groups.

4 Are there differences between men and women as leaders?

5 Are people who were leaders at school more likely to be leaders later in life?

6 What makes a bad boss? Draw up a profile of factors.

7 What is the difference between a *manager* and a *leader*?

**Ⓑ Think of someone in a position of power. List three positive and three
negative things about them. Then compare ideas with a partner.**

Vocabulary
Describing character

A Which adjectives below describe positive aspects of someone's character? Which describe negative aspects? Write + or - next to each one.

decisive	open	passionate	energetic	balanced
charismatic	ruthless	impulsive	straight	careful
motivating	informal	flexible	accessible	thoughtful
adventurous	uncaring	lunatic	moderate	aggressive

B Can you think of adjectives with opposite meanings to the ones above?

C Jack Welch is Chief Executive Officer of General Electric. In the extracts below he talks about leadership. Before you read what he says, try to predict which of the adjectives above describe his idea of a good leader.

D Read what Jack Welch thinks and check your answers. Do you agree with him?

'I simply dislike the traits that have come to be associated with "managing" – controlling, stifling people, keeping them in the dark, wasting their time on trivia and reports. Breathing down their necks. You can't manage self-confidence into people. You have to get out of their way and let it grow in them by allowing them to win, and then rewarding them when they do. The word "manager" has too often come to be synonymous with control – cold, uncaring, passionless. I never associate passion with the word "manager", and I've never seen a leader without it.'

'Above all else good leaders are open. They go up, down, and around their organisations to reach people. They don't stick to established channels. They're informal. They're straight with people. They make a religion out of being accessible.'

'One of the things about leadership is that you cannot be a moderate, balanced, thoughtful, careful articulator of policy. You've got to be on the lunatic fringe.'

'(The future) will not belong to "managers" or those who can make the numbers dance. The world will belong to passionate, driven leaders – people who not only have enormous amounts of energy but who can energize those whom they lead.'

Adapted extracts from *Jack Welch Speaks*, by Janet Lowe

Listening
Running a large company

A Discuss these questions. Imagine you are the leader of a large company.
1 What qualities do you need to run a large company effectively?
2 Which business leaders do you admire? Why?
3 What do business leaders actually do?
4 As a leader, how do you motivate your employees?
5 Do you think leaders are born or made?

B 14.1 Listen to an interview with Marjorie Scardino, Chief Executive of the media group Pearson plc. What answers does she give to the questions in Exercise A? Make notes as you listen.

C Discuss these questions.
1 Do you agree with Marjorie Scardino's ideas?
2 Would you like to work for her? Explain your reasons.

Reading
Leadership
qualities

A Douglas Ivester is Chief Executive Officer of Coca-Cola. Before you read the article about him, discuss what qualities you expect him to have.

B Now read the article and complete the fact sheet on the opposite page.

Focus on Douglas Ivester,
CEO of Coca-Cola

Ivester, a factory foreman's son and former accountant, stepped in smoothly to run Coca-Cola as CEO following the death of champion wealth creator Roberto Goizueta.
5 Early in his job as Coke's chief, Goizueta had recognised Ivester's drive, commenting that he was the hardest-working man he had ever met. Together the two changed the company's operations and capital structure to maximize
10 shareholder value.

Both of Ivester's parents were factory workers from a tiny mill town in Georgia. His parents were children of the depression, he recalls, 'strong savers, very strong religious
15 values,' and had very high expectations for their only son. If he got an A, his father would say, 'They give A pluses, don't they?'

Doug Ivester is the guy who for nearly two years worked constantly to provide essential
20 support to Roberto Goizueta as he not only turned Coca-Cola around but made it into a powerhouse. If you want to know just how driven Ivester is, know that more than a decade ago he set himself the goal of
25 becoming the CEO and chairman of Coca-Cola. Then he put on paper the dates by which he intended to do that.

By comparison with Goizueta, Ivester is an accountant by training, an introvert by nature.
30 He worked systematically to obtain the breadth needed to be a modern chief executive – getting media coaching and spending three years' worth of Saturdays, six hours at a time, being tutored in marketing. He is a straight
35 arrow, constantly encouraging his executives to 'do the right thing', yet he is fascinated with Las Vegas, which he visits once a year, gambling and people-watching a lot.

He is big on discipline, which to him
40 means: be where you're supposed to be. Dress the part (he is opposed to casual Fridays). Return phone calls promptly (employees know never to get too far away from their office voice-mail, even on
45 weekends). Still, when directing his troops, he asks them to set 'aspirations' (difficult targets).

Hierarchy is out – it slows everything down; he communicates freely with people at
50 all levels. The 'conventional' desk job is also out. Ivester prefers that employees think of themselves as knowledge workers – their office is the information they carry around with them, supported by technology that
55 allows them to work anywhere. This really matters when your business is as large as Coke's, which gets 80% of its profit from overseas.

At Coke, business planning is no longer an
60 annual ritual but a continual discussion – sometimes via voice-mail – among top executives. Technology is not just nice; it's *crucial*. Huge volumes of information don't frighten Ivester; he insists that they are
65 necessary for 'real-time' decision-making. With past-generation executives, their style was more 'don't bring me your problems, bring me your solutions,' says Tim Haas, Senior Vice President and Head of Latin
70 America. 'Doug thrives on finding the solutions.' 'In a world this complicated and fast-moving, a CEO can't afford to sit in the executive suite and guess,' Ivester says. He believes that many of America's executives 'are getting terribly isolated.'

From *Fortune Magazine*

Douglas Ivester

Parents' background/values:

Present position:

→

Previous job:

accountant

Previous boss:

Roberto Goizueta

Personal qualities:

driven, hard-working, introvert, systematic, determined, straight.

Management style/beliefs:

big on discipline – encourages employees to set themselves diff. targets – anti-hierarchy communicates freely at all levels – no desk jobs – bus. planning = continual technol.' disc. personal contact

Achievements at Coca-Cola:

helped change companies operations & capital structure.

Hobbies:

gambling / people-watching

C **Answer these questions about the article.**

1 The writer says that 'Goizueta had recognised Ivester's drive' (paragraph 1). What does *drive* mean? How did Ivester show that he had this quality? *energy, self-motivation. hardest working man he had...*

2 'They give A pluses, don't they?' (paragraph 2). *Teachers,* Who is Ivester's father referring too when he says *they*?

3 How did Ivester prepare for the position he now holds?

4 Explain the meaning of this sentence: 'Dress the part (he is opposed to casual Fridays)' (paragraph 5). Do you agree with this policy?

5 Why does Ivester want employees to think of themselves as 'knowledge workers'?

6 Ivester believes that many American executives 'are getting terribly isolated.' What is Ivester doing to avoid becoming cut off from his staff?

D **Find words and phrases in the article which mean the following:**

1 Someone who has greatly increased the company's profits (paragraph 1).

2 A time of high unemployment and poverty (paragraph 2).

3 A very successful, profitable company (paragraph 3).

4 Very determined to succeed (paragraph 3).

5 Carefully, following a fixed plan (paragraph 4).

6 Organising people into different levels of importance (paragraph 6).

7 Something that happens regularly each year (paragraph 7).

8 Gets a feeling of satisfaction from doing something (paragraph 7).

E **Discuss these questions.**

1 What do you think Douglas Ivester's main objectives should be as leader of Coca-Cola?

2 What sort of problems do you think he has to deal with when running the company?

Language review
Relative clauses

Defining clauses provide essential information about the subject or object of a sentence. Without this information the sentence often doesn't make sense or has a different meaning. For example, *Managers* **who trust their staff** *often become good leaders.*

- Defining clauses have no commas.
- *Who* or *that* are used for people.
- *Which* or *that* are used for things.
- You can leave out the relative pronoun if the clause defines the object of the sentence. For example, *The person* **I spoke to** *was very helpful.*

Non-defining clauses provide *extra* information about the subject or object of a sentence. The sentence still makes sense without this information. For example, *The President,* **who is 64**, *is retiring next year.*

- The extra information is contained between commas.
- *Who* (not *that*) is used for people.
- *Which* (not *that*) is used for things.
- You cannot leave out the relative pronoun.

 page 140

A Complete the sentences in the job advertisement below with *who* or *which*.

Chief Executive

Highly successful quoted company

London Area   c. £300,000+Bonus+Benefits

Our client is a medium-sized publicly-quoted group of businesses ....¹ are engaged in distribution and engineering. The group, ...² had a record turnover last year, is looking to continue its expansion. The outgoing Chief Executive ....³ has led the company successfully for the last 10 years, is due to retire at the end of the year. The new Chief Executive, ...⁴ will have an excellent track record in the industry, will need to fulfil a role ....⁵ requires a variety of leadership skills. Our client is looking for an outstanding leader ....⁶ will drive the group forward using a mix of strategic, financial and commercial skills.

Send a full CV in confidence quoting reference number 315J.
Executive Recruitment, 23–25 Hill Street, London W1X 7BB.

B Use the relative pronouns below to complete these quotations. Which gap does not need a relative pronoun?

who   which   that   where

1 'The job for big companies, the challenge .... we all face as bureaucrats, is to create an environment .... people can reach their dreams.' *Jack Welch (US business leader)*

2 'He .... has never learned to obey cannot be a good commander.' *Aristotle (Greek philosopher)*

3 'A leader shapes and shares a vision, ... gives point to the work of others.' *Charles Handy (British writer and philosopher)*

4 'A leader should be humble. A leader should be able to communicate with his people. A leader is someone .... walks out in front of his people, but he doesn't get too far out in front, to where he can't hear their footsteps.' *Tommy Lasorda (US sports personality)*

5 'A leader is someone .... knows what they want to achieve and can communicate that.' *Margaret Thatcher (British politician)*

C In the text below, all the relative pronouns have been taken out.
Put them back in, where appropriate.

A leader among men

Carly Fiorina, has been called America's most powerful business woman, is Chief Executive of the huge Hewlett Packard group, manufactures computers and printers. Ms Fiorina, has spent most of her working life in the telecommunications industry, started out as a sales representative with AT&T, she rose rapidly through the ranks. Later she was a key player in the creation of the equipment and components company Lucent Technologies, she was in charge of the sales and marketing of networking products. Ms Fiorina now oversees an organisation is one of the 30 leading companies in the Dow Jones Industrial Average.

Skills

Leading a team

A Role play this situation. Take turns to be the team leader. Use expressions from the Useful language box.

You are senior managers at a computer graphics company. Your business has expanded rapidly: your workforce has doubled from 60 to 120 in two years. You urgently need to move from your small city-centre location to a new suburban development area with bigger offices.

Hold a meeting to discuss what needs to be done, and by whom. For example: drawing up a schedule; predicting problems; liaising with the union; informing customers and suppliers; keeping staff informed; dealing with negative feelings; hiring a removal company. Then draw up an action plan to ensure that the move goes smoothly.

B Work in small groups. Choose a *planning activity* related to your work or place of study. Decide who will lead your team, and what the other roles and tasks will be. Then role play the meeting.

Useful language

Stating goals
Our main objective is to ...
Our aims will be to ...

Highlighting factors for success
If we're going to be successful, we need to act quickly.
To succeed, we'll have to take into account several factors.

Indicating priorities
Our first priority will be to contact our customers.
It's also essential that we brief our suppliers.

Defining roles and delegating
I'd like you to prepare a report.
Could you please liaise with Sales and Marketing?

Motivating the team
It's a challenge, but it's also an opportunity to develop the business.
We'll all benefit because new orders will follow.

Reporting back
I'd like you to keep me up-to-date by e-mail.
I'd like to have your report by Tuesday.
I suggest we set up another meeting in two weeks' time.

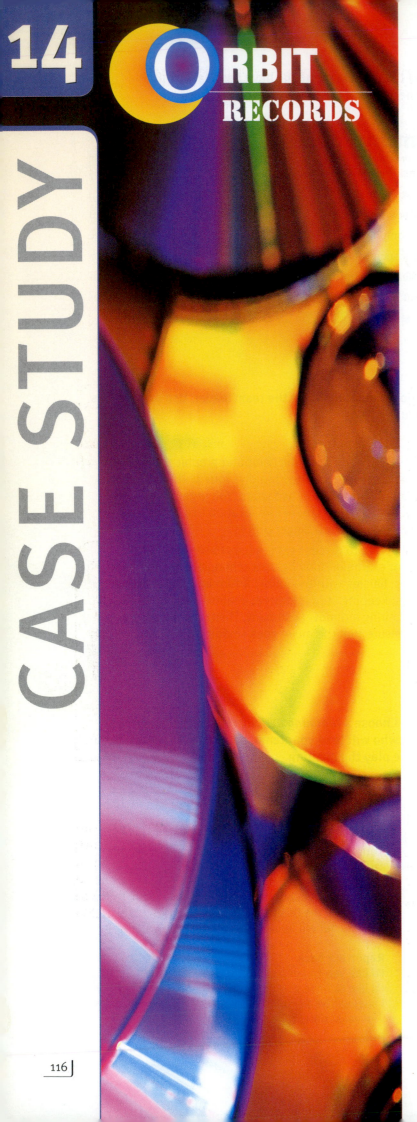

CASE STUDY

ORBIT RECORDS

Background

Orbit Records was founded in London 20 years ago, and now has 12 large stores in the UK and five in Germany. The company grew at a fast rate because it had a successful marketing strategy. The stores offer a wide range of CDs which they sell at reasonable prices. Their record stores carry over 80,000 titles – about three times more than their main competitors. What's more, if a customer asks for a CD which is not in stock, the store will get it for a customer within two weeks, if it's available.

About two years ago, Orbit stores diversified into selling computer games, videos, tee-shirts, adventure holidays, concert tickets, books and comics. Not all the new areas of business were profitable, and as a result the company's profits fell sharply.

A change of leadership

After the founder of Orbit records died, a new Chief Executive, Sheldon Drake, took over. However, he failed because he lacked leadership qualities. He was unable to develop a strategy for improving profits and had no clear vision of where the company was going. Also, he did not communicate well with employees, who started to lose confidence in the business. They began to worry about losing their jobs and their morale suffered.

Three months ago, Sheldon Drake resigned, and his place was taken by someone from outside the company.

Task of the new Chief Executive

One of the new CE's main tasks is to motivate staff and raise morale, so that staff will be more productive. He has asked Personnel to carry out a survey of staff attitudes. Questionnaires were sent to all employees below senior management level. The results are summarised in the chart on page 117.

He has also jotted down ideas for raising motivation and morale, and has asked employees to do the same. The best ideas will be implemented throughout the company.

STAFF ATTITUDES (%)	Yes	No	Don't know
1 Do you feel you participate fully in decision-making?	12	70	18
2 Do you feel 'valued' by the company?	48	46	6
3 Do you understand the company's objectives and overall strategy?	16	20	64
4 Do you have enough contact with senior management?	18	50	32
5 Do you have enough opportunities to express your ideas / make suggestions?	42	26	30
6 Are you paid adequately?	48	45	7
7 Do you think you will be working for this company in five years' time?	25	14	61
8 Do you have enough opportunities to meet each other socially?	55	42	3

Chief Executive's ideas

1 Build morale through teamwork outside the office – in sports activities. Form company teams for soccer, squash, basketball, etc. Get employees to participate in inter-company competitions, e.g. athletics, swimming events and so on.

2 Introduce regular staff meetings which will enable staff at all levels to participate in decision-making.

3 Set up regular small-group meetings to share ideas, develop plans and help prepare budgets. Also, start an 'Employee of the Month' scheme. Everyone has to nominate someone, giving reasons why they should be nominated.

4 Make sure that the CE gets out of his/her office frequently during the first year and drops in on staff at different Orbit stores.

5 Encourage staff through meetings and a newsletter (to be edited on a monthly rotating basis by different senior managers) to give ideas and suggestions. There would be cash rewards for the best ideas.

6 Set up a profit-sharing scheme for all employees related to increased productivity and profits.

7 Cancel the end-of-year bonus scheme. Spend some money instead on a spectacular Christmas dinner and party at a luxurious hotel.

8 Organise one-to-one meetings with senior managers to build morale and generate ideas. Agree targets and objectives with senior managers, who share them with other staff members at regular seminars.

9 Have an open-door policy in every store. Employees can see the manager whenever they are available.

10 Create career development plans for all staff, which would involve consultation with each employee.

Task

1 Work in small groups. Choose six ideas from the Chief Executive's list which you think would be worth implementing. Note down the reasons for your choices.
Then think of three other ideas, which are not on the list, for improving staff motivation and morale.

2 Meet as one group and discuss your ideas, giving reasons for your choices.

3 As one group, try to agree on the six best ideas (from the Chief Executive's and your own list) which should be put into effect.

Writing

You are the manager of an Orbit Records store in the UK. Write a persuasive letter to a famous recording star or their agent inviting them to visit your store. Explain why you want the star to come to the store and what you expect them to do if they accept your invitation. Offer a suitable fee for the visit. Lay out your letter correctly.

➡ *Writing file* page 142

15

Competition

> ' *Competition brings out the best in products and worst in people.* '
>
> David Sarnoff (1891–1971), American business leader

Starting up

Answer the questions in the quiz. Then turn to page 155 to find out your score. Compare your score with a partner.

How Competitive are you?

1 Which of the following statements do you agree with?

a) Winning is everything.
b) It's not the winning that counts, it's the taking part.
c) We are in this world to help each other.

2 Which of the following would satisfy you?

a) Earning more than anyone else you know.
b) Earning more than most of your friends.
c) Earning enough to have a comfortable life.

3 You have just won $40,000 and need to buy a new car. Do you:

a) spend $9,000 on a reliable car that will get you from A to B?
b) spend $16,000 on a middle-range car?
c) spend $40,000 on a top-of-the-range car that will impress your friends?

4 If a colleague did something very successful, would you feel:

a) pleased for them?
b) pleased for them, but a bit jealous?
c) very jealous and unhappy?

5 If you lose at something, do you:

a) forget about it immediately?
b) think about it for a while?
c) never forget?

6 How do you feel when you win? Do you:

a) boast about it and tell everyone?
b) feel good, but keep it to yourself?
c) feel sorry for the person who lost?

7 What do you want for your children? Do you want them:

a) to be happy?
b) to achieve more than you did?
c) to be the best at everything?

8 You are at the traffic lights next to another car. The lights change to 'go'. Do you:

a) let the other car go first?
b) move away slowly, without being aware of the other car?
c) try to be the first away?

9 You are waiting to check in at a crowded airline counter. There does not seem to be a system of queuing. Would you:

a) push your way to the front?
b) insist loudly that a fair system is adopted?
c) keep quiet and wait?

10 How do you feel about doing this quiz? Do you want to:

a) show you are the most competitive person in the group?
b) show you are the least competitive person in the group?
c) find out something about yourself?

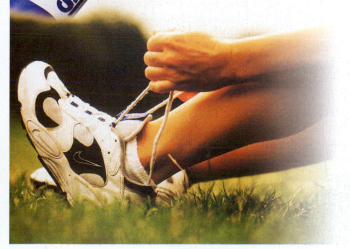

Vocabulary
Describing competition

A Match the phrases with the definitions.

1 market leader:
2 market challenger:
3 market follower:

A company or product ...

4 market nicher:

a) with the second largest market share
b) with the largest market share
c) that focuses on a small segment of the market
d) that is not a threat to the leader

B Complete the chart with companies or products in your own country (for example, cars, soft drinks, sports shoes, jeans). Then compare your table with a partner.

PRODUCT TYPE	market leader	market challenger	market follower	market nicher

C Which products do you buy that are not market leaders or market challengers? Why do you buy them?

D Choose one adjective from each pair to make word partnerships with *competition*. Then use them to comment on industries or companies. For example, *There is strong competition between Coke and Pepsi.*

strong/hard
fierce/aggressive
dirty/unfair   competition
heavy/tough
intense/deep

E Match the verbs with the prepositions (where necessary) to make phrases with *competition*. Then make sentences using some of the phrases. For example, *Our company welcomes competition — it keeps us alert.*

respond
cope
face
ignore   up to
welcome   with   competition
adapt   to
avoid   —

119

Reading
Competitive advantage

Lexus

A The text below presents three strategies for firms to achieve above-average performance. Before you read it, discuss what strategies companies in the following sectors might use to compete with their rivals:
a) supermarkets   b) construction equipment   c) luxury cars.

B Read the *first sentence only* of each paragraph. What three strategies does the text mention? Do you think they are similar to any of the ideas you discussed?

C Match the words below to the definitions. Then read paragraph one.

broad scope	saving money by producing goods in large quantities
breadth	wide range
segment	width
economies of scale	a section of a market or industry

D Match the words below to the definitions. Then read paragraphs two and three.

attributes	see, realise
perceive	ability to last a long time
uniqueness	something very unusual and special
durability	qualities

E Match the words below to the definitions. Then read paragraphs four and five.

tailors	making the best use of
to the exclusion of	adapts
optimizing	the opposite of wide
narrow	not including

Three Strategies to gain a competitive advantage

Cost leadership is perhaps the clearest of the three strategies. In it, a firm sets out to become the low-cost producer in its
5 industry. The firm has a broad scope and serves many industry segments, and may even operate in related industries; the firm's breadth is often important to its
10 cost advantage. The sources of cost advantage are varied and depend on the structure of the industry. They may include the pursuit of economies of scale,
15 technology, preferential access to raw materials and other factors.

The second strategy is differentiation. In a differentiation strategy, a firm
20 seeks to be unique in its industry along some dimensions that are widely valued by buyers. It selects one or more attributes that many buyers in an industry perceive as
25 important, and uniquely positions itself to meet those needs. It is rewarded for its uniqueness with a premium price.

30 The means for differentiation are peculiar to each industry. Differentiation can be based on the product itself, the delivery system by which it is
35 sold, the marketing approach, and a broad range of other factors. In construction equipment, for example, Caterpillar Tractor's
40 differentiation is based on product durability, service, spare parts availability, and an excellent dealer network.

The third strategy is focus.
45 This strategy is quite different from the others because it rests on the choice of a narrow competitive scope within an industry. The focuser selects a
50 segment or group of segments in the industry and tailors its strategy to serving them to the exclusion of others. By optimizing its strategy for the
55 target segments, the focuser seeks to achieve a competitive advantage in its targets segments even though it does not possess a competitive advantage overall.

60 A firm that engages in each strategy but fails to achieve any of them is 'stuck in the middle'. It possesses no competitive advantage. This strategic position
65 is usually a recipe for below-average performance. A firm that is stuck in the middle will compete at a disadvantage because the cost leader,
70 differentiators, or focusers will be better positioned to compete in any segment. In most industries, quite a few competitors are stuck in the middle.

From *Competitive Advantage*, by Michael Porter

F **Answer these questions about the text.**

1 Which sentence best expresses the main idea in paragraph one?
A firm can get a competitive advantage by:
a) selling goods in many markets.
b) making as wide a range of goods as possible.
c) producing goods more cheaply than its rivals.

2 Which sentence best expresses the main idea in paragraphs two and three?
When a firm uses a *differentiation* strategy:
a) it tries to persuade consumers that its products have special qualities.
b) it tries to reach a small group of loyal customers.
c) it wants to attract as many buyers as possible.

3 Which of these sentences best expresses the main idea in paragraph four?
If a firm chooses *focus* as its strategy, it tries to:
a) do better than its rivals in a small part of the market.
b) prevent other firms from entering the market.
c) do business in a large number of narrow markets.

4 In the final paragraph, does the writer say it is a good or bad thing for firms to be *stuck in the middle*? Why?

G **Discuss these questions.**

1 Can you think of companies which use one of the strategies in the text?
What about your own company or a company you know well?

2 Can you think of any companies which are *stuck in the middle*?
What do you think they could do to improve their competitive position?

Listening

Competition and the market

A 🎧 **15.1 Kevin Warren, a Vice President at Coca-Cola and Schweppes Beverages (UK), is talking about competition.**

Answer the questions below. Then listen to the first part of the interview and check your answers.

1 How many servings of Coca-Cola are sold worldwide?
a) one billion a day   **c)** one billion a year
b) 47 billion a day   **d)** 47 billion a year

2 Complete the chart.

To be successful you need:

a portfolio of pr _ _ _ _ _ _

an efficient manu _ _ _ _ _ _ _ _ g and dist _ _ _ _ _ _ _ n operation

the best br _ _ _ _

the most recognisable pack _ _ _ _

3 Choose the correct answer. Kevin thinks the way to stay ahead is to focus on:
a) the actions of your competitor.   **b)** your own products and customers.

B 🎧 **15.2 Listen to the second part of the interview.**
Which of these statements more accurately reflects Kevin's views?

1 Price is the most important element when you are talking about value.

2 Value for money is not only about price. Cheaper is not always better.

C **Do you think competition always leads to better products and better value?**

D 🎧 **15.3 Listen to the third part of the interview.**
What changes in consumer habits does Kevin predict?

Language review
Talking about the future

We can use different verb forms to talk about the future.

1 We use *going to* to talk about what we intend to do and have already decided to do: *We're **going to** launch our new product in January.*
2 We use *'ll* to talk about something we have decided to do at the time of speaking: *'The photocopier's broken.' 'I'**ll** call the engineer.'*
3 We use the present continuous tense to talk about a fixed arrangement: *I'**m meeting** our agent next week.*
4 We use the present simple tense to talk about a timetable or programme: *The flight **leaves** at 2pm tomorrow.*

 page 141

A Find examples in the conversation below of language which is used to talk about the future.

The CEO and the Production Manager of a small but successful PC lap top firm are discussing some sudden news from their Sales Manager, Steve Andrews. Steve has been negotiating an important contract.

CEO   I've got bad news from Steve about that contract he's been negotiating with Ambros plc. He's heard that another company's putting in their own bid in three days' time.

Manager   Oh no! We're counting on that contract. What can we do?

CEO   Well, we're going to fight it. Our rivals say they'll match us for price and beat our deadlines so we'll have to concentrate on those two issues. Steve says we're going to beat them on every other detail, but price and deadlines are the crucial items.

Manager   Well, you can make the decision to cut prices but, in terms of deadlines, our assembly lines are already working to capacity except at the weekends.

CEO   I know. I can cut prices slightly but do you think you can beat our rival's deadlines?

Manager   Well, the union meets later this afternoon for their regular monthly meeting. I'll raise this with them as a matter of priority.

CEO   Can you persuade them to work extra hours at the weekend?

Manager   Yes, I think so. Can you authorise overtime payment in advance so it's not an issue when I'm talking to the union?

CEO   Yes, I'll do that once we finish this meeting. What else?

Manager   We have to contact Steve so he can tell Ambros that we're going to respond with an improved bid. We've only got two days to prepare.

CEO   Right. You prepare for the meeting. Tell the staff that we're relying on their cooperation. I'll authorise the overtime payments.

B Work in pairs. Take turns to add comments to the sentences below. Use *will*, *going to*, the present continuous, or the present simple.

1 I'm sorry, I can't attend the sales meeting tomorrow ...
2 We've decided how to cut costs next year ...
3 The line's engaged ...
4 Don't worry if you can't drive me to the airport ...
5 I've got the details about your flight to Turkey ...
6 Oh no. The computers have crashed again ...
7 I've made up my mind ...
8 Oh John, you asked me about the time of your presentation tomorrow ...

Discussion
Competitve strategy

Read the two texts below. Discuss the questions that follow.

Blues Fight The Reds

In 1996, after over 100 years of rivalry, Pepsi launched 'Project Blue' to challenge Coca-Cola's position as market leader in the soft drinks market. At a cost of £330 million, Pepsi changed the colour of their can to blue as well as painting a Concorde airliner blue. They also used supermodels Claudia Schiffer and Cindy Crawford, and tennis star Andre Agassi in the campaign. It was felt that blue was a trendy, futuristic colour which would differentiate Pepsi from the red of Coca-Cola. However the campaign failed to achieve its main aim.

1 Why do you think the campaign was unsuccessful?
2 Can you suggest ways for Pepsi to compete more successfully with Coca-Cola?

Fly Me, I'm Cheap

In autumn 1995 Easyjet and Ryanair, two small North European airlines, introduced budget flights on UK domestic routes. Other carriers responded with similar services but British Airways decided not to. Later, British Airways changed its mind and in May 1998 it launched its successful airline *Go*. This offers low-cost flights with no on-flight food or entertainment on certain domestic and European routes.

1 Why do you think British Airways changed its strategy?
2 How do you think its decision affected the small airlines? What can they do to respond?

Skills
Negotiating

Useful language

Match the sentences on the left with the more diplomatic sentences on the right.

1 We must talk about price first.
2 There's no way we can give you any credit.
3 I want a discount.
4 I won't lower my price.
5 Can you alter the specifications?
6 Your price is far too high.

a Your price seems rather high.
b Unfortunately, I can't lower my price.
c Could you give me a discount?
d I'm afraid we can't give you any credit.
e I think we should talk about price first.
f I wonder if you could alter the specifications.

A Being diplomatic often brings the best results when negotiating. It is important not be too aggressive. Think of other ways to express sentences 1–6 in the Useful language box more diplomatically.

B Role play the situation below. Be diplomatic.
A shop owner is placing an order with a chocolate manufacturer.

Shop owner	Chocolate manufacturer
• You want to order 50 boxes of deluxe chocolate at the quoted price. • You want a 20% discount. • You want 30 days' credit. • You want delivery in two weeks.	• You get a bonus if the order is over 100 boxes. • You don't give a discount for orders of less than 100 boxes. • You want payment on delivery. • You can deliver in three weeks.

City Plaza Hotel

Background

City Plaza Hotel is situated in downtown Toronto, Canada. A few years ago it was the leader in its segment of the market. There is no official star system in Toronto, but travel guides always place it in the four-star category. Nowadays City Plaza has become a market follower instead. It has been losing money, and its traditional customers have been going to rival hotels such as the Majestic and Belvedere. Reasons for this include: competition; the increasing cost running the hotel; the lack of capital to improve its accommodation and facilities (these have fallen well below standard in recent years).

City Plaza needs a new strategy. Fortunately, the management now has sufficient capital to finance that strategy. City Plaza was recently bought by the dynamic hotel group, Price Inc., who have allocated C$2.75 million to make the hotel more profitable and competitive. The Chief Executive of Price Inc. believes that City Plaza will make a good contribution to group profits if it positions itself correctly in the market.

Facts and figures

The following tables give information about City Plaza Hotel and its rivals in the area, Majestic, Belvedere and Mount Charlotte.

Table 1

HOTEL	DESCRIPTION	TARGET MARKET	FACILITIES
Majestic ****	• Market leader • 300 rooms • 5 large conference rooms • Luxurious and very customer-orientated • A 'yes I can' attitude	High-income. Tourists, business people, conventions and special events, e.g. golf tournaments, concerts, etc.	A wide range, including: bar and night-club, 2 restaurants, swimming pool, fitness centre, gift shop and hairdresser. Guest rooms have many facilities, e.g. coffee-maker, air-conditioning, safe, minibar; fax machine and voice-mail, if required.
City Plaza ****	• Market follower • 250 rooms • 3 conference rooms • Needs to redecorate, modernise and improve its service.	Tourists, business people, group bookings and organisers of conventions (as above).	One large restaurant and bar, shop, sauna; tour organiser. Guest rooms have good basic facilities, e.g. coffee-maker, hair dryer, iron, minibar.
Belvedere ***	• Market nicher • 190 rooms • 1 conference room • Inexpensive for its three-star rating	Middle-income tourists. Package tour visitors.	One restaurant and bar, newsagent/ gift shop. Health care studio and small swimming pool. Guest rooms have similar facilities to City Plaza.
Mount Charlotte **	• Budget hotel • 360 rooms • No conference room • A large breakfast room • Cheap prices, friendly staff	People looking for cheap, 'no frills' accommodation.	No restaurant. A small bar. Comfortable rooms, with few facilities.

Table 2: Convention facilities

	Number of halls	Capacity (each hall)	Day rate per person*
Majestic	5	500	C$95
City Plaza	3	100	C$70
Belvedere	1	60	C$75
Mount Charlotte	0	—	—

* (including equipment and meals)

Table 3

	*Repeat business	Annual average occupancy rate	**Average room rate C$
Majestic	55%	75%	240
City Plaza	32%	35%	170
Belvedere	44%	72%	130
Mount Charlotte	35%	92%	90

* i.e. customers returning   ** The rates exclude a charge for breakfast and sales tax.

Table 4: Financial information

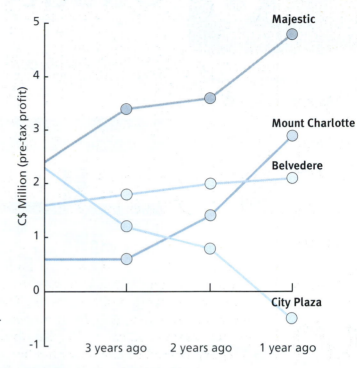

Task

To choose the right strategy, the Chief Executive of Price Inc. has called in a team of consultants, Maple Leaf Associates (MLA). The group will consider the options and advise Price Inc. on the correct positioning of the hotel. MLA has formed small teams within its organisation to study the problem.

You are one of MLA's consultants. Work in teams and do the following:

1 Analyse and interpret the data. Decide what facts and figures are important to help you work out a new strategy for City Plaza.
2 Discuss each option, considering its advantages and disadvantages. If you wish, you may add other options.
3 Decide on a strategy for City Plaza and note down your reasons. Then present your recommendations to the other groups.
4 Working as one group, agree on a strategy and action plan for City Plaza.

Options

The management are considering four options before deciding how to use the C$2.75 million. They estimate that the cost of redecorating a room to 'market leader' standard would be approximately C$12,000. The options are as follows:

1 Take City Plaza Hotel up-market so that it is clearly seen as market leader.
2 Reposition the hotel as a budget hotel with either low prices and limited service, or higher prices and a basic range of services.
3 Stay in its present position as a market follower, but improve the hotel.
4 Aim at a niche market, for example, middle-income older tourists, family groups, or young visitors.

Writing

As Head of Maple Leaf Associates (MLA), write a short report outlining the new strategy you recommend for the City Plaza Hotel. Your report should contain these sections:

1 Background to the problem
2 Analysis of the data
3 Recommended action, with reasons

➡ *Writing file page 146*

Quality

" Quality is the elimination of variation. "

W.E. Deming (1900–1993), American quality expert

Starting up

A Which of the words and phrases below best represents the idea of quality?

reliable   value for money   long-lasting
well-known expensive   well-made

B Give examples of high quality products or services. Explain your choices.

C There is a saying 'You get what you pay for.' What does it mean?
Do you agree with this idea?

Vocabulary
Quality control and customer service

A Use the words in the box to complete the flow chart.

identified	re-launched	reliability
modified	durability	tested
failed	recalled	~~launched~~

A DEFECTIVE PRODUCT

The product was ...*launched*... two years ago.

Shortly after that, complaints were received about its .... and ....

Because of market feedback, it was .... so that any faults could be investigated. At the same time, it was withdrawn from sale.

After extensive tests, a fault was .... by engineers.

As a result, they were able to correct the fault and the product was ....

It was then .... under controlled conditions.

Finally, the redesigned product was .... in the market.

Unfortunately, it .... due to lack of consumer confidence caused by bad publicity.

B Match the words and phrases in the box to the correct headings. Use a good Dictionary to help you.

after sales care	consumer satisfaction questionnaire	compensation
faults	monitoring	defects	~~routine checks~~	flaws	inspection
minimum standard	goodwill payment	warranty	zero defects

PROBLEMS

QUALITY CONTROL
routine checks

CUSTOMER SERVICE

C Think of a product or service that you have complained about.
Tell your partner what the problem was and whether it was solved.

Reading

Defining quality

A Read the first paragraph of the article. Then complete the sentence below.

In the past, quality meant .... ; nowadays, business people believe that quality means ....

B Read the article. Then correct the five factual mistakes in the summary at the top of the opposite page.

New-style quality

Old-style excellence got a bad name, says **Tony Jackson**. The aim should be to provide a product consistently and make it the best you can.

The term 'quality' is one of the most misused in the business world. What exactly does it mean? Our grandparents would have been in no doubt. Quality meant excellence: a thing was the best of its kind, and that was that. A Stradivarius violin had quality, a tinker's fiddle did not. In business, however, the word has acquired a very different meaning. As defined by the American statistician Edward Deming some 50 years ago, quality means consistency, a lack of defects.

Around 1970, it is said, a group of investment analysts visited a world-famous UK engineering company. They asked the questions of their trade: about profit margins, stock control and balance sheets. The company's executives seemed honestly puzzled. They did not see the point of all this, they said. Their products were the finest in the world. Why all these detailed questions about numbers?

Rolls Royce, the company in question, duly went bust in 1973. The trouble with old-style quality, it seemed, was that it encouraged supply-driven management. The engineers would make the product to the highest possible standard and price it accordingly. If the public was so uncultured that they turned it down, so much the worse for the public. And so old-style quality got a bad name in business circles. It was all very well for artists to produce masterpieces. The job of companies was to please the market.

Further damage to old-style quality was done by the rise of Japan. When Japanese cars, toys and television sets first reached the market in the US and UK, local manufacturers considered them cheap trash. In the beginning, they were. But under the teaching of Edward Deming, the Japanese were learning about the second definition of quality. Western customers then began to realise that while Japanese cars might be tin cans, they did not keep breaking down, as did British and American cars.

In time of course, Japanese cars stopped being tin cans, and became stylish and comfortable vehicles instead. That is, they achieved old-style quality as well. As western manufacturers discovered to their cost, that was in some respects the easy bit. New-style quality was harder.

Quality has a third meaning: that of value for money. To qualify for that meaning, a product must be of certain standard; and it should convey a sense, not of outright cheapness, but of being sold at a fair price.

The US fast foods group McDonald's, for instance, talks of its 'high quality food'. But at 99c or 99p, its hamburgers are as close to absolute cheapness as any person in the developed world could desire. They are also highly consistent. Eat a McDonald's anywhere around the world and the results will be roughly similar. But as anyone who has eaten a really good American hamburger knows, a McDonald's is also a long way from quality in its original sense.

From the *Financial Times*

FINANCIAL TIMES
World business newspaper.

New-style quality: summary

According to the article, quality used to mean that a product was well-made and high-priced. Nowadays, quality has a different meaning for business people. It means a product is reliable and does not have things wrong with it. In 1980, a group of analysts visited Rolls Royce. They asked many questions about finance, but few about quality. It is not surprising that Rolls Royce went bankrupt; they sold their cars too cheaply in their markets.

The old-style idea of quality became popular with business people because it emphasised the importance of good production methods. The Japanese learned a lot from Edward Deming. Their products sell well in western markets because they are low-priced. The US company, McDonald's, sells products which are cheap and excellent value for money. According to the writer of the article, McDonald's hamburgers are the best in the world.

C Discuss these questions.

1 Why were the Rolls Royce executives 'puzzled' when the analysts asked their questions?

2 According to the writer, what mistake caused Rolls Royce to go bankrupt?

3 What advantage did Japanese cars have compared with British and American cars?

D Complete the definition below.

Nowadays, high quality products have three essential features:

1 ....

2 ....

3 ....

E Match these phrases from paragraph two to the definitions.

1 profit margins   a) checking supplies of goods

2 balance sheets   b) the difference between manufacturing cost and selling price

3 stock control   c) statements of the amount of money a company has, including money it owes or is owed

F Find words or phrases in the article which mean:

1 reliability (paragraph 1)

2 went bankrupt (paragraph 3)

3 management focus on production (paragraph 3)

4 refused to buy the product (paragraph 3)

5 badly-made goods sold at low prices (paragraph 4)

G Which sentence means the same as these quotations from the article?

1 *And so old-style quality got a bad name in business circles.* (paragraph 3)
   a) Business people did not try to produce well-made products.
   b) Business people no longer accepted this idea of quality.
   c) Business people tried to find another name for quality.

2 *It was all very well for artists to produce masterpieces.* (paragraph 3)
   a) It was right that artists should try to produce masterpieces.
   b) Artists don't have to produce masterpieces.
   c) All artists produce masterpieces at some time.

H Can you think of products that are made according to:
a) old-style quality? b) new-style quality?
Make two lists. Then compare lists with a partner.

Language review
Prepositions of time

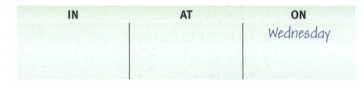

We can use the prepositions below in the following ways:

at with times of the day: *The meeting's **at** two o'clock.*

on with days and dates: *I'm leaving **on** Tuesday.*

in with longer periods: *She started work **in** June.*

by with a deadline: *We need to decide **by** tomorrow.*

for to say how long something lasts: *They've been on strike **for** three weeks.*

during for a period in which something happens: ***During** the meeting he had to leave to make a phone call.*

since to describe a point in time up to now: *I haven't seen her **since** Monday.*

➜ page 141

A 🎧 16.1 **Listen to the words and phrases on the recording. Write them under the correct headings.**

IN	AT	ON
		Wednesday

B 🎧 16.2 **Listen to Enid Wong, a business executive based in Hong Kong. Make notes about the problems she had with a new laptop computer.**

C 🎧 16.2 **In these extracts from Enid's story the prepositions of time are used incorrectly. Correct the mistakes. Then listen again and check your answers.**

1 I had a bad experience on June last year. At the Monday my office bought me an expensive American laptop computer. I had been waiting for it since two months.

2 ... the technician tried to fix it. He worked during seven hours on the Friday and it still wouldn't work. I didn't have time to take the laptop to the Computer Centre as I had to fly in the Saturday morning.

3 I tried to install the software. No luck! My brother-in-law tried. No luck! During two months, I had no e-mail at a busy time in my life.

4 When I returned to Hong Kong in the end of August, I sent the machine to the Computer Centre. It was a faulty modem on a brand-new machine. Fortunately, it was working properly since the end of September.

D 🎧 16.3 **Lisa Soares, an Argentine student studying for an MBA in London, had problems when she bought a second hand car. Complete her story below with prepositions of time. Then listen and check your answers.**

........¹ the summer last year, I think it was ....² August, my car kept breaking down. I bought it second hand. I went to the same garage that I'd bought it from. The car salesman said that it would take five days to get it fixed. This was ....³ the Monday and we agreed that I would be back to pick it up ....⁴ the Friday. So I went to pick the car up ....⁵ the Friday – and I had to take time off work. I turned up ....⁶ 9.30 in the morning. The salesman hadn't arranged for any of the work to be done and he was on holiday ....⁷ a week. So we agreed that the work would be done the following Tuesday. I dropped the car off ....⁸ the Tuesday ....⁹ 9.30 on the way to work. Fortunately, when I turned up ....¹⁰ the evening, all the repairs had been finished. Three weeks later, they had the cheek to send me a customer service evaluation questionnaire — and they wanted the answers ....¹¹ the end of the week!

Skills
Telephone complaints

Useful language

COMPLAINING

Making the complaint
I'm ringing to complain about ...
I'm sorry, but I'm not satisfied with ...
Unfortunately there's a problem with ...

Explaining the problem
The CD player doesn't work.
There seems to be a problem ...
We haven't received the ...

Insisting
It really isn't good enough.
I'd like to know why ...

Threatening
If you don't replace the product, I'll complain to the manager.
If you can't deliver on time, we'll have to contact other suppliers.

DEALING WITH COMPLAINTS

Showing understanding
Oh dear! Sorry to hear that.
Mmm, I see what you mean.
I'm sorry about the problem/delay.

Getting the facts
Could you give me some details please?
What happened exactly?
What's the problem exactly?

Making excuses
It's not our policy to replace items.
It's not our fault that it hasn't arrived.
I'm afraid that's not quite right.

Promising action
OK, I'll look into it right away.
I promise you I'll check the details and get back to you.

**A Study the Useful language in the box above.
Then complete the dialogue below with appropriate phrases.**

Salesperson	Hello. Electrical goods department.
Customer	Oh, hello. I'm .... [1] the video recorder I bought from your store six months ago.
Salesperson	Oh, ... [2]. Could you give me some details, please?
Customer	There .... [3] when you try to take the video out of the machine. I want to exchange it for a new video recorder.
Salesperson	I'm afraid it's not .... [4]. We'll send it to the manufacturer for repair.
Customer	It really .... [5]. It's the second time it's happened. .... [6] exchange it for a new machine, ... [7] have to take further action.

B One of you is Production Manager for a power tools manufacturer. The other is a supplier of components. Role play the following telephone call.

Production Manager

Ring your supplier to complain about some electric motors (order No PV205) which have a number of defects (don't fit, not up to usual standard, etc.).

Supplier

- Deal tactfully with the complaint.
- Show understanding.
- Get the facts.
- Promise action.

Background

Western Airport, in the British Midlands, is operated by the Western Airport Authority (WAA). In the last five years the number of passengers it handles has greatly increased. Many airlines now use the airport for long-haul flights to North America and the Far East.

Unfortunately the growth in business has brought problems. A recent survey showed that passengers had many complaints about the terminal. Several airlines have threatened to route their aircraft through other airports unless WAA take action to improve the situation.

WAA must decide how to deal with the complaints and consider what action should be taken. Changes should not require great expenditure as WAA have cash flow problems at present.

Complaints about the terminal

1 The terminal is hot and noisy. Queues at check-in are long, and delays are common.

2 Some of the gates are a long way from the Departure Area. 'We walked miles to get to our plane.'

3 After disembarking, passengers couldn't find the luggage collection hall. 'We wandered around for ages.'

4 The baggage conveyor system often breaks down. 'When this happens, the staff just look worried and shout into their mobile phones.'

5 The ground staff don't know enough about the terminal. 'They can't answer a simple question like, "Where's the BA check-in?".'

6 Some passengers say the security officers are too strict. Because they are so thorough, flights are sometimes delayed. Also, when they search passengers and luggage the scanning equipment does not work properly. 'One officer thought the Christmas pudding in my hand luggage was a bomb!'

Complaints about the restaurant and bars

The restaurant and bars are run by Airfare, a food company which has a five-year contract with the airport. They are used by four types of customers: business people, tourists, airport employees, and groups (sports teams, clubs, associations, etc.).

Complaints made by customers were as follows:

1 'The restaurant menu is unimaginative. The main dishes are either steak, ham or chicken. Surely the airport can do better?'

2 Airport staff, who use the restaurant frequently, say the meals are too expensive.

3 Smoking areas are not large enough, and there is no clear division from non-smoking areas.

4 Passengers can't relax because they don't know when they have to board their planes.

5 There is nowhere for passengers to put their hand luggage. 'I was afraid someone would steal it, so I couldn't enjoy my drink.'

6 The bar staff look unhappy and overworked. Some are rude to passengers. 'Bar staff seem to expect a tip after serving every drink.'

Task 1

You are a representative of one of the following:
• The Customer Relations Department of WAA   • A major airline   • Airfare

1 Consider the complaints and come up with ideas for dealing with them.
2 Hold a meeting of all three groups. Decide what action to take to improve customer service. The meeting should be led by the Manager of the Customer Relations Department.

Task 2

You are either:
• The Manager of the Customer Relations Department   • A dissatisfied customer

The Customer Services Department Manager telephones an important customer who often uses the airport to tell them about the plans for improvements. The customer is very unhappy with the poor customer care at the terminal. They are tired of listening to excuses for the delays, noise, poor food, etc. This time, they expect to receive more than promises. An expensive free offer is the least they expect. Role play the situation.

Writing

You attended the meeting as a representative of either the Customer Relations Department, an airline or Airfare. Write a memo to the General Manager of your company. Inform them of the decisions that were taken to improve the service at the airport.

➡ *Writing file* pages 144 and 145

Grammar reference

1 Comparing

Comparatives

1 If we compare two things using a one-syllable adjective, or a two-syllable word ending in -y we add the ending -er.

   Women live **longer than** men.
   We need an **earlier** date **than** that.

2 If we compare two things using long adjectives we put *more* or *less* in front of the adjective.

   Advertising on television is **more effective than** on the radio.
   She is **less experienced than** he is.

3 Adverbs of degree can make the comparison stronger or weaker.

   Their services are **far/a lot/much/a little/no** cheaper than their rivals'.

4 If the two things being compared are equal we can use *as* + adjective + *as* or *the same as*.

   I hope the product is **as good as** the advertisement says it is.
   Japanese firms expect all employees to look the same, and think **the same as** other members of staff.

Superlatives

We use the superlative to describe something that ranks number one.

Tokyo is **the most expensive** city in the world.
December is our **busiest** month.
His **greatest** success was winning the Nobel Peace Prize.

Irregular adjectives

There are a number of irregular comparative and superlative forms.

She's a **better** driver than him.
What's **the farthest/furthest** distance you've ever driven in one day?
The worst experience I have ever had was when I was attacked in New York.
Those with **the least** money pay **the least** in taxes.

2 Past simple and present perfect

Past simple

1 We use the past simple to refer to events that took place in the past.

   A pharmacist called John Pemberton **invented** Coca-Cola.
   '**Did** you **go** to Berlin last week?' 'Yes, and I **met** Herr Gnuchtel.'

2 We frequently use a time adverb to situate the event in finished past time.

   Rolls Royce went bust **in 1973**.
   A few years ago, the City Plaza hotel was a leader in its segment of the market.
   Some people made fortunes on the Stock Exchange **during the 1980s.**

3 We use the past simple in annual reports to describe the company's performance over the last year.

   Last year **was** a good year for our group.
   Sales **rose** by more than 11% and we **made** substantial gains in market share in a number of countries.

Present perfect

1 We use the present perfect to say that a finished past action is relevant now.

   They **have developed** a new brand of toothpaste.
   The chairman **has** recently **resigned**.

2 We use the present perfect when we are thinking of a period of time continuing up to the present.

   For over 50 years, Stirling Cars **has made** a classic English sports car.
   Calvin Klein **has been** one of the leading fashion designers since the mid-1970s.

3 We often use this tense to talk about our life experiences.

   She **has had** a number of interesting jobs.
   He**'s worked** for a variety of firms.

3 Uses of *will*

1 We use *will* to make predictions about the future or to give information about events that have been organised.

*There **will** probably **be** some turbulence during the flight.*
*The Queen **will open** the new airport extension on 1 April.*

2 We use *will* and *'ll* to make promises.

*When we receive your form we **will** send you a free flight voucher.*
*Everyone entering the competition **will** receive a prize.*
*I'**ll** get in touch very soon.*

3 We use the future progressive to indicate that something will be in progress at a future time.

*The plane **will be landing** in a few minutes' time.*
*You'**ll** soon be **enjoying** the comfort of our business class cabins.*

4 It is also used to refer to future events that have been arranged or which are expected to happen if everything goes according to plan.

*I've arranged your accommodation and **you'll be staying** in the Carlton Hotel.*
*If all goes well **we'll be living** in luxury in a couple of years' time.*

5 We use the future perfect to say that something will be over by a certain time in the future.

*The meeting **will have finished** by 4 o'clock.*
*If you don't hurry up the flight **will have left** before you get to the airport.*

6 *Will* can also be used with a verb in the passive form.

*The winner **will be offered** a free holiday in San Francisco.*
*All business passengers **will be given** VIP treatment.*

4 Articles

The indefinite article: *a/an*
We use *a/an* in the following ways:

- before unspecified singular countable nouns.
  *She works in **an** office.*

- with the names of professions.
  *She's **an** executive and he's **a** waiter.*

- in expressions of measurement.
  *We charge $500 **an** hour.*
  *It sells at €1.75 **a** litre.*

- before a noun to mean all things of the same type.
  ***A** loss leader is **an** article that a store sells at a low price to tempt customers to buy other goods.*

The definite article: *the*
We use *the*:

- when it is clear from the context what particular thing or place is meant.
  *I'll meet you in **the** reception area.*

- before a noun that we have mentioned before.
  *They had **a** villa in Cannes and **a** chalet in Innsbruck but they sold **the** villa.*

- before adjectives to specify a category of people or things.
  ***the** rich, **the** poor, **the** French, **the** unemployed, **the** world wide web*

Zero article : (Ø)
1 We do not put an article before mass nouns used in general statements.

(Ø) Money is the root of all (Ø) evil.

2 There is no article before the names of places and people.

(Ø) Poland　　(Ø) Japan　　(Ø) Dr. Spock
(Ø) President Clinton

5 Questions

1 In questions which can be answered with either *yes* or *no*, we put an auxiliary verb before the subject.

Is your present job interesting?
Are you willing to relocate?
Would you have to give notice?
Have you applied for any other jobs?
Do you have a clean driving licence?
Does your partner work?

2 We use questions beginning with *wh-* or *how* when asking for information.

Where were you born?
What did you study at college?
How long did you stay there?
How many people finished the course?

3 When *who*, *what* or *which* is the subject of a sentence, an auxiliary is not used.

Who gave you the information?
*(NOT * Who did give you ...)*
What happened at the meeting?
*(NOT * What did happen ...)*
Which costs the least?
*(NOT * Which does cost the least?)*

4 Requests and questions can be made more polite by making them less direct.

Would you mind if I smoked?
Do you mind if I use your phone?
Could you tell me how you found out about our firm?
I'd like to know what you don't like about your present employer.

5 Note that in reported questions, as in indirect questions, the word order is the same as for a statement.

'How soon will you be able to start?'
He wanted to know how soon he would be able to start.

6 Conditions

1 We use conditional sentences when discussing the terms of an agreement, making hypothetical proposals, bargaining and making concessions.

If you order now we will give you a discount.
We will reduce the price by 10% if you give us a firm order in advance.
If we give you 90 days' credit instead of 60 will you give us the interest you would have paid?
The use of *if* + *will* + base form of the verb suggests that the acceptance of the condition is the basis for a deal.

2 If the proposal is more tentative and possibly less feasible we use past verb forms.

If we said we were prepared to deliver in March would you make a firm order?
If you agreed to create more jobs we might think about a productivity deal.
If the Government found some extra money would you be prepared to create a subsidiary in our country?

3 We use *unless* in conditional sentences to mean *if not*.

We won't be able to start construction unless you train our personnel.

4 *As long as* and *provided that* are also used to state conditions.

We will sign the contract as long as you guarantee prices for the next eighteen months.
We can reach agreement on a joint venture provided that our firm has a representative on your board.

7 Passive

1 We use a passive structure when we are not interested in who carries out an action or it is not necessary to know.

*The company **was founded** in 1996.*
*Some changes **have been made**.*
*He **has been promoted** to the post of Sales Director.*
*A new low-alcohol lager **is being developed**.*

2 If we also want to mention who performs the action we can use a phrase beginning with *by*.

*The self-extinguishing cigarette was invented **by Kaj Jensen**.*
*The prototype is being checked **by the design team**.*

3 In a passive sentence, the grammatical subject receives the focus.

You will be met *at the airport by a company driver.*
(You receives the focus of attention.)

Compare with:
A company driver will meet *you at the airport.*

4 The passive is often used to describe processes and procedures.

*First of all an advertising agency **is contacted** and the aim of the campaign **is discussed**. Then a storyboard **is created** and, if acceptable, the TV commercial **is filmed** and **broadcast** at prime time.*

5 We also use the passive in a formal or impersonal style.

*It **was felt** that our design should be more innovative.*
*Company procedures **must be respected** at all times.*

8 Noun combinations

1 We use *'s* to express a relationship between a person or organisation and another person or thing.

*Mr Blake**'s** secretary   her husband**'s** car*
*BA**'s** employees   Volvo**'s** reputation*

The *'s* very often means that the relationship can be expressed using *have*.

*Mr. Blake **has** a secretary.*
*Volvo **has** a reputation.*

2 When two nouns are used together, the first noun functions as an adjective and describes the second noun.

a business card   a job description
an office complex a travel agency
Sometimes three or more nouns occur together.

a company credit card (a credit card issued by a company)
a management training programme (a training programme designed for management)

3 Two nouns are joined by *-of* when the ideas are more abstract.

*the cost **of** living*
*independence **of** mind*
*the joy **of** working and lifelong learning*

4 Some compound nouns are written as one word.

database   answerphone
letterhead   headquarters

5 When compound nouns are used with a number in expressions of measurement, the first noun is singular.

a six-lane motorway   a four-day week

9 Trends

1 To describe changing circumstances we can use verbs of movement.

improve   increase   recover   rise (↗)
decline   decrease   drop   fall (↘)

A dramatic movement may be expressed by:

rocket   soar   (↗)
dive   plummet   (↘)

A slight movement can be indicated by:

edge up   (↗)
edge down   dip   (↘)

The amount of increase can also be indicated using these verbs:

halve   (/2)
double   (x2)
triple   (x3)
quadruple   (x4)
increase tenfold   (x10)

Or with a preposition:

*Our business grew **by** 15% last year.*
*Sales have increased **from** €5 million **to** €5.8 million.*

2 Changes which have not reached their end-point are expressed using *-ing*.

*Profits are fall**ing**.*
*Unemployment has been ris**ing**.*

If the change is complete we use a perfect tense.

*The Government has privatis**ed** the rail network.*
*Sales have increas**ed** and that has meant higher profits.*

10 Narrative tenses

1 The past simple is common when we describe a sequence of events or tell a story in chronological order about events that happened in the past.

*On Monday 3 December 1984, a poisonous cloud of gas **escaped** from a pesticide plant in Bhopal, India. Eye witnesses **described** a cloud in the shape of a mushroom which **rose** above the plant and then descended over the town.*

2 We use the past perfect to situate an event that happened before another past event.

*By the end of the week, 1,200 people **had died** and at least 10,000 **had been affected** very seriously.*

3 The present perfect is used to describe past events of current significance.

*A major problem for doctors in Bhopal was lack of information on how to treat the chemical's effects. A pathologist said: 'Why **hasn't** Union Carbide **come forward** to tell us about the gas that **has leaked** and how to treat it. Is it not their moral duty? They **have not come** forward.'*

4 We use the past continuous to describe unfinished events which were in progress around a particular past time.

*By Monday 10 December, the death toll had risen to 2000 and American lawyers representing Indian families **were suing** Union Carbide for $12,500 million in compensation. Meanwhile journalists **were asking** the company difficult questions about its safety procedures and the share price **was dropping** sharply as investors became worried about the billions of dollars compensation that the company might have to pay.*

(Adapted from Ian Marcousé, *Business Case Studies*, Longman 1990)

11 Reporting

1 We use reported speech to say what someone else said at a different time or place. The tense used depends on the time when the report is made.

*I've just seen Kevin and he **says** he wants to change the specifications.*
(The situation is present, therefore the verb is in the present.)
*I saw Kevin last week and he **said** he wanted to change the specifications.*
(The situation is past, so a past verb form is used.)

2 There are no *absolute* rules for moving the verb one tense back.

*I saw Kevin last week and he said he **wants** to change the specifications.*
(He still wants to change them.)

If someone says, 'I'm going to resign', this can be reported as:

*He said he **is going** to resign.*
(This is still his intention.)
Or
*He said he **was going** to resign.*
(This may still be his intention but he may have changed his mind.)

3 In reported speech *will* becomes *would*.

*She said the meeting **would** start at 10.00.*
However, *could*, *might* and *should* do not change.

She said you could / might / should try to contact a different supplier.

4 *Yes/no* questions are reported using *if* or *whether*.

'Do you like managing change?'
*He asked me **if** I liked managing change.*

5 Note the word order in reported questions.

'When do you think you can start?'
He asked me when I thought I could start.
*(NOT *When did I think ...)*

12 Dependent prepositions

1 Some verbs always or typically have a particular preposition after them.

insure /plot /react	**against**
profit /stem /suffer	**from**
believe /invest /result	**in**
concentrate /insist /rely	**on**
amount /object /refer	**to**
deal /part /sympathise	**with**

2 Other verbs may be followed by one or another preposition, depending on the meaning.

*Our problems result **from** past errors.*

*The change has resulted **in** chaos.*

*Our success consists **in** our ability to react rapidly to changing circumstances. (i.e. is based on/depends on)*

*The team consists **of** four Europeans and two Americans. (i.e. is made up of)*

*We've agreed **on** a date for the meeting.*

*We've agreed **to** see her later today.*

*I agree **with** you entirely.*

*We're still thinking **of** a name for the new product.*

*I'll think it **over** for a while.*

*Having thought the idea **through**, I listed the pros and cons and made a decision.*

*Things have changed **for** the better.*

*I'd like to change my money **into** euros.*

*We've changed **from** traditional methods of work organisation.*

3 Many verbs are followed by a noun group beginning with a preposition. The nouns are objects of the preposition.

*The American market **accounts for** 40% of our sales.*

*I'd like to **ask for** some information.*

*We're **counting on** her support.*

*They **jumped at** the opportunity.*

13 Modal verbs

Ability

We use *can* to say that someone or something is able/not able to do something.
Could is used for a past ability.

*She **can** speak three languages fluently.*
*He **can't** find his briefcase.*
*The browser **can** find hundreds of related web sites.*
*He **could** write computer programs when he was ten years old.*

Obligation

We use *must* or *has/have to* to indicate what is compulsory.

*All travellers to the US **must/have to** be in possession of a visa.*

Permission and requests

May and *could* are a little more formal than *can*.

***Can** I use your mobile phone?*
***May** I sit here?*
***Could** I just make one more point?*

Possibility

We use *can* to say that something is possible and *cannot* if it is not.

*Other cultures **can** be really interesting.*
*You **can't** visit the museum on Mondays because it's closed.*

Probability

We use modal verbs to express the degree of likelihood.

*He left an hour ago so he **will/must** be there by now.* (100% certain)
*He left 45 minutes ago so he **should** be there by now.* (reasonably certain)
*He left 30 minutes ago so he **may/might** be there by now.* (possible)
*He only left 15 minutes ago so he **can't/won't** be there yet.* (impossible)

14 Relative clauses

1 We use *who* or *that* in a relative clause to identify people.

*The people **who/that** we employ are very highly qualified.*
As *people* is the object of the clause the relative pronoun can be left out.

The people we employ are very highly qualified.
If the relative pronoun defines the subject of the sentence, it must be included.

*A counterfeiter is a person **who** copies goods in order to trick people.*

2 We use *that* or *which* in a relative clause to identify things.

*Have you read the report **that/which** I left on your desk?*

If *that* or *which* identifies the object of the clause it can be left out.

Have you read the report I left on your desk?

If *that* or *which* defines the subject of the sentence, it must be included.

*Organisations **that** are flexible can respond to change.*

3 Non-defining clauses provide extra information about the subject or object of a sentence. The extra information is separated by commas.

*Philip Condit, **who** is chairman of Boeing, wants the airline to become a global company.*

Note that it is not possible to use *that*.

*The Dorfmann hotel, **which** is situated 30 kms outside Vienna, charges US$ 1400 per person.*

Again, it is not possible to use *that* in a non-defining clause.

15 Talking about the future

1 We use *going to* to talk about what we intend to do or what someone else has already decided to do.

*I'm **going to** buy a new car.*
*She's **going to** tell us about the ideas they've come up with for the ad campaign.*

Both *going to* and *will* are used for predictions.

*There's **going to** be a flight of capital from the West towards India and China.*
*The Fortune Garment Company **will** continue to lose market share unless it solves its problems.*

2 We use *'ll* to make a spontaneous promise or offer to do something.

*'I haven't got time to do this myself.' 'Don't worry. I**'ll** give you a hand.'*

3 We use the present continuous to talk about fixed plans or arrangements.

*I**'m meeting** Mrs da Silva next week. She's **arriving** on Wednesday.*

4 We use the present simple to talk about a schedule.

*The flight **leaves** at 15.50 tomorrow.*

In time clauses, we use the present simple to refer to future time. It is incorrect to use *will* in a time clause.

*We won't start until everyone **gets** here.*
*I'm going to go round the world when I **retire**.*
*As soon as I **have** the results, I'll give you a ring.*
*Come and see me before you **go**.*

16 Prepositions of time

at	is used with clock times, feast days and certain periods of time.

*The train leaves **at** two o'clock.*
*We have a holiday **at** Easter and Christmas.*
*I relax **at** the weekend.*
*She got married **at** the age of twenty.*

on is used with days and dates.

*I'll see you **on** Tuesday.*
*She was born **on** 2 July 1956.*

in is used for longer periods.

*Commerce developed **in** the seventeenth century.*
*The stock market boomed **in** the eighties.*
*The weather is good **in** summer.*

by is associated with a deadline.

*We will know **by** the end of the week.*

for refers to a period of time.

*She's staying here **for** three weeks.*
*I worked in Chicago **for** two years.*

during can be used instead of *in* with periods of the day, months, seasons, years, decades and centuries.

*Production will begin **during** September.*
***During** the 19th century Britain was an empire.*

It can also be used more generally, to indicate that one event occurs while another is taking place.

*I'll be in Prague **during** the festival.*

since is used if we say when something started in relation to the present.

*I haven't seen her **since** I left the firm.*
*We've sold 100,000 units **since** the beginning of the year.*
*They've been publishing books **since** 1908.*

Writing file

Letters

FAR EASTERN AIRWAYS COMPANY LIMITED

Regent House, 5th Floor,
12/16 Haymarket, London W1V 5BX
Administration: 020 7285 9981
Reservations: 020 7564 0930
Fax: 020 7285 9984

15 February 2000

Mr Roberto Garcia
Universal Imports
28 Whitechapel Court
London E10 7NB

Dear Mr Garcia

Re: Roxanna Garbey

Roxanna Garbey has been accepted for a position as Passenger Service Agent with Far Eastern Airways at Gatwick Airport.

In order for Roxanna to work at Gatwick, she must have a special PASS which would permit her to visit high security areas. She has given your name as a reference.

I would appreciate it if you could complete the enclosed form and return it to us as quickly as possible. She is due to start work with us on 15 March, but can only do so after we receive your reference.

Thank you for your cooperation. I enclose a stamped addressed envelope.

Yours sincerely

J. P. Dent

J. P. Dent
Personnel Manager

British (Canadian)
Open Punctuation =
no colon after
salutation or
comma after
closings.

American (Canadian)
Dear Sirs :
colon
Sincerely , comma

Faxes

FALCON HOTELS

FAX

TO	Alice Wong
Fax No	00 852 7514329
FROM	Zofia Nadstoga,
Fax No	020 7945 2647
	Reservations Dept. Falcon Hotels
Date	5 July

No of pages (including this)   1

Dear Ms Wong
This is to confirm your booking for a single room from
20 July to 27 July inclusive
at a rate of £150.00 per night (excluding Sales Tax).
As requested, you we will hold your room until
midnight on the day of your arrival.
We look forward to meeting you shortly.

Yours sincerely

Zofia Nadstoga

Zofia Nadstoga
Reservations Manager

> Information transmitted by fax may be presented in various formats, for example in letter, memo or note form.

> Faxes may contain the following headings: To / From / Date / Subject / No. of pages / Fax numbers

> The style of a fax message may be formal, informal or neutral depending on the subject and recipient.

E-mails

cc:mail for: Tom Hunt

Subject:	Friday's meeting
From:	Harry King at MHATG_HSN_MACO1
To:	tom.hunt@promoworld.com
cc:	mary.fowler@audiovision.com
bcc:	claudia.stahnke@audiovision.com

Tom
Just to confirm that we will be able to attend
the meeting next Friday.
I'll be with our Sales Director, Mary Fowler.

Harry

> Be careful to type in all e-mail addresses accurately.

> bcc means blind copy (a copy will be sent to this person but other people will not know this).

> In general e-mails tend to be less formal than a letter and are often used for brief communication.

Memos

Memos are usually for internal communication.

They should include the following headings:
To / From / Subject / Date

They should be short and include only relevant information.

Points should be arranged in logical order.

In longer memos, it is common to number points.

The tone of a memo may be formal, informal or neutral.

It is usual to end with your initials rather than a signature.

MEMO

To: **All department heads**
From: **Patricia Marchand,**
General Manager
Date: **18 April**

Subject: **Visit of German agent**

Please note that Katya Schmidt, our German agent, will be visiting the company on Friday, 26 April.

There will be a meeting on that day at 11.30 am in the Boardroom, which you should all attend. Ms Schmidt will be presenting her marketing plan for expanding sales in the German market.

If you wish to join us for lunch at a local restaurant, please let me know as soon as possible.

Agendas

Always put the title, date, time and venue (place).

Larger meetings and committee meetings may also include the following:
a) Apologies for absence
b) Matters arising from last meeting
c) Correspondence
d) Date of next meeting

A.O.B. means *any other business*. This is for other relevant issues that were not included in the agenda.

Management meeting

AGENDA

Date: 1 March
Time: 14.00
Venue: Room 23M, Shaw House

1. Complaints about reception staff.

2. New brochure.

3. Price list for next year.

4. New product presentation.

5. A.O.B.

Action minutes

Minutes of the management meeting

Date	1 March, 14.00
Venue	Shaw House, Room 23M
Present	Chris Glover, Bill Brace, Gill Winstanley, Iwona Pawlowska, Gareth Massey

1   Guidelines for reception staff
Following recent complaints about the attitude and professionalism of the reception staff, we all agree that it is essential to produce a set of written guidelines.   IP   8 March
The Human Resources Department will also arrange additional customer service training to take place over the next two months.   IP

2   New brochure
The Marketing Department is speaking to all senior managers about this on an individual basis. A draft brochure will be circulated so that it can be approved and sent to the printers by 15 March to be ready for next month's trade fair.   BB   5 March

3   Price list
We agreed that our new prices this year will be contained in a separate booklet, rather than as part of the New Product Brochure. An updated list is being compiled.   BB   15 March

4   New product presentation
A presentation to the sales team is being given on 11 March to familiarise all sales representatives with our new products. Individual meetings with team members will be arranged so that everyone is fully briefed for next month's trade fair.   GM

Next Meeting: 18 March, 11.00am
Venue: To be confirmed

For most business meetings, action minutes are more useful than full minutes.

Action minutes are intended to make sure that decisions of the meeting are understood and carried out.

There is a brief summary of the discussion for each item on the agenda.

The initials of the person responsible for carrying out any action required are given in the margin, along with any deadline.

Reports

Report on staff lateness

Terms of Reference

Louise Dawson, Personnel Manager has requested this report on staff lateness at the new London office. The report was to be submitted to her by 20 April.

Procedure

Out of 24 members of staff, 23 were surveyed about:

1. Their method of transport.
2. Time taken to get to work.
3. Problems encountered.

Findings

1. All staff are late at least once every two weeks.
2. Fifteen members of staff use the Underground, two use the bus and six travel by car.
3. Travelling time varies between 20 minutes and one hour.
4. All staff experienced problems.
   (i) All members of staff experienced delays on the Underground (Circle, Central, Northern and District lines) due to:
      1. Signal problems
      2. Engineering work
      3. Overcrowding
      4. Poor train frequency on some lines
   (ii) Members of staff who use the bus experienced delays due to traffic jams.
   (iii) Members of staff who travel by car also experienced delays due to traffic jams and two had problems parking, particularly on Mondays and Tuesdays.

Conclusions

1. All staff using public transport are late because the Underground and bus services are unreliable.
2. A minority of members of staff who travel by car experienced problems with parking.
3. The office opens at 9.00am and so staff are forced to travel during the rush hour.
4. Members of staff are not leaving sufficient time for their journeys which are extended due to delays.

Recommendations

1. Members of staff should leave longer for their journeys in order to allow for delays.
2. Staff should investigate alternative routes and means of transport.
3. It is recommended that staff who travel by car and experience parking problems use the new car park in Commercial Road, which opens next week.
4. It is recommended that the Personnel Director investigates the possibility of introducing a flexitime system so staff do not have to travel during the rush hour.

John Atkinson

Office Manager

18 April

1 A report should be well organised with information presented in a logical order. There is no set layout for a report. The layout will depend on:
   a) the type of report (for example, it may be the result of an investigation or a progress report; it may be short or long, formal or informal, etc.)
   b) the particular style that a company uses for its reports.

2 The format used for this example is common for many *formal* reports:
   • Title
   • Terms of reference
   • Procedure
   • Findings
   • Conclusions
   • Recommendations

3 Another common structure for a short report is:
   • Title
   • Introduction
   • Main body (Findings)
   • Conclusions
   • Recommendations

4 Formal reports normally contain:
   • Sections and subsections
   • Headings and subheadings
   • A numbering system
   • Indented information
   All these help to make the report easy to read.

5 *Terms of reference/Introduction* usually includes:
   • who asked for the report
   • why the report is being written
   • the purpose/subject of the report
   • when it should be submitted by
   The introduction to the report sometimes contains the *Procedure* (also called *Proceedings*) – where/how you got the information.

6 *Findings* are the facts you discovered.

7 *Conclusions* are what you think about the facts and how you interpret them.

8 *Recommendations* are practical suggestions as to what should be done to solve the problem, remedy the situation, etc.

Notices

Notices are used to inform people about changes of plan, instructions or warnings.

A notice needs a clear heading.

Information must be presented in a clear, concise form.

The tone of notices is usually rather formal and impersonal.

It must have the name and position of the person who wrote it, and the date.

AURIC BANK

CUSTOMER NOTICE

This branch will be closed until 10.30 am on Tuesday 7 November for staff training.

We apologise in advance for any inconvenience caused.

Antonia Valdes
Branch Manager
2 November

AB

The social-cultural game

What do you say?	**1** You have forgotten the name of the person you are talking to. Find out their name politely.	**2** You are late for a meeting.
6 You are in an important business negotiation. The other person asks you if he/she can smoke.	**7** The waiter in a restaurant has just given you the bill. You are sure it is much too high.	**8** You are having dinner with a foreign colleague in their country. The food is unfamiliar to you and you do not know what to choose.
12 An important client invites you to the theatre. You cannot attend because you have already accepted another invitation.	**13** At a conference you meet someone you think you've met before.	**14** You have just spilled red wine on a client's dress.
18 Spell your name.	**19** Give your telephone number.	**20** In which country is chewing gum forbidden by law? a) Iran b) Iraq c) Indonesia d) Singapore
24 Give directions from your office to the closest station or airport.	**25** In which country is it illegal to drink anything alcoholic and drive? a) Sweden b) France c) UK d) US	**26** Recommend a restaurant to a client.
30 In which country is it common to go out to eat after 10pm? a) UK b) Sweden c) Japan d) Spain	**31** You arrive for an appointment with your bank manager. Introduce yourself to the person at the reception desk.	**32** You are visiting a company and you want to use their telephone.

3 You are at a party. You want to get away from someone who will not stop talking.	**4** You are offered some food that you hate.	**5** You should not point the sole of your foot towards your hosts. Which area does this refer to? a) Arab world b) West Indies c) Scandinavia d) Australia
9 You are at a cocktail party and the host/hostess has just handed you a glass of champagne. You do not drink alcohol.	**10** In which country would it be a grave insult to touch someone on the head? a) Thailand b) Japan c) Pakistan d) Iraq	**11** You have been invited to your colleague's house for dinner. He/She telephones you to ask if there is anything you don't eat.
15 In which country is it quite likely that you will be asked to sing a song during the celebrations following a successful business negotiation. a) Italy b) Austria c) Japan d) Germany	**16** A visitor wants to buy some local souvenirs.	**17** A visitor wants advice on how to spend an evening in your town.
21 Talk about today's weather.	**22** You are on the phone. Describe yourself to someone you are going to meet at the airport, so they can recognise you.	**23** You are at an international conference. Complain about your hotel room.
27 You are on an plane. Introduce yourself to the person sitting next to you.	**28** Introduce your boss to a person visiting your organisation.	**29** You are having a small dinner party. Introduce two friends of yours to each other.
33 You see an attractive person at an international conference. Start up a conversation.	**34** You meet a business contact at a railway station. Offer to carry some of his luggage for him.	*Finish!*

Activity file

1 Globalisation, Skills, Exercise D 1, page 11

> **Buyer Donatelli SpA**
> The details of the order are as follows:
>
> | Quantity | Order no. | Comment |
> |---|---|---|
> | 1000 | 2850 EPX | The parts sent are too short and the wrong size. |
> | 40 | 105 GJ | Incorrect amount, 400 were sent. |
> | 680 | 189 PTZ | Wrong product and amount. 500 198 PYZ were sent. |
> | 1200 | 204 RD | Correct amount sent but the wrong price quoted in the invoice. The amount should be £2,500 not £25,000. |
>
> The replacement parts must be delivered within one week – they are urgently needed by an important customer.

11 Change, Skills, Exercise F, page 91

> **L Dickinson, Sales Director**
> You know it is not the topic of the meeting, but you wish to let everyone know that you are unhappy about your present salary. You believe that the long waiting list for Sterling cars is due to your excellent sales skills and that you should be paid a lot more. You think that the company should raise the price of the car by at least 40%–50%. Full automated production should be introduced so that 4000 or more cars could be made each year. If necessary, the car could be manufactured by an overseas company.

14 Leadership, Starting up, Exercise A, page 110

From left to right:

Top row: Mikhail Gorbachev, born 1931, Stavrapol, Russia, Secretary General of the Communist Party and Soviet Leader 1985-1991, began the policy of Perestroika which brought greater freedom the Soviet Union and eventually led to democratic governments in Central and Eastern Europe; **Carly Fiorina**, born 1955, Austin, Texas, taught English in Italy before joining AT&T in 1980 as a sales representative, appointed Chief Executive of Hewlett-Packard 1999; **Nelson Mandela**, born 1918, Transkeu, South Africa, South African President 1994-1999, leader of the African National Congress, imprisoned for life 1964 for his campaign against apartheid, released 1990; **Bill Gates**, born 1955, Seattle, USA, founder of Microsoft, left Harvard University without a degree, now believed to be worth over $100 billion.

Bottom row: Aung San Sui Kyi, born 1945, Burmese political opposition leader, educated in India and Oxford, returned to Burma 1988 and elected President but blocked by the military and put under house arrest; **Akio Morita**, 1921-1999, co-founder, with Masaru Ibuka, of Sony Corp. in 1946, inventor of the Walkman, introduced the world's first all-transistor TV in 1960; **John Lennon**, 1940-1980, co-founder of The Beatles pop group, 1960, one of the key figures in music and youth culture of the 1960s, assassinated outside his apartment block in New York; **John F Kennedy**, 1917-1963, Captain in the US Navy in World War II, elected US President 1961, assassinated Dallas, Texas, 22 November 1963; **Margaret Thatcher**, born 1925, Grantham, England, British Prime minister 1979-1990, her policies transformed the UK economy, emphasising the importance of the free market and privatisation of the public sector.

3 Travel, Case study: Team-building seminar, page 28

Stage 1: Manager, IDP's travel service

No of participants	20 (Male 12 / Female 8)
Ages	25–48
European participants	German, Spanish, French, Swiss
Arrival	Registration: 5pm, Friday 12 November
Departure	Preferably late Sunday evening
Type of hotel	Either 4 or 5 star
Equipment required	Overhead projector, flip chart, PowerPoint, VCR
Meals required	Friday: dinner; Saturday: breakfast, lunch, dinner; Sunday: breakfast, lunch
Special requirements	Two participants are vegetarian. Four do not drink alcohol. One participant uses a wheelchair. Six participants are smokers.

Stage 3: Manager, IDP's travel service

You must arrange a suitable date to meet the Universal Airline executive. Here is your diary for the week.

	morning	afternoon
Monday	All-day meeting to discuss the department's budget	
Tuesday	Meeting & dental appointment	Free
Wednesday	All-day training session	
Thursday	Interviewing candidates until 4pm	
Friday	Department meeting until 2.30pm	

Stage 4: Manager, IDP's travel service

You will only decide which hotel to choose after further negotiation. You want value for money, but it is essential that the executives enjoy themselves and get to know each other. Also, a friend has strongly recommended the Dorfmann because of its excellent location.

You expect the seminar to finish at 5pm on Sunday and participants will probably fly home that evening. However, they could fly early Monday morning, if necessary.

You need information about the following:
- the facilities at each hotel
- exactly what is included in the prices quoted to you
- when payment must be made
- details about the location of the hotels
- transport to and from the airport
- meals
- secretarial and other support services, for example, interpreters

3 Travel, Reading 2, Exercise F, page 27

Customer Relations Manager
You must try to stop this kind of behaviour. It harms the image of Alpha Airlines. However, the university is a very good customer. If possible, you do not want to lose its business. Deal with the situation politely, but be firm. Try to get the Sports Director on your side.

1 Globalisation, Skills, Exercise D1, page 11

Production Manager Rod Engineering
A buyer from Donatelli SpA will phone you concerning incorrect spare parts sent by your firm.
1 Apologise for the mistakes made by your firm.
2 Write down details of the incorrect order. Check to make sure your notes are correct.
3 Promise to take appropriate action.

You will need two weeks to deliver replacement parts as stocks of most items are very low at the moment.

9 Money, Case study: Angel Investments, page 76

Briefing notes: AI investors

Before the meeting
1 Study the proposals that the entrepreneurs have chosen and discuss which appeal to you most. Consider which are the most risky and which have the greatest potential profits.
2 Prepare questions which you wish to ask each person/company.

During the meeting
1 Listen to the presentation of each person/company. Ask questions to help you decide which projects to invest in.
2 Discuss the projects. Decide which to invest in, and how much money you will give to each.

Remember: You have a maximum limit of £5.5 million to invest, but can invest less.

11 Change, Skills, Exercise F, page 91

J Stirling, Managing Director
You chair the meeting. You want everyone to have their say. You respect the Finance Director's judgement. However, the Sales Director often gets off the point in meetings. You hope that the members of the meeting will not want to change the company too much. You don't want to do anything to harm the firm's image and reputation.

3 Travel, Case study: Team-building seminar, page 28

Stage 1: Head of Corporate Travel, Universal Airlines

You need the following information:
- Participants: male? female?
- Ages?
- Nationality of non-American participants?
- Any special habits? For example, do they smoke?
- Arrival and departure dates/times?
- What class of hotel do they want?
- Any special equipment?
- Meals: When? How many?

Stage 3: Head of Corporate Travel, Universal Airlines

You must try to arrange a suitable day and time for your meeting with IDP's travel service Manager. Here is your diary for the week.

	morning	**afternoon**
Monday	all-day visit to a conference centre	
Tuesday	Free	Appointment with your son's headmaster at 3pm
Wednesday	Free after 10.30am	Free
Thursday	Entertaining foreign visitor all day (including the evening)	
Friday	Presentation to Board	Free after 3pm

Stage 4: Head of Corporate Travel, Universal Airlines

Read the information about the two hotels. You must try to persuade the IDP manager to choose the Monarch hotel because you will make 40% more profit. Your price for this hotel includes accommodation for Sunday night.

MONARCH HOTEL	**DORFMANN HOTEL**
Location City centre, near top restaurants, Opera House and shopping. 18th century hotel	**Location** 30 kms outside Vienna, lovely countryside, forest, lake. Modern hotel (1952)
Transport Hotel 'shuttle' cars	**Transport** Luxury bus provided by the hotel.
Facilities Health club, gym, pool, sauna, shop. Facilities shared with other hotel guests	**Facilities** Health club (used *only* by IDP's executives), pool sauna, running track through countryside
Meals Outstanding cooking	**Meals** Healthy family-style cooking
Payment By 31 December	**Payment** On/before 12 November: 10% discount
Departure Monday *	**Departure** Sunday evening
Secretarial help/interpreter $40 an hour	**Secretarial help/interpreter** free of charge

* Use of hospitality suite at the airport

6 Trade, Case study: Ashbury Guitars, page 53

Information file: Ashbury Guitars

Models	You want KGC to supply three models: Ashbury SG1000, SG500 and SG200. The SG1000 has some special additional features.
Quality	All the guitars should be manufactured in KGC's own factory, or quality may suffer. There are alternative suppliers in Korea but the quality of their products is probably not as good as KGC's.
Quantity	You want to place the following first order: Model Quantity SG1000 750 SG500 500 SG200 300 You are sure that demand will be good for the SG1000. The cheaper guitars *may* sell well. However, there is strong competition in the lower price ranges. If all the guitars sell well, you will place a larger order in three months' time.
Price	KGC have quoted these prices: SG1000 US$ 920 SG500 US$ 550 SG200 US$ 475 All prices are FOB Pusan, Korea. Your normal profit margin is 33%, but for the SG1000, it will be 40%.
Delivery	By June 1. A later date will affect sales. (Music festivals in California in May always stimulate demand.)
Discounts	Although this is a first order, you hope to negotiate a discount of at least 6% off the quoted price and 10% on further orders of over 1,000.
Payment	Letter of credit 60 days. This will give you time to sell some of the guitars before paying for them.
Guarantee	At least two years, three if possible.
Exclusivity	You would like to have a non-exclusive contract so that you can order from other Korean guitar manufacturers.
Transport	By sea in containers. Prices should be CIF San Francisco. If prices are FOB, Pusan (Korea), it will add 5% to your purchase price.

11 Change, Skills, Exercise F, page 91

F Densham, Sales Manager

You have strong feelings about how the company can increase its profits. You want to subcontract the manufacture of the car's engine to another company. The workers who did this job before could then be retrained to make the bodies of the cars. You do not want the car to be produced in another country – it would no longer be a British car. You are sure that workers in another country could not produce cars of the same quality. You want to increase output in England by about 10% a year.

11 Change, Skills, Exercise F, page 91

B Reilly, Production Manager
You are worried about the labour situation. Older workers are retiring and it is becoming difficult to hire new workers at the current wage rates. The workers are unhappy and are demanding higher wages. They are threatening to strike. If the car is produced in another country, you will lose your job. You want to move to a larger factory and to produce 4000 cars a year, with full automation in the manufacture of the body and engine. This will increase profits and give you more status and a higher salary. In your opinion, the price of the car cannot be greatly increased – it is already in the higher price range.

1 Globalisation, Skills, Exercise D 2, page 11

Reception Manager
Your are the Reception Manager of the Belvedere Hotel. You will receive a call from someone confirming a hotel reservation. Note the caller's name, company and telephone number. Note also the name of the guest and all other details concerning the booking e.g. how the caller will pay, and any special requirements of the guest. Your restaurant closes at 10pm each evening, but other restaurants in the area stay open later. You do not normally hold a room later than 8pm, as in the past several guests have failed to arrive.

3 Travel, Reading 2, Exercise F, page 27

Sports Director
You are not too worried about the team's behaviour on airlines. They are young women and men, full of energy and the joy of youth. Why shouldn't they make a little noise and have a drink or two? Be polite to the Customer Relations Manager, but be loyal to your students and support them.

15 Competition, Starting up, page 118

Key

	1	2	3	4	5	6	7	8	9	10
a)	3	3	1	1	1	3	1	1	3	3
b)	2	2	2	2	2	2	2	2	2	2
c)	1	1	3	3	3	1	3	3	1	1

Over 26:   Highly competitive. You want to be first, best, always.

18–26:   Fairly competitive. You are ready to compete in a number of areas.

12–17:   Not very competitive. Running is more important than winning for you.

11 or 10:   The rat race is not for you. Relax!

6 Trade, Case study: Ashbury Guitars, page 53

Information file: KGC

Models	You want to supply three models in the first year: Ashbury SG1000, SG500, and SG200. The SG1000 will be costly to produce because it has advanced technical features.
Quality	To reduce costs of production, at least 40% of the order will be manufactured by other Korean firms.
Quantity	You want Ashbury Guitars to place a first order for 3000 guitars. You need a large order to cover the costs of setting up the production lines. Try to persuade Ashbury to buy a large number of the SG200 model because your profit margin on this guitar is high.

List price (US$)		Estimated cost of production	Prices quoted to Ashbury
	SG1000	700	920
	SG500	220	550
	SG200	140	475

Payment	By bank transfer, as soon as the goods have been dispatched.
Guarantee	One year.
Delivery	June 30. If an earlier delivery is required, production costs will increase by 10% because of overtime payments to workers. Before June 30, the factory will be fulfilling orders for other customers.
Discount	Your company policy is to offer new customers 3% off list price for a first order, and 5% for second and further orders.
Exclusivity	You want an exclusive contract because Ashbury is a big distributor. It could be very profitable to do business with them in the future.
Transport	Prices are FOB, Pusan (Korea). If CIF San Francisco is required, your prices must be increased by 5%.

11 Change, Skills, Exercise F, page 91

S Dubois, Production Controller
You have strong feelings about how to increase the company's profits. You believe it must produce the cars in a lower-cost country such as Korea or China. This would enable the price of the car to be kept at a competitive level. You are worried because labour costs have been increasing and this has reduced the profit margin on the cars. In your opinion, the price of the car should not be raised. You think that production could be increased by 10% a year if more power-driven tools were used to make the body of the car.

2 Brands, Starting up, Exercise C, page 14

Top 10 global brands

1	Coca-Cola	5	Ford	8	McDonald's
2	Microsoft	6	Disney	9	AT&T
3	IBM	7	Intel	10	Marlboro
4	General Electric				

Source: *Interbrand/Citibank 1999*

Companies ranked according to:

Weight (market share)	35%
Breadth (cross section of society reached)	30%
Depth (brand loyalty)	20%
Length (brand-stretching ability)	15%

11 Change, Skills, Exercise F, page 91

C Bristol, Finance Director
You have received the offer of a better job at a competitor's company. You will probably accept the job as you think you are overworked and underpaid. You think that the cost of producing the car will increase greatly in the future because the factory workers are asking for a large pay increase. You think the financial future of the company is poor. The car appeals to customers because it is mostly hand-made. If it greatly increases its production, the car will lose its image of quality and craftsmanship. You are not sure what the company can do to increase its profits.

1 Globalisation, Skills, Exercise D 2, page 11

Personnel Manager
You are a Personnel Manager of a publishing company. Your telephone number is 01753 320492, extension 1209. Call the Belvedere Hotel to confirm a reservation for your overseas visitor, Malin Johansen for 3 nights from Friday 22 April – Sunday 24 April. She will be arriving late on Friday (approximately 11.30pm), so ask the hotel to hold the room for her until that time. She may also want to have a late meal at the hotel. However, she will not require breakfast or any other meals. She will want coffee-making facilities in her room, a fax machine and a safe for keeping valuables. You will pay the accommodation with your Visa Card, No. 4209 1802 3853 8620.

9 Money, Case study: Angel Investments, page 76

Briefing notes: Entrepreneurs

Before the meeting
Choose one of the proposals or present your own idea for a product or service.

1 Prepare a presentation of your product/service. Use the Key Points as a guide for structuring the presentation.

2 Your aim will be to persuade AI to give you the money you need. Try to predict what questions they will ask you.

During the meeting

1 Give your presentation and answer the AI team's questions.

2 While waiting to hear AI's decision concerning your request for finance, discuss these questions:
   a) Was your presentation effective?
   b) Do you think you will be successful?
   c) How well did you answer their questions?
   d) What problems did you have, if any ?

1 Globalisation

🎧 **1.1 (I = Interviewer, SH = Stephen Haseler)**

I   Could you tell me about the advantages and disadvantages of globalisation?

SH The great advantage of globalisation in my view is that it increases competition. Companies and firms have to be careful and have to order their affairs so that they compete in a global market. But I think that is outweighed by a large number of disadvantages.
The first one is that it does hurt the local government's ability to deal with issues like welfare benefits, wages and taxes mainly because the corporation is able to say to the British Government or the French Government or the American government, 'Look unless you lower your taxes on us, we'll be moving off to South East Asia or Latin America', and so on. And so it takes out of the hands of government the ability to control their own welfare systems and provide a decent infrastructure for their people. Now this is not so bad as long as there is some negotiation between governments and companies. But more and more in recent years, companies have started to rule the roost. The corporation … some commentator said the other day, 'The corporation is the most important institution in our lives,' and I think there's a lot of truth in that. They can now dictate to governments and I want to see some kind of give-and-take between governments and corporations. Now that's the first problem.

The other problem that I see, of course, is one of unemployment in the Western world. As companies want to improve their profitability, they're going to be looking for the low-cost, low-wage centres. And we're just about to see a major change in the global economy, because of the addition of China and India to the global labour market. There are great advantages in this but there's a lot of problems as well because China and India are going to provide a skilled population. Also, they're going to provide fairly good infrastructures for the companies that are going to go out there. So we're going to see a flight of capital from the West which is going to be sudden and dramatic. If this is too sudden and is not managed properly we could find very severe employment problems in the Western world.
So that is, I think, the kind of issue we've got to deal with as this process of globalisation gathers pace.

🎧 **1.2**

A survey has come up with some interesting information about the cost of living in our major cities.
Tokyo is still the most expensive city in the world. Osaka is second and Moscow third, on a par with Hong Kong. Many European cities have gone down the rankings because their exchange rates have become weaker against the US dollar. Moscow's exchange rate has also become weaker, but Russia has a much higher inflation rate than many European countries. So prices in Moscow are among the highest in Europe. But there is one advantage of living in Moscow. The underground is excellent – very cheap and much more comfortable than the one in London.
New York is the most expensive US city. This is because the US dollar is stronger than many other currencies. Some European countries that used to be far more expensive than New York are now much cheaper. London is the 10th most expensive city in the world, according to the survey. A year ago, London was 5%–10% cheaper than many French and German cities. This is no longer so. Now London is 15% dearer than the German and French cities mentioned in the survey. However, London is a good city to live in. Business people said that London was the most exciting of all the major cities in the world. Londoners also claim that it is cleaner than it used to be, and safer than many other European cities. If you're hard up, don't go to Oslo – it's Europe's most expensive city. Meals at restaurants cost a fortune and drinks are very pricey.

🎧 **1.3**

Conversation 1
A Yes?
B Could I speak to Mr Smith?
A Er … I don't know erm I think he's out.
B Do you know when he'll be back?
A Well, I'm not quite sure. You could maybe try tomorrow.
B OK. Bye.

Conversation 2
A Hello. Is that Janet, Bill's secretary?
B Yes, that's right.
A It's John Blake. I'm just phoning to give him an invoice number.
B Yeah. What is it?
A Oh, let me see, where is it. Yeah, I've got to have it here somewhere.
B Look phone me back when you find it. I'm rather busy just now.

Conversation 3
A Hello. I'd like to speak to Bob Graham.
B He's not here.
A Could you tell me when he'll be back?
B Later this afternoon.
A Well, could you take a message for me?
B Sorry, I don't have time. I'll have to ring off, I'm going to lunch.

Conversation 4
A Hello, it's Susan here. I'm just phoning to check my appointment with Chris tomorrow.
B Yeah?
A Could you look it up for me?
B Oh, I don't know … where's the diary? … Yes, got it. So it was the 16th was it?
A No, the 18th.
B No, I can't find anything. I didn't write it down.

Conversation 5
A Hello Bilk Ltd.
B Hello, this is Jack Johnson. I'm phoning about the delivery. Has it arrived yet?
A No it hasn't. We've been waiting a week. It still isn't here yet.
B I'm really sorry about that.
A Well, we've been waiting for too long. It's not good enough. You're wasting our time.
B Oh, I'm sure your order will be …

2 Brands

🎧 **2.1 (I = Interviewer, LF = Lynne Fielding)**

I   What is branding and why do we need brands?

LF A brand can be a name, a term or a symbol. It is used to differentiate a product from competitors' products. The brands guarantee a certain quality level. Brands should add value to products. It's a synergy effect whereby one plus one equals three. But customers must believe they get extra value for money.

🎧 **2.2**

LF There are different types of brands. There are what we refer to as the stand alone brands or individual brands, for example Ariel, Haagen Daaz ice-cream, Direct line insurance, or Marlboro cigarettes. They require separate marketing support. There's also the corporate branding, or family brands such as Heinz or Virgin, Marks and Spencer, Levis.

🎧 **2.3**

LF We need new brands because, well, customers want new brands. They want choice. They want a selection of different products. They like to rely on the quality levels guaranteed by the company. They like to trust products. It makes shopping so much easier for them. And also, they like to identify with brands.

3 Travel

3.1 (R = Receptionist, PK = Philippa Knight, MB = Maria Bonetti)

R Good morning CPT. How may I help you?

PK It's Philippa Knight here. Could you put me through to extension 281 please?

R Certainly. Putting you through.

MB Hello. Maria Bonetti speaking.

PK Hello Maria. It's Philippa Knight from *The Fashion Group* in New York.

MB Hi Philippa, how are things?

PK Fine thanks. I'm calling because I'll be in London next week and I'd like to make an appointment to see you. I want to tell you about our new collection.

MB Great. What day would suit you? I'm fairly free next week, I think.

PK How about Wednesday? In the afternoon? Could you make it then?

MB Let me look now. Let me check my diary. Oh yes, that'd be no problem at all. What about 2 o'clock? Is that OK?

PK Perfect. Thanks very much. It'll be great to see you again. We'll have plenty to talk about.

MB That's for sure. See you next week then.

PK Right. Bye.

MB Bye.

3.2 (R = Receptionist, PK = Philippa Knight)

R Good morning, CPT. How may I help you?

PK I'd like to speak to Maria Bonetti, extension 281, please.

R Thank you. Who's calling please?

PK It's Philippa Knight, from *The Fashion Group*.

R Thank you. I'm putting you through. Hello, I'm afraid she's engaged at the moment. Will you hold or can I take a message?

PK I'll leave a message please. The thing is, I should be meeting Ms Bonetti at 2pm, but something's come up. My plane was delayed, and I've got to reschedule my appointments. If possible, I'd like to meet her tomorrow. Preferably in the morning. Could she call me back here at the hotel please?

R Certainly. What's the number please?

PK It's 020 7585 3814. I'll be leaving the hotel soon, so if she can't call me back within, say, within the next quarter of an hour, I'll call her again this morning. Is that OK?

R Right. I've got that. I'll make sure she gets the message.

PK Thanks for your help. Goodbye.

R Goodbye.

3.3 (I = Interviewer, DC = David Creith)

I Could you introduce yourself please?

DC Certainly. My name's David Creith and I'm the Customer Service Teaching Manager for British Airways in Terminal 4 at Heathrow.

I What problems do you have to solve for business travellers?

DC A lot of problems. Probably the main one is seating requests. A lot of business travellers have specific seating requests. Some people want an aisle, some people want a window, some people want to sit next to their colleague. It's not always possible to give everyone the exact seat they want due to the aircraft being fully booked. Certain passengers may say this is going to disrupt their business trip because they can't discuss things with colleagues – that sort of thing.

One of the other things we get is downgrading. Sometimes, like all airlines, due to commercial pressure we have to oversell flights. Occasionally we miscalculate and have to downgrade passengers to a lower class – for example from First to Business Class or Business to Economy. Obviously passengers aren't happy about this at all.

The opposite thing is an upgrade. Passengers may request an upgrade for countless reasons – for anything that has happened to them in the past and they perceive that British Airways has done wrongly. Or just because they think they're a very important person or very commercially important as regards British Airways. And so they demand an upgrade for the smallest of reasons.

For example, we have Gold Card holders – that's part of the British Airways frequent flights scheme – who like to see their status recognised and will request an upgrade almost habitually.

There are also problems with baggage. Passengers' baggage may have been lost or damaged on previous flights and it may mean a lot of running around on my part and trying to trace where a bag may have gone missing or how it was damaged. And it's quite an exhausting process trying to find out things because obviously Heathrow and British Airways is a very large organisation.

3.4 (I = Interviewer, DC = David Creith)

I How do you deal with people who complain by phone?

DC The very first thing you've got to do is listen very carefully because they may have a very valid cause for complaining. But the important thing is to listen carefully enough to find the actual cause of the complaint and not just the symptoms of the complaint.

For example, a passenger may have been on a delayed flight. From our point of view it's important to find out what actually caused the delay – because it may have been factors completely out of the airline's control. And if it was something to do with the airline then we obviously have to try and redress that so that it doesn't happen again and offer an apology if it's due.

4 Advertising

4.1

1 There's one about a car with lots of children and people dancing. They're all playing around. I like it because it's colourful, I like the music and it's chaotic. But I can't remember what car it is. Oh, and I hate all the ads for banks and insurance companies. They're so boring.

2 The one I liked was Levi Strauss, when a very good looking boy dives into a pool. And everyone thinks he looks marvellous. And there's a great tune they play – 'Mad about the boy'.

3 I liked the Renault Clio ad so much that I went out and bought the car. My husband hadn't passed his driving test and it was totally my decision. I thought it was a funny ad. It just appealed to my sense of fun and actually it was a bit of a joke to say that I'd bought something as big as a car purely on the basis of the advert.

4 I remember watching a Dairy Box chocolate advert very late at night with some college friends and there was an all-night garage round the corner. Suddenly I just felt that I had to have those chocolates and I went out and bought them. It was an immediate response to an advert. Normally you don't allow yourself to be influenced strongly by ads but sometimes it's fun just to go along with it.

5 I liked the French Connection ad where this really pretty girl walks into the Tube with her French Connection bag and then begins to undress, and she's looking really cheeky, you know, sort of mischievous. Everyone in the Tube is staring at her and she changes into her French Connection clothes in front of everyone, and there's this really great playful music, and she ends up walking out of the Tube at the next stop leaving everyone behind her. It was a really sexy ad, it was great.

4.2 (I = Interviewer, AP = Andrew Pound)

I Andrew, could you tell me what has been your most successful advertising campaign?

AP Er, I did a campaign for a marmalade product called Frank Cooper's marmalade, in Britain. It was a campaign we organised with a radio station, Classic FM, which concentrates on classical music. We targeted the morning, the breakfast programme, and we had a series of regular adverts, we had a sponsorship tie-up and we had a competition. And the response was tremendous. We had a huge increase in sales of our marmalades, especially in the key retailers who we were targeting, and since then we had many more listings in retail outlets. So the campaign was extremely positive, but the key thing that made it successful was the amount of money we spent – very little money – and in terms of sales results, as a percentage of the amount of money we spent, it was a huge success.

I So it was very cost effective.

AP It was very cost effective and at the end of the day, that's what we're looking for.

I Why do you think it was so successful?

AP Targeting. We had a very good match between the types of people who we knew bought marmalade and the types of people who we knew through research listened to that radio station. And we fitted them together in a way that made sense. In the morning, at breakfast time, marmalade is a product eaten mainly by older people, so they were listening to this radio station. Everything fitted together – that's what made it a success.

I   Is there another piece of TV advertising you can think of, which was very successful?

AP Well, er … I was very proud once of an advert I did for Kraft Cream Cheese Spread. It was very simple. We demonstrated what the product did. Three glasses of milk went into this cheese spread, we said why mothers would need it – it was for the kids to help them grow up, it was a growing up spread – and we created an advert that was fun. And so the kids liked watching it, and so obviously when they were in the supermarket with their mothers, they'd say, 'Mum, mum, I like that product, can we get it?' And so the kids like it, the mother feels OK because she's being reassured that it's got health and nutrition benefits, and the sales have done very well. That's the key thing about advertising. If it doesn't generate sales, then it's no good.

4.3 (I = Interviewer, AP = Andrew Pound)

I   Andrew, a lot of people think advertising is a waste of money. Is that your view?

AP No, not at all. I would say that, wouldn't I? Advertising is one of many ways in which manufacturers persuade customers to buy their products. You've got public relations, you've got sponsorship, you've got price promotions, you've got all sorts of promotional techniques. It's one element of what we call the marketing mix. In today's world, people are bombarded with advertising, with calls on their time, with picking up the kids from school, taking the dog for a walk, paying the gas bill. They haven't got time to make judgements on which can of tomatoes is the best one for me, or which brand of coffee gives me the best flavour. And if you can be constantly telling people why they should choose your brand, rather than another one, they're going to remember that. So when they're shopping, and they see your product on the shelf, they'll remember it. It's 'front of mind', as we say. It means that the person knows, ah coffee, I need coffee, which brand am I going for, ah Jacobs, yes I've seen that, that's good isn't it – and they just buy it. It's an automatic response, they don't spend more than two or three seconds making a choice, and unless you're front of mind in those two or three seconds, they're going to choose another brand.

4.4

Presentation 1

Good morning everyone, on behalf of myself and Focus Advertising, I'd like to welcome you. My name's Sven Larsen, I'm Commercial Director. This morning, I'd like to outline the campaign concept we've developed for you. I've divided my presentation into three parts. First, the background to the campaign, next the results of our market study, thirdly, the concept itself. If you have any questions, please don't hesitate to interrupt me.

Presentation 2

Hi, I'm Dominique Lagrange. Good to see you all. As you know, I'm Creative Director of DMK. I'm going to tell you about the ideas we've come up with for the ad campaign. I'll give you the background and talk you through the results of the market study and tell you all about our concept. If you're not clear about anything, go ahead and ask any questions you want.

5 Employment

5.1 (I = Interviewer, AL = Alan Lawson)

I   Alan, how can a candidate impress an interviewer?

AL Well, David, I feel it's basically all down to good preparation. First of all find out about the job. You could ring up the Press Officer or the Marketing Department and get the latest press releases or perhaps an annual report. The annual report, for example, will say where the company operates and the products it sells. Then, when you get there, you perhaps could congratulate the interviewer on a recent success the company's had. In a nutshell, find out about that company. Show that you've taken an interest in the company and show enthusiasm for the job because, after all, that's what they're looking for in the candidate. They want somebody not only who's qualified for the job but will want to do the job, and will be interested and enthusiastic about the job. Secondly, you could go to the company maybe a few days before the interview, talk to the receptionist, get a company newspaper – you can always pick up literature on the products maybe you'll be involved in. A very good tip – find out what the dress code is. You need to fit in and you need to make a good impression. Finally, your CV. Make sure it's easy to read, it's well written, but it's concise – don't ramble. I must say that I have done all of this, I've prepared my CV, it was really good. I left it behind – I didn't get the job!

5.2 (I = Interviewer, AL = Alan Lawson)

I   Alan, are there any key questions that you regularly use when interviewing candidates?

AL Yes, there are and it's almost a ritual with me. Following the CV tells you about the person and their qualifications. What you also want to know is their personality. So key questions I ask – what do they like most and what do they like least about their present job? They might say that they like travelling and they like meeting new people. These are standard answers. I think more interestingly perhaps are what don't they like about the company. They might not like working weekends at their current company. You might have the same problems with yours, working weekends might be something essential for the job. Also, ask them what their weaknesses are. They're usually, generally I would say, quite honest when they're giving their weaknesses. And ask them what their strengths are. It gives you an in-depth, if you like, feeling about their personality rather than just the straightforward qualifications that they have on their CV. Do they fit in? That's what you're really looking for.

5.3

A   Good, everyone's here now. There's coffee if you want it. Right, can we start please? As you all know, Roberto's been working as assistant to Carla Nuñez for six months now. He's just finished his probationary period. How do you feel about offering him a full time contract?

B   I'm not sure we should do it really. It says in this report that he's been late to work a few times and he can be rather …

C   Oh I don't think that's too important …

A   Could you let her finish please?

C   Oh, sorry, I didn't mean to butt in …

C   Another thing about Roberto I'm not happy about. He leaves exactly on time every day. Also he doesn't have lunch with us very often, you know, he goes off on his own …

A   I'm not sure that's relevant.

C   Mmm, maybe.

A   I think we should move on now if we're going to finish by 11 o'clock. We do have other promotions to consider.

B   But what about his actual work? In my opinion, it's fine. He's done some really good things.

A   Well, I think we should discuss this a bit more. What exactly do you mean by 'good things'?

A   Well, thanks very much, Maria. You've made your views very clear. OK, let's go over what we've agreed. Roberto will have a further probationary period of three months. After that …

5.4 (I = Interviewer, IR = Isabella Rosetti)

I Now let me ask you a question we ask all our candidates. Why should we hire you?

IR Why hire me? Simple. I get along well with people. I'm used to dealing with people from all walks of life. That's vital for this job. And I've got lots of ideas for making Slim Gyms more profitable. Want to hear them?

I Not just now, if you don't mind. We'll come back to that later. Um, about your attendance record. Could you tell me why you've had quite a bit of time off?

IR Hmm, you've been talking to my boss, I see. Let's get this clear. I've taken a day off now and then, true, but it's always to go to some family celebration – a marriage, a christening, a family reunion sometimes.

I Uh huh.

IR Anyway, I've got a great assistant at work – she looks after things if I'm away. It's no problem at all if I have a day off now and then.

I Right. Can we look into the future now. I'm interested to know where you see yourself in a few years.

IR In a few years I suppose I see myself … um, working for your organisation, running the whole business.

I I hope you achieve that objective.

5.5 (I = Interviewer, MB = Michael Bolen)

I Right, a question now about your managerial skills. You're currently with a sporting goods firm. Do you enjoy working on a team – with other managers

MB I enjoy working with colleagues a lot, especially when developing a project, let's say, working on a new product. It's exciting, often tiring, you're working long hours sometimes, but everyone's working together, to make a success of things.

I So would you say you're a good team player?

MB Definitely. But, let me say this, I like to be on my own from time to time. Especially if there's some problem to be worked out. I guess some people would say I keep to myself too much, but it's not true really.

I OK, let me follow that up. Um, I'd like to know what your colleagues would say about you. How would they describe you?

MB Huh, that's a difficult one. Mmm … I think they'd say I know my own mind, I'm a decisive person. Sometimes, you have to do things that you don't like, for example, fire an employee. Well, if I have to do it, I do it, and then forget about it.

I What else would your colleagues say?

MB They'd say that I'm a friendly person, when I get to know people. Some of them think I'm too friendly.

I Really?

MB Well, you know, a few of the women in the company, they get a little jealous because I take out my administrative assistant, Sue, from time to time, give her a nice lunch, you know, say thanks for all her hard work. Nothing wrong in that, is there?

5.6 (I = Interviewer, BW = Bob Wills)

I You're obviously eager to get this job. Could you tell me what your strengths are? What do you think you're good at?

BW Main strengths? Good at managing people, I'd say. I suppose it's my army training. I know how to set goals for people. Objectives. And I make sure they meet them.

I Hmm, don't you think some people might get upset, you know, lose their motivation if they don't achieve the goals you set?

BW Not at all. You don't get anywhere in this life if you're too easy on people. You've got to make an effort to get anywhere. Like your health club customers. If they want to get fit, they've got to have discipline. Do all the exercises, eat properly, give up alcohol and smoking. Change their lifestyle – that's what it's all about.

I Mmm, interesting! A final question. Maybe a difficult one. Could you tell me how you've changed in the last … oh … five years, let's say.

BW Sure. I think I'm more realistic now than I used to be. I know it'll be difficult for me to get a good job – being in the army most of my life. So, I'm trying to learn new skills, update my knowledge. Like in marketing and finance. So I'll have more to offer an employer. I'm not going to sit around waiting for the big job to come to me – it's not my style.

5.7 (I = Interviewer, SG = Stephanie Grant)

I Right. Can you tell me why you want to leave your present job. TV announcer. Well paid. Everyone knows you. Admires you. You've got everything you want, don't you?

SG Huh, I guess it does look like that. I do love the job. But I'm thirty now. I know the management is looking for younger talent. It wants sparky, glamorous twenty-year-olds in the job. To increase the ratings. I'm on the way out, I know that. So … I'm going before I'm pushed.

I Oh surely not. Someone with your reputation.

SG People come and go in my profession. Think of all the stars of ten years ago. Where are they now?

I Mmm, I take your point. Um, looking at your CV, your earlier career. You gave up competitive swimming when you were … er … twenty-four. Rather early to do that, wasn't it? I mean, don't swimmers go on competing …?

SG Look, I'm sure you read the papers. You must know, when I won the big races, some of the swimmers accused me of taking drugs. You know, to improve my performance. It was horrible. All a bunch of lies. I got really upset, I thought, oh, I don't need this nonsense. I just gave it all up. I'd had enough.

6 Trade

6.1 (BF = Bella Ford, PH = Pierre Hemard)

BF If we buy more than 500 cases of the Reserve, what discount can you offer us?

PH On 500, nothing. But if you buy 1000 cases, we'll offer 15%.

BF Let me think about that. Now, if I place an order for 1000, will you be able to despatch immediately?

PH I don't know about immediately, but certainly this month.

BF Well, if you get it to us before the Christmas rush, it'll be OK. I take it your prices include insurance?

PH Actually, no. You'd be responsible for that. If you can increase your order, then we'd be willing to cover insurance as well.

BF I'll need to do some calculations.

PH Let's look at methods of payment. Since we've not dealt with you before, we'd like to be paid by banker's draft.

BF Well, this is a large order. We've done business with many well-known wine producers and we've always paid by letter of credit.

PH OK. If we agree to you paying by letter of credit, then you'll have to pay us within 30 days.

BF That should be fine.

6.2 (I = Interviewer, KW = Kevin Warren)

I When you go into a negotiation, do you always expect to win?

KW I guess the honest answer is that I always have a clear expectation of what I expect to achieve, and I guess I would like to always win. Let me illustrate that for you. Something that was sort of shared with me early in my career was the mnemonic L-I-M and that's Like, Intend, Must. What would I like to do, what would I intend to do, and what must I do? And this is probably well illustrated by a recent contract that we negotiated in the UK with a major leisure company. And, I guess our 'like' was, we would like to win the business there and then, in the negotiation on that day. I guess our 'intend' was that we must leave that group thinking that we are a very professional and competent outfit who can best meet their needs. And I guess our 'must' was, we must have done enough to keep the dialogue open and ensure that our competitor didn't win the business on that day. So, the short answer is you don't always win. I always want to win, but I don't always expect to win – but I certainly expect to deliver the objective that we went in to achieve.

6.3 (I = Interviewer, KW = Kevin Warren)

I Could you give me some tips for negotiating?

KW Yes. I think everybody has their own tips. But these are things that have worked for myself and the people I've worked with, and it's more around avoiding classic errors. And I guess the first one is to identify who the decision maker is. I've lost count of the occasions at every level, from first-line salesman through to board director, board to board negotiations, where I've seen fantastic presentations, superb dialogue and the person that's been sitting across the table, so to speak, is not the decision maker. So that's the first tip, make sure you know who you're talking to. The second one is that all salesmen, if they're good salesmen, tend to be very enthusiastic about what they're selling. That could be a product or a service, or even a social occasion, but it's all selling at the end of the day. And in their enthusiasm they focus on their need, rather than the buyer's need. So, for example, in our own case I've seen on many, many occasions people basically go straight to the point – We're here to sell you Coca-Cola, it's the world's number one brand, you must want it. What they haven't done is establish the buyer's need. So, for example, the buyer's need may be in a grocery store that they want to supply the world's number one brand to encourage consumers to come in and purchase their range of products. The manager of a ball bearing factory might want a vending machine because if he supplies a free, or discounted refreshment service it keeps his union employees happy. So the important thing is to understand the buyer's need. Now, it's not impossible to sell without establishing that need. But it tends to mean you'll never have a long term relationship. So, for example, again the workplace example, I could come in, bang, sell you a Coca-Cola vending machine, pay you maybe a small royalty. Because I never established your need, if another soft drinks supplier walks through the door and just offers you more money, you will probably switch. Whereas if we'd established the fact that all you were interested in was offering a service and you wanted it to be as hassle free as possible, we could have tailored our offering. So I think that's very important. My favourite one, and I'm probably in danger of doing it myself now, is once you've made the sale, shut up. I think it's very important: close the sale, reinforce the buyer's decision – everybody likes to feel they've made a good decision – and then leave.

7 Innovation

🎧 7.1 (PP = Pamela Pickford)

PP The key is preparation. So the first step is to find out who you're going to be presenting to. Now you need to do this on two levels. Firstly, how much does the audience know about the subject? Are they experts or do they know very little? Secondly, are you presenting to a group from the same or from different countries? And adjust your language so that everybody can understand.
If possible, visit the room where you'll be giving the presentation beforehand and organise it precisely to your own requirements. Check you're familiar with the equipment, re-arrange the seating, and try to make yourself feel comfortable and relaxed in it.
So once you know who you're presenting to and where, you're ready to start preparing what exactly you're going to say. OK? So stage one is the opening – that all-important first few moments that can make or break the presentation. Then stage two, a brief introduction about the subject of your talk. Then three, the main body of the presentation. And four, the conclusion, which should include a summary of your talk and your final opinion or recommendations. Finally, the question and answer session.
Now the most important stage is the opening minute or so and I'd suggest that people memorise it exactly as if they were actors. Write down the opening with all the pauses and the stress clearly marked, and then record it, listen to it, and practise it again and again. This is so important because if it's properly done, you not only get the audience's attention immediately, but you feel confident during what can be the most frightening part of the presentation. After that, you can start using your notes.
So the first step is to write those notes. Write the whole presentation out just like an essay. Then select the key points. But read the full version over and over again until it's imprinted on your mind. The next step is to buy some small white postcards and write no more than one or two of the key points or key phrases onto each one.
Now visual aids, like overhead transparencies, are very important of course. But most people put far too much information on them. Don't – because it's difficult to read and it bores the audience. Limit yourself to a maximum of five points on each. Remember to turn off the projector when you're not actually using it. And don't talk to the machine, or the transparency, which again, lots of people do. Face the audience at all times.
Finally, remember that it's not just what you say. How you say it is just as important. Quite unlike meetings and negotiations, a good presentation is very much a performance.

🎧 7.2

Good morning everyone, thanks for coming to my presentation. I know you're all very busy, so I'll be as brief as possible. OK then, I'm going to talk about the new chocolate bar we're putting on the market, the St Tropez premium bar. I'll tell you about the test launch we carried out in the south west of England a few weeks ago. My presentation is divided into three parts. First I'll give you some background about the launch.
After that, I'll tell you how we got on and assess it's effectiveness. Finally, I'll outline our future plans for the product. If you have any questions, don't hesitate to ask.
Right, let's start with the background to the launch. As you know, St Tropez is a mint and nut bar with a distinctive taste. It's been thoroughly tested in focus groups and special attention was paid to packaging. It's wrapped in a metallic foil. The colours are rich, strong, to give high visual impact. OK everyone? Yes, Johan, you have a question ...
So, that's the background. Right, let's now move on to the test launch. How successful was it? Well, in two words, very successful. If you look at the graph, you'll see the bar's actual sales compared with forecast sales. Quite a difference isn't there? The sales were over 20% higher than we predicted. In other words a really good result. Well above our expectations. The sales show that the pricing of the product was correct. And they show that as a premium line, the St Tropez bar should be successful nationwide. To sum up, a very promising test launch. I believe the bar has great potential in the market.
Right, where do we go from here? Obviously, we'll move on to stage two and have a national advertising and marketing campaign. In a few months, you'll be visiting our sales outlets and taking orders, I hope, for the new product. Thanks very much. Any questions?

8 Organisation

🎧 8.1 (I = Interviewer, CB = Chris Byron)

I Chris Byron, you're the project manager for British Airways' new office complex at Waterside. Could you please tell us what your job involves?

CB My job was to make sure that the building got built on time, was built inside budget and that we moved in smoothly and successfully. I had a further role to also make sure that we were able to change the culture of British Airways through a relocation because British Airways see very clearly that the quality of office that you give somebody affects their performance.

I Now Waterside has some unusual features. Could you tell us about some of those and their purpose.

CB It was designed specifically to make sure that we encourage teamwork. So we have a street, we also have open plan offices, and the whole design is built around the idea that people should be able to bump into each other, meet each other easily and frequently, and manage each other's conversations in a very informal way. So that's one feature.
A second key feature was that we cut down on paperwork, we reduced that to the minimum by the way in which we've introduced electronic forms and electronic e-mails and electronic manuals.
And a further component was that we also encouraged flexible working, so that quite literally from virtually nobody working flexibly, what we now have is out of 2,800 people who work here, 700 people neither have an office nor their own desk. They are very much mobile, but we do support them with the technology that we provide them.

🎧 8.2 (I = Interviewer, CB = Chris Byron)

I So this is the practice of hot-desking.

CB Yes, it includes hot-desking, it also includes home-working, which is why we tend to call it flexible working. And we've laid out certain of our offices very much with the concept of flexible working in mind. So what we do is that we identify a person's task, and we try to provide a space in the building to meet that task. So instead of one single space that you occupy, you can come into a wing of this building, of which there are six, you can come in, you can read your e-mails at what we call a 'drop-in point', you can have a conversation and a meeting with somebody in a relaxed informal club setting. Or at another part of the wing, you can find space where there's a quiet area where you can either read your manuals or whatever you want to study, or alternatively sit in, in effect, a library environment and write a paper to somebody.

I What other advantages does Waterside offer BA's employees?

CB Waterside's a very flexible building but at the same time, it's very much driven by trying to make it easy for you and informal for you to actually work within. So the … what we like to feel is that when you go home at night, you really do feel valued. And to take you into a bit more detail on that, the sort of facilities we provide you is a very ready access to education – we have open-learning piped through to your desktop; we've introduced electronic shopping so you can literally shop at one of the local supermarkets and it gets delivered here … or your weekly shopping. Thirdly, there's video conferencing. So there's accessibility to other people in other parts of our building. We've also introduced I believe very high quality catering arrangements with a very pleasant look from our restaurant overlooking a lake. We also provide you with car parking down in the basement, so it's very easy to come to Waterside. And we also have a gymnasium as well. So there's a whole variety of facilities all designed to get the best out of our people.

I It sounds a marvellous environment. Have there been any problems for the staff moving in to Waterside?

CB Surprisingly few given the size of the organisation and the task. But I do think that was largely down to some very good planning, and I hasten to say that's by all my team rather than just myself. We did a lot of planning, we thought through very carefully the move, we trained people very well, and we communicated with people … erm … to death, you could say. So that nobody had any surprises when they came in here, and they had a lot of confidence that things would be up and running.

9 Money

🎧 9.1

The French Government yesterday approved a Ff4.6bn urban development project east of Paris, co-ordinated by EuroDisney, and designed to create 22,000 jobs by 2015.

Yule Catto, the chemicals group, launched a £240m bid for Holliday Chemical. Yule shares fell 32p (about 10%) to 274 in response to the news. Holliday's shares dropped 8p to end at 225p.

The worldwide fall in stock markets last month encouraged Prince Alwaleed bin Talal to invest in media and technology companies. The Saudi prince spent $400m on a 5% stake in News Corporation, $300m on 1% in Motorola and $150m on 5% of Netscape Communications.

A beach scene painted in 1870 by French impressionist Claude Monet when he was desperately short of money made £3.8m at Christie's Auction House in London.

Sales of the *Financial Times* hit an all-time record in November. Worldwide sales were 12.4% up on November, last year.

New car registrations in Western Europe in November rose 10.4% to 991,800 from 898,400 a year ago, said the European Auto Manufacturers Association.

🎧 9.2 (P = Peter, J = John, K = Kate)

P I'm glad you managed to make it today. I'd like to start by taking a look at the year's sales and profit figures. First of all John, could you summarise the sales figures?

J Well, we had a good January – 5.2 million. January's a difficult month because sales always drop after Christmas. In February we launched the new children's line and it went very well. Total sales rose to almost 8 million, which was nice. Unfortunately they then plummeted after the fire in the main factory. But by the end of April we had recovered – 10.2 million was the figure – and since then sales have gone up steadily month by month. The December figures aren't in yet, but it looks like we will probably reach 15 million this month.

P Good. I've got a couple of questions, but I'll save them for later. Kate, sales have increased, but has that meant higher profits?

K Yes, it has. We're waiting for the final figures, but we already know that overall, in the first three quarters of the year, profits rose by 15% compared to last year, from 960,000 to 1.1 million. In fact since April, profits have increased every single month and

they are still going up.

P What about next year?

K Well, as you know, next year we're going to centralise distribution so costs will decrease. Even if sales level off, profits will improve.

🎧 9.3 (I = Interviewer, GG = Gerard Gardner)

I Gerard, how do you decide who to lend money to and who not to?

GG One of the most important elements is to consider the individual or individuals. Frankly, if they're prepared and know what they want and can demonstrate an understanding of those requirements, it's far more impressive when they explain with clarity the purpose for which the money is required. It is essential that they're confident, not brash, just confident – usually the sign of someone who is well prepared. But the individual alone isn't the only important factor. The business itself clearly is extremely important in deciding whether it can provide the means of repaying the money that it's borrowed. A quality business plan should be capable of demonstrating this. It should include the details of the business structure as well as financial information. It's often clear that logical thought processes produce good financial structures. The third key element is intuition. Frankly, if it doesn't sound right, it probably isn't.

🎧 9.4 (I = Interviewer, GG = Gerard Gardner)

I Can you give me some examples from your experience?

GG Well, yes, someone who has demonstrated in the past that they have been successful is often quite important in agreeing a future structure. One such occasion was a gentleman who had financed his business in the past, he'd been successful and had then had the opportunity to leave the business to someone else, having sold on his interest. Sometime later, when the business had not been successful, he returned and wanted to buy the business back. Even though in his absence it had deteriorated. Our faith in him was rewarded and the second time around the business was more successful and more profitable than it had been previously. Sometimes, you also just feel that a transaction is right even though it may be presented badly. Once such an opportunity arose on the financing of an entirely new product which was extremely badly presented. With considerable assistance a successful business structure was created and today the firm is a well-known UK company.

I Have you ever missed any really big opportunities?

GG Yes, some years ago I was given the opportunity of financing a business which screen-printed business logos on umbrellas. This was before the current craze for golf umbrellas and although the individual was impressive, and, although the business plan also showed considerable foresight, I thought intuitively that no one would ever buy an umbrella with a business logo on and therefore turned down the opportunity.

10 Ethics

🎧 10.1 (I = Interviewer, CB = Claire Bebbington)

I Why should companies be ethical or what are the advantages of a company in behaving ethically?

CB Mm, I think the whole issue of ethics is a very complex one. Companies are made up of people. Multinationals are made up of many different nationalities. I think that companies are part of society and as such they should reflect society's standards. Companies, especially multinational ones, do have responsibilities in the world and should try to be a positive influence and I think if a company is not ethical, then it will not survive as a company.

I Should a company have a code of ethics?

CB I think from my point of view it's useful on two counts. Firstly, it makes a commitment to certain good behaviour and so it's a way of communicating the importance of good behaviour to all of it's employees and partners. Secondly, if a company has a code of ethics and spends time communicating it, it does actually contribute to it's ethical behaviour. If you express these things in writing, especially, then you can be held accountable for them. This tends to mean that you are much more likely to act on them as well. I think following up that code is difficult. People tend to have different ethical standards, and defining the term 'ethics' can I think be a problem. But I think generally to express what your ethics are is a positive thing to do.

🎧 **10.2 (I = Interviewer, CB = Claire Bebbington)**

I What kinds of moral dilemmas do large companies face? Can you think of any examples?

CB I think if you were to look at any company's ethical code you would usually find in it a section about offering bribes and this can be an area where I think people can get themselves into hot water. Facilitation payments are part of doing business in many countries, and bribes are something which most companies are not going to want to get involved in. But when does a facilitation payment become a bribe? And that is a question that can be quite difficult to answer.

I Can you think of an example where a facilitation payment is clearly a facilitation payment and not a bribe?

CB I think that there are many examples. When you are paying consultants to make introductions to new business contacts, obviously the reason you choose these consultants is because they are well placed to give that kind of advice in a particular country. And you're paying for that introduction.

I Can you give an example of a facilitation which is closer to a bribe?

CB I would say size is important. Sometimes facilitation payments are out of proportion to the kind of business that you are expecting to win. I think there are many instances. Also, you have to be careful with issues such as nepotism.

🎧 **10.3**

A I'll never forget the trouble we had with that face cream. We launched it and you know it was a real winner. I mean, it was going really well.

B Hmm, great.

A When suddenly people started phoning and complaining it was burning their skin.

B Burning their skin? You mean, like a kind of allergy.

A Yeah, it was making red marks on their faces. The newspapers heard about it and wanted to know what we were doing about it.

B Huh typical. They don't exactly help, do they? So what did you do?

A We didn't know what to do. You see, we'd tested it for over six months, and you know, there'd been no bad reaction to it.

B Well, so what was the problem?

A Well, we'd invested a lot in the product and the launch. I mean, you know what advertising costs are these days, then suddenly the number of complaints doubled in the space of a week or so.

B Doubled? Incredible? Did you manage to keep it quiet?

A No, our Managing Director got more than a bit worried. Said all this was harming the company's image. So we recalled the product and lost a lot of money. I tell you, the only people with red faces were us. Since then, we've kept away from skin care products.

🎧 **10.4**

A OK, we agree then, we know Louisa has a drink problem, but we don't know why. Anyway her drinking is definitely affecting her work. And her relations with staff.

B Yes, so what are we going to do about it? In my opinion there are several ways we could deal with this.

A Oh yes?

B Well, we could have a talk with her and suggest she gets some professional help or we could do nothing and hope the problem goes away. Having said this, I think we should give her a verbal warning. I think it's a serious matter.

A Mmm, let's look at the pros and cons of giving her a verbal warning …

B I agree with you. Maybe it's too soon for a verbal warning. Let's look at this from a different angle. We don't want to make the problem worse, do we? So, how about this? It might be worth asking a friend to have a quiet chat with her. It could help a lot, I think …

A OK, let's think about the consequences of doing nothing. The drink problem could get worse or in time we may find she solves her personal problems. Who knows …

B OK then, we've looked at all the options. And we agree, I think. The best way forward is to advise her to get professional help.

A Right. So it's decided. So the next thing to do is to contact our medical officer. He'll give us some suitable names …

🎧 **10.5 (BD = Bob Dexter, NT = Nikos Takakis)**

BD A bit of information now, Nikos, I think you ought to know. Carl often has lunches with Monica Kaminsky, the design manager for Rochester Electronics, our main competitor.

NT Monica Kaminsky? Really? That's something I didn't know.

BD Yes, and she often phones him at work. She has long, cosy chats with him. I've no idea what they talk about.

NT Are you saying, you mean … you think there's something going on between them? You know …

BD I'm not saying anything.

NT You don't really like Carl, do you, Bob?

🎧 **10.6**

A Bob Dexter's awful to work for, you know. I'd much prefer to work for Carl Thomson.

B Yeah, me too.

A Carl is so charming and nice to everyone. I think he's a great manager.

B Mmm. What I like about him, you know, he treats everyone the same. He speaks to everyone. Always smiling and joking. The canteen staff just love him, and the cleaners too. Do you think there's a chance his PA, Valerie, will move on – I'd love her job.

A Maybe, they're not getting on very well, I hear.

B Well, you never know. Wonder why Bob Dexter doesn't like Carl. Do you think he's a bit jealous because Carl is so popular?

A Mmm, could be.

11 Change

🎧 **11.1 (I = Interviewer, JK = Jeremy Keeley)**

I OK Jeremy, let me start by asking you, why do people resist change?

JK Resistance to change is the most natural of human reactions and is based on uncertainty and it's based on fear – fear of losing your job, fear of, perhaps, not being able to cope with a new situation. It's based on lack of trust in the decision-makers and it's based on a complete feeling of lack of control over the situation. All of those are very natural reactions, and the way to manage resistance is not to completely ignore it but actually to manage it as if it were natural.

🎧 **11.2 (I = Interviewer, JK = Jeremy Keeley)**

I Can you think of an example where change was handled well?

JK One of my favourite examples. I was working for a client a number of years ago, and a new Chief Executive came on board and the client had to significantly reduce it's costs. It had been trying to compete with it's major competitor on a basis of volume and was trying to be cheaper. And it's major competitor was four or five times it's size and there was just no way that could happen. And the new Chief Executive came in and within three weeks had published exactly what he was trying to achieve. And every single person in the organisation knew this chap's vision. They knew they were going to segment the market – they were going to go for corporate, high spend, high profile customers, and they were going to ignore the mass volume residential market which was a lot bigger, and with much larger margins. And the company was going to go for much more value-added. And the Chief Executive made absolutely clear, right from the beginning, exactly what he was going to do. He talked about the number of heads he was going to have to take out of the organisation. So he talked about the pain – he was absolutely honest about it. But he also talked about the gains and explained his vision in a lot of detail to everybody but in a number of face-to-face communications and in a weekly letter that he wrote to everybody in the organisation. Every week a letter came out from this chief executive saying exactly what progress had been made, exactly what he was still aiming to do – what the next steps were. And this happened week after week after week.

He was a very effective manager. And the second thing he did was move very quickly on the painful stuff. So he very quickly took out the people who didn't fit. So sometimes the decisions were hard, but he made them and he made them quickly.

Skills, Exercise D

11.3 (C = Carl, N = Nancy, M = Max, S = Stefan)

C Can we move on to the third point on the agenda, the open plan office? I know there are different opinions about this, so our main purpose will be to explore your views and see if we can reach agreement. Nancy, would you like to begin as I know you're in favour of the idea.

N It's good for communication, people see each other at the office. It's er, I think good for team spirit too. I think there's more interaction between people but what's important is productivity, people work harder when they're on display.

M I really can't agree with you there. I think that with open plan offices there is the problem of privacy.

C OK Max, thanks. Em, Stefan, what do you think?

S I agree with Max about privacy. What if you want to make a private phone call?

C We could use meeting rooms.

S Meeting rooms? Yes, that's true I suppose, but …

M I don't think that works.

C Let Stefan finish please, Max.

S I'm just not happy about this proposal. I hope we're not going to have a vote about this. I mean, I really think we need a report or some extra survey done on this.

C You've got a point there. Do we all agree?

N/S Yes./OK with me.

C Right, so Max, would you prepare a short report please? Ask staff how they feel about the open plan idea, and report back to me by, say, August 1, OK? Now, can we go to the next item on the agenda?

M I was shocked to see hot-desking there. I think this is totally ridiculous. This will really upset people. It just won't work.

C How do you feel about this, Nancy?

N I'm pretty sure that hot-desking won't work unless we go open plan. I think one depends on the other. I don't think that hot-desking in closed offices works. But I think open plan without hot-desking is OK.

S I don't understand your point. Can you explain it a bit more clearly?

11.4 (I = Interviewer, HW = Hugh Whitman)

I I imagine you'll be making some changes, Mr Whitman, now that you're in charge at Metrot.

HW Yes, there will certainly be some changes, there always are when you acquire another company. Metrot is a fine company, that's why we bought it. It has a skilled work force and excellent products. We think we can help Metrot to become more dynamic and efficient. We want it to compete successfully in European markets where there are big opportunities for us.

I You say, more efficient. Does that mean reorganisation? Job losses? I believe that the staff at Metrot are worried about this.

HW It's too early to say. But there could be some staff cutbacks in the short term. We shall see. Our plan is to expand the company and create as many job opportunities as possible.

I What about the factories? Some people say you're thinking of relocating some of the factories and selling off some of the land you've acquired.

HW I don't want to comment on that. Our aim is to build Metrot and make it a strong company at the leading edge of technology, with an image for quality, reliability and good service.

I I see. Thank you Mr Whitman. I wish you the best of luck in your new position.

12 Strategy

12.1 (I = Interviewer, MS = Marjorie Scardino)

I How do you develop a strategy for a large company?

MS There are lots of ways to go about it. I think the way we've done it is to first think about what assets we have – what's unique about those assets, what markets we know about and what markets are growing, and which of those markets can make the best use of our assets. We then put that into a bowl, heat it up, stir it around, and come out with a strategy.

I And in broad terms, what is your strategy at Pearson?

MS Well I, we have approached our strategy … Let me answer it this way, by looking at it as three simple steps. When I joined Pearson a couple of years ago, we needed to improve our operations. We needed to just run the companies we had, and the businesses we had better. So our first step in our strategy was simply to operate better. To create better profits, and better cash generation, and better long term value for the shareholders. We then … the second step which was not happening in a serial way but happening at the same time, the second step was to look at the assets we had and see which ones we should keep and which ones we should dispose of. Those we disposed of, we did because they would be worth more to other companies than to us because they didn't fit with the rest of our company, or were things we didn't actively control – we had a passive interest in – so those disposals were an important part. And then the third step was to stitch together all our businesses, so that they were able to use each other's assets, to make a greater whole.

12.2 (I = Interviewer, MS = Marjorie Scardino)

I What trends do you see emerging in the strategy of large companies?

MS I'm not a great student of everybody else's strategy, but I would suspect they are trends towards globalism, toward having more international operations, rather than simply having a national business. They are probably trends towards more focus on people, and more focus on the people who work in a company as the company. And probably more a change in the management style of companies towards more teamwork and more collegiality and less sort of authoritarian ways of running the company, and therefore the ideas that come from that kind of an organisation.

I What strategies have influenced or impressed you?

MS There's one … Strategies that impress me are strategies that are extremely clear, and define a very unique goal. I think one of the strategies that impresses me is Coca-Cola's. And I'm sure it's strategy has several levels. But it is encompassed in what they call their 'goal' or their 'mission', which is something like: Put a cold bottle of Coca-Cola within arm's reach of every thirsty person in the world. So that means: here's what their main product is – and they're going to focus on that; they're going to focus on international markets, not just parochial markets; and they're going to focus on distribution, wide distribution and promotion. And so that sort of encompasses everything. That's a good strategy, very clear, I'm sure nobody who works in Coca-Cola doesn't understand what they're after.

12.3 (C = Chairman, M = Michel, P = Paula, T = Tom, S = Susan)

C OK, the main item on the agenda is whether we should sell our store in Paris. I'd like to hear your opinions about this. But first of all, can you give us the background, Michel?

M Yes. As you all know, we opened the store in Boulevard Jordan five years ago. We hoped it would be a base for expansion into other areas of France. But it hasn't been a success. It hasn't attracted enough customers and it's made losses every year. As I see it, it's going to be very difficult to get a return on our investment.

P I agree. There's no possibility it'll make a profit. It's in the wrong location, there's too much competition, and our products don't seem to appeal to French people. We should never have entered the market – it was a mistake. We should sell out as soon as possible.

T I don't agree with that at all. Things have gone wrong there, it's obvious. The management's let us down badly – they haven't adapted enough to market conditions. But it's far too early to close the business down. I suggest we bring in some marketing consultants – a French firm, if possible, and get them to review the business. We need more information about where we're going wrong.

S I totally agree with you. It's too early to close down the store, but I am worried about the store's location. We're an up-market business, but most of the stores in the area have moved down-market, selling in the lower price ranges. That's a problem. I think we have to make changes – very soon. I mean, our losses are increasing every year, we just can't go on like this. We may have to revise our strategy. Maybe we made a mistake in choosing France for expansion.

C Well, thanks for your opinions. I think on balance we feel we should keep the store going for a while. So, the next thing to do is to appoint a suitable firm of marketing consultants to find out what our problems are, and make recommendations. Personally, I'm convinced the store will be a success if we get the marketing mix right. We've got to get the store back into profit, we've invested a lot of money in it.

🎧 12.4 (I = Interviewer, E = Expert)

I What's going wrong with Texan Chicken, Susanna? It used to be a star performer. Now, no one seems to want to buy their shares. What's it all about?

E There are a number of problems, as I see it. First, demand has fallen for their food. I'm not sure if it's because people are eating less chicken these days. But certainly there's lots of competition from the fast food chains. McDonald's, Burger King, Kentucky Fried Chicken and so on.

I But I thought Texan Chicken was a bit special? Different from the others? Spicier, better tasting, and so on?

E That may be true. But it's rather expensive. You pay a lot more than a similar meal at, say, McDonald's.

I So is that the problem, pricing?

E It's not just that. They've been expanding very fast, probably too fast, and they've run into financial problems. They couldn't pay back some of their loans on time – the banks don't like that – and the word gets round. Investors don't like it either.

I Mmm, no wonder the share price fell.

E Another thing. They've built up the business by franchising. But some of the franchisees aren't running their restaurants properly. Customers are complaining about long queues, poor service and dirty restaurants. The decor is also dull and unexciting.

I So what's the solution? What are they going to do about it?

E I called Eva Martinez yesterday and asked her what plans they had to turn the business round. She didn't tell me much, but she did say they had called in a team of management consultants to advise them on their future strategy.

13 Cultures

🎧 13.1 (I = Interviewer, CB = Claire Bebbington)

I Can you tell me any problem you've had of a cross culture nature?

CB Understanding what the aspirations of people in different cultures are is important. In my previous job where I was looking after BP's publications, we selected images to go with particular stories, especially in developing countries. We were quite keen to show what we would consider the more photogenic aspects of a particular lifestyle, culture, society. But the society was much more keen to show the more dynamic, international, forward-looking western images that it wanted to present to the outside world.
For example, images of Malaysia. We wanted to show images of the countryside, the old systems of agriculture, people using oxen. But they wanted to show the downtown, suburban, western, highly developed, highly sophisticated aspects of Malaysian life.

I That's interesting. Can you think of any other examples, apart from Malaysia?

CB We came across the same issues when we were doing articles on Turkey, Colombia – many of the countries that were on the edge of quite rapid economic development, maybe for the first time, who were very sensitive towards how they were presenting themselves to the outside world.
Also you shouldn't assume that because you understand the culture of the capital city that you also understand the culture in the provinces and other areas in the country. For example, in Colombia where you have a very sophisticated group of people working in Bogota, their lifestyle, their way of life, their culture if you like is quite different from, for example, one of the provinces a long way from the city where the Government and the Government culture in the capital has had very little chance to spread.
And even maybe, if you think of, say, somewhere like Papua New Guinea where you have 700 different … 'tribes' is probably the wrong word, but say 'groupings' – and each of them is subtly different, and certainly from, say, the people and the tribes that live at high altitude, it's going to be very different from the coastal inhabitant.

🎧 13.2 (CB = Claire Bebbington)

CB I think it's very important to be as open-minded as you possibly can. You come across different kinds of cultures and they affect business in different ways. You should be aware of a number of things. There are different attitudes towards work, and towards resolving problems and working in teams and so on. In an Anglo-American culture, they emphasise action, doing things and achieving things. But when you're dealing with people who are much more comfortable with consensus, in discussion, then you shouldn't dismiss that as time-wasting. You should have a very open attitude to how people approach work. The simple things like inappropriate food, alcohol, that sort of thing, are much easier to deal with than these more subtle things.

14 Leadership

🎧 14.1 (I = Interviewer, MS = Marjorie Scardino)

I Marjorie Scardino, you are leading one of the top companies in the UK, and you've been voted businesswoman of the year. What qualities do you need to run a large company effectively?

MS Well, I think different companies probably require different qualities, but for me there are only a few simple qualities that cut across all requirements, and those are courage and imagination and empathy. And by empathy I mean, having the ability to put yourself in other people's positions and understand how they feel about situations and ideas.

I Which business leaders do you admire and why?

MS I think the best business leaders are probably ones we don't know about, not the stars we read about in the newspapers. I think they're probably the ones who have had a great business idea and have seen it through to fruition. So the business leaders I most admire right now are those managers in Pearson who are achieving our goals of double-digit earnings growth.

I What do business leaders actually do?

MS My staff would probably say this was a really excellent question they ask themselves every day! I think what they do is just what I've said the business leaders I admire do. They create a business idea, and they see it through.

I As a leader, how do you motivate your employees?

MS I'd like to think we motivate each other. I think my job is to make sure the company has a purpose, because I think people like to work for a company that has a reason for being, that they can identify with and feel good about. I think that I have to communicate well with them everything that's going on – and everything I'm trying to do – in a clear way. And then in return I think they inspire me to think more adventurously and to think more carefully about how to stimulate them and how to build a better business. So it's a sort of a circular operation.

I Do you think leaders are born or made?

MS I think it's probably a bit of both. All human beings obviously are born with certain qualities, and certain genetic traits. But I've seen so many people in my life who have, using those basic qualities, re-invented themselves several times as they've gone into new situations. You know, you're a certain kind of person when you're in school, and your friends know who you are, and you get slotted in. And then as you grow up you go into new situations and become somebody else. So people who were never leaders in school become the great business leaders of our time. So I would have to say, mostly it's made, but you have to use what you're born with.

15 Competition

🎧 15.1 (I = Interviewer, KW = Kevin Warren)

I The soft drinks market is one of the most competitive in the world. How do you stay ahead of your competitors?

KW Well, the Coca-Cola company this year reached the point where, world-wide it sells a billion servings of it's product every day. However, the world still consumes 47 billion servings of other beverages – again, every day. The key point here is to understand what the opportunity actually is. Which in our case is to grow the whole soft drinks category. To be successful we believe you need a portfolio of products which include the best brands and the most recognisable packages, for example the icon bottle. It needs to be supported by excellent market place execution, in other words, attention to detail. We grow our business one bottle at a time. Now behind this you need an efficient manufacturing and distribution operation. All the glamorous TV advertising in the world won't sell your product if Tesco's has run out. And of course advertising, especially for a company like the Coca-Cola Company has a major part to play in ensuring the consumer is aware of the intrinsic values of our brands, a good example of which is refreshment. So, in summary, the way to stay ahead is to focus on delivering to the consumer a product that adds value to their lives rather than simply focusing upon the actions of your perceived competitor.

🎧 15.2 (I = Interviewer, KW = Kevin Warren)

I Does competition always lead to better products and better value for customers?

KW I think it does but it's important to remember that value is not just a function of price. Now a good example of this might be to look back at some of the history of the travel industry. I would guess this country enjoys some of the least expensive holiday flights and in the main I would think they offer excellent value for money. I'm equally sure that on occasions the consumer's desire for low prices has led to compromises. Who hasn't suffered the 2am flight time, the delayed departure and so on? Dependent on your needs as a consumer, you will therefore have a different view on whether you think this is better value. So I guess the point is that better doesn't necessarily mean cheaper. Although price as an element of value is very important, and the key challenge is to maintain a balance.

🎧 15.3 (I = Interviewer, KW = Kevin Warren)

I How do you see competition affecting the way your business operates in the future?

KW Well firstly, we assume our competition will improve in every thing they do. This focuses our team on the task ahead. However, we spend far more time preparing for shifts in consumer behaviour – in driving our programmes to increase overall soft drink consumption – than we do worrying about specific competitors. So, for example, I see major changes coming in terms of the purchase environments in which the consumer can access our product. Some examples of this would be: How will they do their shopping? Will frequency increase or decrease? Will they not even go to the store? i.e. Will they shop from home? There will definitely be continued increase in leisure time, so we need to be where the consumer is, whether that be the sports centre or the multiplex cinema, for example. Will the increase in out-of-home eating, especially snacking, for example, sandwich bars, continue? We think it will. So clearly, whilst it's important to keep improving our core offerings, our product portfolio, our packaging, our operational efficiency, most importantly we have to prepare for the needs of our future consumer.

16 Quality

🎧 16.1

Wednesday, Wednesday afternoon, the afternoon, the morning, 29th July 1962, 1962, July, 3 o'clock, Christmas, Christmas Day

🎧 16.2 (EW = Enid Wong)

EW OK, let me tell you my story now. I had a bad experience in June last year. On the Monday my office bought me an expensive American laptop computer. I had been waiting for it for two months. I wanted to use it for e-mail when I was in Europe. I wanted to install software so I could read my Hong Kong e-mail anywhere in Europe. I travel a lot there on business. OK, I wanted a reliable, quality laptop so they bought me a top-of-the-range model.

On the Friday morning, one day before I flew to London I installed the software. It wouldn't work. I took the laptop and the software into the office and the technician tried to fix it. He worked for seven hours on the Friday and it still wouldn't work. I didn't have time to take the laptop to the Computer Centre as I had to fly on the following Saturday morning.

The technician phoned me in England, from Hong Kong, the following Monday. He said he would send new software by courier. It arrived two days later on the Wednesday. I tried to install the software. No luck! My colleague tried. No luck! My brother-in-law tried. No luck! For two months, I had no e-mail at a busy time in my life.

When I returned to Hong Kong at the end of August, I sent the machine to the Computer Centre. It was a faulty modem on a brand new machine. Fortunately, it was working properly by the end of September. I'd wanted that particular laptop because I had always used that brand and they have always been reliable. Although they are expensive, I agree that they usually provide reliability, consistency and value for money. This time, however, I was exceptionally unlucky.

🎧 16.3 (LS = Lisa Soares)

LS During the summer last year, I think it was in August, my car kept breaking down. I bought it second hand. I went to the same garage that I'd bought it from. The car salesman said that it would take five days to get it fixed. This was on the Monday and we agreed that I would be back to pick it up on the Friday. So I went to pick the car up on the Friday – and I had to take time off work. I turned up at 9.30 in the morning. The salesman hadn't arranged for any of the work to be done and he was on holiday for a week. So we agreed that the work would be done the following Tuesday. I dropped the car off on the Tuesday at 9.30 on the way to work. Fortunately, when I turned up in the evening, all the repairs had been finished. Three weeks later, they had the cheek to send me a customer service evaluation questionnaire – and they wanted the answers by the end of the week!

Adjective *(adj)* Headwords for adjectives followed by information in square brackets [only before a noun] and [not before a noun] show any restrictions on where they can be used.

Noun *(n)* The codes [C] and [U] show whether a noun, or a particular sense of a noun, is countable (an agenda, two agendas) or uncountable (AOB, awareness).

Verbs *(v)* The forms of irregular verbs are given after the headword. The codes [I] (intransitive) and [T] (transitive) show whether a verb, or a particular sense of a verb, has or does not have an object. Phrasal verbs *(phr v)* are shown after the verb they are related to.

Some entries show information on words that are related to the headword. Adverbs *(adv)* are often shown in this way after adjectives.

Region labels The codes *AmE* and *BrE* show whether a word or sense of a word is used only in American or British English.

---

above board *adj* [not before a noun] honest and legal

acquire *v* [T] if one company acquires another, it buys it

acquisition *n* [C] when one company buys another or part of another company, or the company or part of a company that is bought

advertising campaign *n* [C] an organization's programme of advertising activities over a particular period with specific aims, for example an increase in sales or awareness of a product

agenda *n* [C] 1 a list of the subjects to be discussed at a meeting
2 the things that someone considers important or that they are planning to do something about

aggressive *adj* 1 an aggressive plan or action is intended to achieve its result by using direct and forceful methods
2 an aggressive person or organization is very determined to achieve what they want

alliance *n* [C] an agreement between two or more organizations to work together

AOB *n* [U] any other business; the time during a meeting when items not on the agenda can be discussed

application *n* [C] 1 a formal, usually written, request for something or for permission to do something
2 a formal request for work
3 a practical use for something
4 a piece of software for a particular use or job

apply *v* 1 [I] to make a formal, usually written request for something, especially a job, a place at university, or permission to do something
2 [T] to use something such as a law or an idea in a particular situation, activity, or process
3 [I,T] to have an effect on someone or something, or to concern a person, group, or situation

approximate *adj* an approximate amount, number etc is a little more or a little less than the exact amount, number etc —**approximately** *adv*

asset *n* [C] something belonging to an individual or a business that has value or the power to earn money

attend *v* [I,T] to go to an event such as a meeting

attribute *n* [C] a characteristic, feature, or quality

awareness *n* [U] knowledge or understanding of a particular subject, situation, or thing

background *n* [C] someone's past, for example their education, qualifications, and the jobs they have had

balance sheet *n* [C] a document showing a company's financial position and wealth at a particular time. The balance sheet is often described as a 'photograph' of a company's financial situation at a particular moment

bankrupt¹ *n* [C] someone judged to be unable to pay their debts by a court of law, and whose financial affairs are handled by a court official until the debts are settled

bankrupt² *adj* not having enough money to pay your debts

bankrupt³ *v* [T] to make a person, business, or country go bankrupt

bankruptcy *n plural* **bankruptcies** [C,U] when someone is judged to be unable to pay their debts by a court of law, and their assets are shared among their creditors (=those that they owe money to), or a case of this happening

bank statement *n* [C] information sent regularly by a bank to a customer, showing the money that has gone into and out of their account over a particular period

barrier to trade also **trade barrier** *n plural* **barriers to trade** [C] something that makes trade between two countries more difficult or expensive, for example a tax on imports

benchmark *n* [C] 1 something that can be used as a comparison to judge or measure other things
2 good performance in a particular activity in one company that can be used as a standard to judge the same activity in other companies —**benchmark** *v* [T], **benchmarking** *n* [U]

benefits package *n* [C] the total amount of pay and all the other advantages that an employee may receive such as bonuses, health insurance, a company car etc

bid¹ *n* [C] 1 an offer to buy something, for example a company in a takeover, or the price offered
2 an offer to do work or provide services for a fixed price, in competition with other offers

bid² *v past tense and past participle* **bid** *present participle* **bidding** 1 [I,T] to offer to pay a particular price for something, for example a company in a takeover
2 [I] to offer to do work or provide services for a fixed price, in competition with others —**bidding** *n* [U]

billboard *n* [C] *AmE* a large sign used for advertising. Billboards are usually called hoardings in British English

blueprint *n* [C] a plan for achieving or improving something

board also **board of directors** n [C usually singular] the group of people who have been elected by shareholders to manage a company

bonus n [C] an extra amount of money added to an employee's wages, usually as a reward for doing difficult work or for doing their work well

boom¹ n [C,U] 1 a time when business activity increases rapidly, so that the demand for goods increases, prices and wages go up, and unemployment falls
2 a time when activity on the stockmarket reaches a high level and share prices are very high

boom² v [I] if business, trade, or the economy is booming, it is very successful and growing

brand¹ n [C] a name given to a product or group of products by a company for easy recognition

brand² v [T] to give a name to a product or group of products

branded adj branded goods or products have brand names

branding n [U] the activity of giving brand names to products, developing people's awareness of them etc

brand leader n [C] the brand with the most sales in a particular market

brand loyalty n [U] the degree to which people buy a particular brand and refuse to change to other brands

brand manager n [C] someone in a company responsible for developing a brand

brand stretching n [U] when a company starts to use an existing brand name on a different type of product, hoping that people will buy it because they recognize the name

bribe¹ n [C] money that is paid secretly and dishonestly to obtain someone's help

bribe² v [T] to dishonestly give money to someone to persuade them to do something that will help you

bribery n [U] dishonestly giving money to someone to persuade them to do something to help you

broker n [C] a person or organization whose job is to buy and sell shares, currencies, property, insurance etc for others

bureaucracy n plural **bureaucracies** 1 [C] a system of governing that has a large number of departments and officials
2 [U] disapproving all the complicated rules and processes of an official system, especially when they are confusing or responsible for causing a delay

buyout also **buy-out** n [C] 1 the act of buying a business
2 the act of buying all the shares in a company of a particular shareholder

cash flow also **cashflow** n 1 [U] the amounts of money coming into and going out of a company, and the timing of these
2 [C,U] profit for a particular period, defined in different ways by different businesses

cash generation n [U] money that a company gets from sales after costs are taken away. Cash generation is often used in talking about the degree to which the company is able to do this

chair n [singular] 1 the position of being the chairman of a company or organization or the person who is chairman
2 the position of being in charge of a meeting or the person who is in charge of it
—**chair** v [T]

Chief Executive Officer (CEO) n [C usually singular] the manager with the most authority in the day to day management of a company, especially in the US. The job of CEO is sometimes combined with others, such as that of president

clock v
clock in/on phr v [I] to record on a special card or computer the time you arrive at or begin work
clock off/out phr v [I] to record on a special card or computer the time you stop or leave work

collapse v [I] if a company, organization, or system collapses, it suddenly fails or becomes too weak to continue —**collapse** n [C,U]

commission n [C,U] an amount of money paid to someone according to the value of goods, services, investments etc they have sold

compensation n [U] 1 an amount paid to someone because they have been hurt or harmed in some way
2 the total of pay and benefits for an employee, especially a high-level manager

competitive advantage n [C] something that helps you to be better or more successful than others

concept n [C] an idea for a product, business etc

conman n [C] someone who tries to get money from people by tricking them

consortium n plural **consortiums** or **consortia** [C] a combination of several companies working together for a particular purpose, for example in order to buy something or build something

consumer behaviour BrE **consumer behavior** AmE n [U] how, why, where, and when consumers buy things, and the study of this

controlling interest n [C,U] the situation where one shareholder owns enough shares to control a company

controlling shareholder also **majority shareholder** n [C] someone who owns more than half the shares in a company

copycat product [C] a product that copies a competitor's idea for a product

core adj **core business/activity/product** the business, activity etc that makes most money for a company and that is considered to be its most important and central one

corrupt¹ adj using power in a dishonest or illegal way in order to get money or an advantage of some kind

corrupt² v [T] to encourage someone to behave in an immoral or dishonest way —**corrupted** adj, **corruptible** adj, **corruptibility** n [U]

corruption n [U] 1 the crime of giving or receiving money, gifts, a better job etc in exchange for doing something dishonest or illegal that helps another person or company
2 when someone who has power or authority uses it in a dishonest or illegal way to get money or an advantage

counterfeit¹ adj made to look exactly like something else, usually illegally

counterfeit² v [T] to copy something so that it looks like something else, usually illegally —**counterfeiter** n [C]

crash¹ n [C] 1 a time when many investments lose their value very quickly, usually when investors lose confidence in the market and sell
2 an occasion when a computer or computer software suddenly and unexpectedly stops working or fails to work properly

crash² v 1 [I] if stockmarkets, shares etc crash, they

suddenly lose a lot of value

2 [I,T] if a computer crashes, or if you crash a computer, it suddenly and unexpectedly stops working

crisis *n plural* **crises** [C,U] 1 a period or moment of great difficulty, danger, or uncertainty, especially in politics or economics
2 a time when a personal problem or situation has reached its worst point

culture *n* [C,U] 1 the ideas, beliefs, and customs that are shared and accepted by people in a society
2 the attitudes or beliefs that are shared by a particular group of people or in a particular organization

customs *n* [U] the government department responsible for collecting the tax on goods that have been brought into the country and making sure that illegal goods are not imported or exported

deceit *n* [C,U] when someone tries to gain an advantage for themselves by tricking someone, for example by making a false statement

deceive *v* [T] to make someone believe something that is not true in order to get what you want

decline *v* [I] 1 if an industry or country declines, it becomes less profitable, productive, wealthy etc
2 if sales, output, production etc decline, they become less
—**decline** *n* [C,U]

defect *n* [C] a fault or the lack of something that means that a product etc is not perfect —**defective** *adj*, **defectively** *adv*

demand *n* [U] 1 spending on goods and services by companies and people in a particular economy
2 the total amount of a type of goods or services that people or companies buy in a particular period
3 the total amount of a type of goods or services that people or companies would buy if they were available

demerge *v* [I,T] if a company or unit demerges from a group, or if it is demerged, it becomes a separate company
—**demerger** *n* [C]

deregulate *v* [T] if a government deregulates a particular business activity, it allows companies to operate more freely so as to increase competition —**deregulation** *n* [U]

devious *adj* using dishonest tricks and deceiving people to get what you want —**deviously** *adv*, **deviousness** *n* [U]

differentiation *n* [U] when a company shows how its products are different from each other and from competing products, for example in its advertising
—**differentiate** *v* [T]

disclosure *n* 1 [C,U] the duty of someone in a professional position to inform customers, shareholders etc about facts that will influence their decisions
2 [U] the act of giving information about someone by an organization or person who would normally have to keep that information secret, for example when a bank gives information about a customer's accounts to the police
3 [C] a fact which is made known after being kept secret

dismissal *n* [C,U] when someone is removed from their job by their employer

disposal *n* 1 [U] the act of getting rid of something
2 [C] an asset that is sold, and the act of selling it

dispose *v* [T] 1 if you dispose of something, you get rid of it
2 *formal* if a company disposes of a particular asset, activity etc, it sells it

distribution channel also **distribution chain** *n* [C]

the way a product is made available and sold, the organizations involved etc

diversify *v* [I] 1 if a company or economy diversifies, it increases the range of goods or services it produces
2 to start to put your money into different types of investments in addition to the investments you already have
—**diversification** *n* [U]

downmarket[1] also **downscale** *AmE adj* involving goods and services that are cheap and perhaps not of very good quality compared to others of the same type, or the people that buy them

downmarket[2] also **downscale** *AmE adv* **go/move downmarket/downscale** to start buying or selling cheaper goods or services

dress code *n* [C] the way that you are expected to dress in a particular situation, as an employee of a particular company etc

drive *n* 1 [U] someone's energy, motivation, and ability to work hard
2 [C usually singular] an effort to improve or increase the level of something

drop[1] *v* 1 [I] to fall to a lower level or amount
2 [T] to stop doing or planning something
drop away/off *phr v* [I] to become lower in level or amount

drop[2] *n* [C usually singular] if there is a drop in the amount, level, or number of something, it goes down or becomes less

dumping *n* [U] the activity of selling products in an export market cheaper than in the home market, or cheaper than they cost to make, usually in order to increase market share

durable *adj* if something is durable, it lasts a long time —**durability** *n* [U]

economies of scale *n* [plural] the advantages that a bigger factory, shop etc has over a smaller one because it can spread its fixed costs over a larger number of units and thus produce or sell things more cheaply

economy drive *n* [C] a planned effort by an organization to reduce costs

endorse *v* [T] if someone, usually famous, endorses a product, they say how good it is in advertisements. People will buy the product because they like or trust the person —**endorsement** *n* [C,U]

ethical *adj* 1 connected with principles of what is right and wrong
2 morally good or correct —**ethically** *adv*

ethics *n* [plural] moral rules or principles of behaviour that should guide members of a profession or organization and make them deal honestly and fairly with each other and with their customers

etiquette *n* [U] the formal rules for polite behaviour

expand *v* 1 [I,T] to become larger in size, amount, or number, or to make something larger in size, amount, or number
2 [I] if a company expands, it increases its sales, areas of activity etc
—**expansion** *n* [U]

extort *v* [T] to illegally force someone to give you money by threatening them —**extortion** *n* [U]

facility *n plural* **facilities** 1 [C] a place or large building which is used to make or provide a particular product or service

2 facilities [plural] special buildings or equipment that have been provided for a particular use, such as sports activities, shopping or travelling

fake¹ *adj* made to look like something valuable or genuine in order to deceive people

fake² *n* [C] a copy of an original document, valuable object etc that is intended to deceive people into believing it is the real document, object etc

fall¹ *v past tense* **fell** *past participle* **fallen** *v* [I] to go down to a lower price, level, amount etc

fall² *n* [C] 1 a reduction in the amount, level, price etc of something
2 when a person or organization loses their position of power or becomes unsuccessful

fiddle *n* [C] *BrE informal* 1 a dishonest way of getting money or not paying money
2 **be on the fiddle** to be getting money dishonestly or illegally

flaw *n* [C] 1 a mistake or weakness in a machine, system etc that prevents it from working correctly
2 a mistake in an argument, plan, or set of ideas

flexible *adj* 1 a person, plan etc that is flexible can change or be changed easily to suit any new situation
2 if arrangements for work are flexible, employers can ask workers to do different jobs, work part-time rather than full-time, give them contracts for short periods etc. Flexible working also includes job-sharing and working from home —**flexibility** *n* [U]

flexitime *BrE* also **flextime** *AmE n* [U] a system in which people who work in a company do a fixed number of hours each week, but can choose what time they start or finish work within certain limits

flight of capital also **capital flight** *n* [U] when money is moved rapidly out of a country, usually because its economy is doing badly or there is political uncertainty

fluctuate *v* [I] if prices, income, rates etc fluctuate, they change, increasing or falling often or regularly —**fluctuating** *adj*

fluctuation *n* [C,U] the movement of prices, income, rates etc as they increase and fall

focus *n* [U] when a company serves particular groups of customers in a market with particular needs, rather than serving the whole market

focus group *n* [C] a group of people brought together to discuss their feelings and opinions about a particular subject. In market research, focus groups discuss their opinions of products, advertisements, companies etc

franchise¹ *n* [C] 1 an arrangement in which a company gives a business the right to sell its goods or services in return for payment or a share of the profits
2 a particular shop, restaurant etc that is run under a franchise, or a company that owns a number of these

franchise² *v* [I,T] to sell franchises to people —**franchising** *n* [U]

franchisee *n* [C] someone who is sold a franchise and operates it

free port *n* [C] a port where import duty does not have to be paid on imports that are to be sent to another country to be sold, or used to manufacture goods that will be sold abroad

gambling *n* [U] the practice of risking money or possessions on the result of something uncertain, for

example a card game or a sporting event such as a horse race

global *adj* 1 affecting or involving the whole world
2 including and considering all the parts of a situation together, rather than the individual parts separately —**globally** *adv*

global economy *n* [singular] the economy of the world seen as a whole

globalization also **-isation** *BrE n* [U] the tendency for the world economy to work as one unit, led by large international companies doing business all over the world

globalize also **-ise** *BrE v* [I,T] if a company, an industry, or an economy globalizes or is globalized, it no longer depends on conditions in one country, but on conditions in the world as whole

goodwill payment *n* [C] a payment made by a supplier to a customer because of a problem the customer has had, for example with quality or late delivery of goods

gross domestic product (GDP) *n* [singular] the total value of goods and services produced in a country's economy, not including income from abroad

gross domestic product per capita *n* [singular] the total value of goods and services produced in a country divided by the number of people living there

grow *v past tense* **grew** *past participle* **grown** 1 [I] to increase in amount, size, or degree
2 [T] if you grow a business activity, you make it bigger

growth *n* [U] an increase in size, amount, or degree

headquarters *n* [plural] the head office or main building of an organization —**headquartered** *adj*

hoarding *n* [C] a large sign used for advertising. Hoardings are called billboards in American English

hot-desking *n* [U] when people working in an office do not each have their own desk, but work where there is one available

incentive *n* [C] something which is used to encourage people, especially to make them work harder, produce more or spend more money

income statement *n* [C] *AmE* a financial document showing the amount of money earned and spent in a particular period of time by a company. This is usually called the profit and loss account in British English

incremental *adj* 1 an incremental process is one where things happens in small steps
2 an incremental amount, sum etc is small when considered by itself

industrial espionage *n* [U] the activity of secretly finding out a company's plans, details of its products etc

infant industry *n* [C] an industry in its early stages of development in a particular country. Some people think that infant industries should be helped with government money and protected from international competition by import taxes etc

infrastructure *n* [C,U] 1 the basic systems and structures that a country needs to make economic activity possible, for example transport, communications, and power supplies
2 the basic systems and equipment needed for an industry or business to operate successfully or for an activity to happen

innovate *v* [I] to design and develop new and better products —**innovator** *n* [C]

innovation *n* 1 [C] a new idea, method, or invention
2 [U] the introduction of new ideas or methods

innovative *adj* 1 an innovative product, method, process etc is new, different, and better than those that existed before
2 using clever new ideas and methods —**innovatively** *adv*

insider trading *n* [U] when someone uses knowledge of a particular company, situation etc that is not available to other people in order to buy or sell shares. Insider trading is illegal

integrity *n* [U] 1 the state of being united or kept together as one whole, and therefore strong, unit
2 complete honesty

interest *n* 1 [U] an amount paid by a borrower to a lender, for example to a bank by someone borrowing money for a loan, or by a bank to a depositor (=someone keeping money in an account there)
2 [U] the interest rate at which a particular sum of money is borrowed and lent
3 [U] the part of a company that someone owns
4 [C] the possession of rights, especially to land, property etc

interpreter *n* [C] someone who translates what someone says from one language into another, especially as their job

inventory *n plural* **inventories** [C,U] *AmE* 1 a supply of raw materials or parts before they are used in production, or a supply of finished goods. Inventories of raw materials or parts are usually called stocks in British English
2 a supply of goods, kept for sale by a shop or other retailer. Inventories of goods are usually called stocks in British English

inventory control *n* [U] *AmE* making sure that supplies of raw materials, work in progress, and finished goods are managed correctly. Inventory control is called stock control in British English

ISO *n* 1 the name used internationally for the International Organization for Standardization, whose purpose is to establish international standards for services, goods, and industrial methods
2 **ISO 9000** the ISO's quality standard for companies producing goods
3 **ISO 9001/9002** the ISO's quality standards for companies providing services

jet lag *n* [U] the tired and confused feeling you can get after flying a very long distance

jingle *n* [C] a short song or tune used in advertisements

joint venture *n* [C] a business activity in which two or more companies have invested together

kickback *n* [C] *informal* a bribe (=money that is paid secretly and dishonestly to obtain someone's help)

KISS *informal* keep it simple, stupid; keep it short and simple. Used to say that a method for doing something should be kept simple, in order to avoid mistakes

knowledge worker *n* [C] someone whose job involves dealing with information, rather than making things

labor union *n* [C] *AmE* an organization representing people working in a particular industry or profession, especially in meetings with their employers. Labor unions are called trade unions in British English

laisser-faire also **laissez-faire** *n* [U] the idea that governments should do as little to the economy as possible and allow private business to develop without the state controlling or influencing them

launch[1] *v* [T] 1 to show or make a new product available for sale for the first time
2 to start a new company
3 to start a new activity, usually after planning it carefully

launch[2] *n* [C] 1 an occasion at which a new product is shown or made available for sale or use for the first time
2 the start of a new activity or plan

letter of credit (l/c) *n plural* **letters of credit** [C] in foreign trade, a written promise by an importer's bank to pay the exporter's bank on a particular date or after a particular event, for example when the goods are sent by the exporter

level[1] *n* [C] 1 the measured amount of something that exists at a particular time or in a particular place
2 all the people or jobs within an organization, industry etc that have similar importance and responsibility

level[2] *v past tense and past participle* **levelled** *BrE* also **leveled** *AmE present participle* **levelling** *BrE* also **leveling** *AmE*

level off/out *phr v* [I] to stop climbing or growing and become steady or continue at a fixed level

liability *n* 1 [singular] an amount of money owed by a business to a supplier, lender, or other creditor
2 **liabilities** [plural] the amounts of money owed by a business considered together, as shown in its balance sheet
3 [U] a person's or organization's responsibility for loss, damage, or injury caused to others or their property, or for payment of debts

liberalize also **-ise** *BrE v* [T] to make a system, laws, or moral attitudes less strict —**liberalization** *n* [U]

limited company also **limited liability company** *n* [C] a company where individual shareholders lose only the cost of their shares if the company goes bankrupt, and not other property they own

logo *n plural* **logos** [C] a design or way of writing its name that a company or organization uses as its official sign on its products, advertising etc

loophole *n* [C] a small mistake in a law that makes it possible to do something the law is supposed to prevent you from doing, or to avoid doing something that the law is supposed to make you do

lose *v past tense and past participle* **lost** *present participle* **losing** [T] 1 to stop having something any more, or to have less of it
2 to have less money than you had before or to spend more money than you are receiving
3 to fall to a lower figure or price
4 **lose something (to sb/sth)** to have something such as a contract or customers taken away by someone or something
5 **lose ground** to become less in value or to lose an advantage

loss *n* 1 [C,U] the fact of no longer having something that you used to have
2 [C] when a business or part of a business spends more money in costs than it gets in sales in a particular period, or loses money on a particular deal, problem etc

loyal *adj* if customers are loyal to a particular product, they continue to buy it and do not change to other products —**loyalty** *n* [U]

margin also **profit margin** *n* [C,U] the difference

between the price of a product or service and the cost of producing it, or between the cost of producing all of a company's products or services and the total sum they are sold for

market challenger *n* [C] an organization or product that may take the place of the organization or product that has the highest sales in its market or industry

marketing mix *n* [C usually singular] the combination of marketing actions often referred to as product, price, place, and promotion: selling the right product, through appropriate distribution channels, at the right price in relation to other products and for the profitability of the company, with the correct support in terms of advertising, sales force etc

market leader *n* [C] an organization or product that has the highest sales, or one of the highest sales, in its market or industry

market nicher *n* [C] a product or service sold in a niche market (=a market for a product or service, perhaps an expensive or unusual one, that does not have many buyers) or the company that sells it

merchandise *n* [U] goods that are produced in order to be sold, especially goods that are sold in a store

merge *v* [I,T] if two or more companies, organizations etc merge, or if they are merged, they join together

merger *n* [C] an occasion when two or more companies, organizations etc join together to form a larger company etc

middleman *n plural* **middlemen** [C] a person, business, organization etc that buys things in order to sell them to someone else, or that helps to arrange business deals for other people

mission statement *n* [C] a short written statement made by an organization, intended to communicate its aims to customers, employees, shareholders etc

model *n* [C] 1 a particular type or design of a vehicle or machine
2 a simple description or structure that is used to help people understand similar systems or structures
3 the way in which something is done by a particular country, person etc that can be copied by others who want similar results

morale *n* [U] the level of confidence and positive feelings among a group of people who work together

motivate *v* [T] 1 to encourage someone and make them want to achieve something and be willing to work hard in order to do it
2 to provide the reason why someone does something —**motivating** *adj*

motivated *adj* very keen to do something or achieve something, especially because you find it interesting or exciting

motivation *n* 1 [U] eagerness and willingness to do something without needing to be told or forced to do it
2 [C] the reason why you want to do something

nepotism *n* [U] the practice of giving jobs to members of your family when you are in a position of power

niche market *n* [C] a market for a product or service, perhaps an expensive or unusual one that does not have many buyers but that may be profitable for companies who sell it

open-plan office *n* [C] open-plan offices do not have walls dividing them into separate rooms

optimize also **-ise** *BrE v* [T] to make the best possible use of something or to do something in the best possible way

overtime *n* [U] 1 time that you spend working in your job in addition to your normal working hours
2 time that a factory, office etc is operating in addition to its normal hours
3 the money that you are paid for working more hours than usual

partner *n* [C] 1 a company that works with another company in a particular activity, or invests in the same activity
2 someone who starts a new business with someone else by investing in it
3 a member of certain types of business or professional groups, for example partnerships of lawyers, architects etc
4 also **economic partner** a country that invests in another or is invested in by another, or that trades with another
5 also **trade partner, trading partner** one country that trades with another

partnership *n* 1 [C] a relationship between two people, organizations, or countries that work together
2 [U] the situation of working together in business
3 [C] a business organization made up of a group of accountants, lawyers etc who work together, or of a group of investors

patent[1] *n* [C] an legal document giving a person or company the right to make or sell a new invention, product, or method of doing something and stating that no other person or company is allowed to do this

patent[2] *v* [T] to obtain a patent, protecting the rights to make or sell a new invention, product, or method of doing something **patented** *adj* [only before a noun]

peak[1] *n* [C] the time when prices, shares etc have reached their highest point or level

peak[2] *adj* 1 **peak level/price/rate etc** the highest level, etc something reaches
2 **peak time/period/hours/season** the time etc when the greatest number of people are doing the same thing, using the same service etc

peak[3] *v* [I] to reach the highest point or level

phone rage [U] angry behaviour on the telephone by people who are not satisfied with the service they are receiving etc

pioneer *n* [C] the first person or organization to do something that other people and organizations will later develop or continue to do —**pioneer** *v* [T], **pioneering** *adj*

plummet *v* [I,T] to suddenly and quickly go down in value or amount —**plummet** *n* [C]

point-of-sale advertising *n* [U] advertising for a product in places where it is sold

prime time *n* [U] the time in the evening when most people are watching television, and the cost of advertising is at its most expensive

product portfolio *n* [C] all of a company's products considered as a group

profit and loss account *n* [C] *BrE* a financial document showing the amount of money earned and spent in a particular period of time by a company. This is usually called the income statement in American English

promotion *n* 1 [C,U] a move to a more important job or

rank in a company or organization

2 [C] also **sales promotion** an activity such as special advertisements or free gifts intended to sell a product or service

protectionism *n* [U] the idea that a government should try to help an industry in its country by taxing foreign goods that compete with it, limiting the number that can be imported etc, and the actions that it takes to do this — **protectionist** *adj*, **protectionist** *n* [C]

prototype *n* [C] the first form that a new design of a car, machine etc has

public limited company (PLC) *n* [C] a limited company whose shares are freely sold and traded, in Britain public limited companies have the letters PLC after their name

qualification *n* 1 [C usually plural] an examination that you have passed at school, university, or in your profession

2 [C] a skill, personal quality, or type of experience that makes you suitable for a particular job

quality circle *n* [C] a small group of employees who meet regularly to discuss ways to improve working methods and to solve problems

quota *n* [C] an official limit on the number or amount of something that is allowed in a particular period

R and D *n* [U] research and development; the part of a business concerned with studying new ideas and developing new products

rationalize also **-ise** *BrE v* [I,T] to make a business or organization more effective by getting rid of unnecessary staff, equipment etc, or reorganizing its structure — **rationalization** *n* [C,U]

real estate *n AmE* [U] land or buildings and the business of buying and selling them

recall *v* [T] 1 if a company recalls one of its products, it asks customers to return it because there may be something wrong with it —**recall** *n* [C]

2 to remember something that you have seen or heard, such as an advertisement —**recall** *n* [U]

receipt *n* 1 [U] the act of receiving something

2 [C] a document given by someone, showing that they have received money, goods, or services

3 **receipts** [plural] money that has been received

recession *n* [C,U] a period of time when an economy or industry is doing badly, and business activity and employment decrease. Many economists consider that there is a recession when industrial production falls for six months in a row

recover *v* 1 [I] to increase or improve after falling in value or getting worse

2 [T] to get back money that you have spent or lost

3 [T] to get back something that was stolen, lost, or almost destroyed

recovery *n plural* **recoveries** 1 [C,U] when prices increase, or when the economy grows again after a period of difficulty

2 [U] the act of getting something back, such as money that you are owed

recruit¹ *v* [I,T] to find new people to work for an organization, do a job etc

recruit² *n* [C] someone who has recently joined a company or organization

recruitment *n* 1 [U] the process or the business of

recruiting new people

2 [C] an occasion when someone is recruited

redundancy *n plural* **redundancies** *especially BrE* 1 [U] when someone loses their job in a company because the job is no longer needed

2 [C usually plural] a person who has lost their job in a company because the job is no longer needed

redundant *adj especially BrE* if you are redundant or made redundant, your employer no longer has a job for you

reference *n* [C] 1 a letter written by someone who knows you well, usually to a new employer, giving information about your character, abilities, or qualifications

2 a person who provides information about your character, abilities, or qualifications when you are trying to get a job

reliable *adj* someone or something that is reliable can be trusted or depended on —**reliability** *n* [U]

relocate *v* [I,T] if a company or workers relocate or are relocated, they move to a different place —**relocation** *n* [C,U]

resign *v* [I,T] to officially leave a job, position etc usually through your own choice, rather than being told to leave —**resignation** *n* [C]

resource *n* 1 [C usually plural] also **natural resource** something such as oil, land, or natural energy that exists in a country and can be used to increase its wealth

2 **resources** [plural] all the money, property, skill, labour etc that a company has available

restriction *n* [C] an official rule that limits or controls what people can do or what is allowed to happen

retailer *n* [C] 1 a business that sells goods to members of the public, rather than to shops etc

2 someone who owns or runs a shop selling goods to members of the public

retail outlet *n* [C] a shop through which products are sold to the public

rise¹ *v past tense* **rose** *past participle* **risen** [I] to increase in number, amount, or value

rise² *n* 1 [C] an increase in number, amount, or value

2 [C] *BrE* an increase in salary or wages. A rise is called a raise in American English

3 [singular] the process of becoming more important, successful, or powerful

rocket also **rocket up** *v* [I] if a price or amount rockets or rockets up, it increases quickly and suddenly

sample¹ *n* [C] 1 a group of people who have been chosen to give opinions or information about something

2 a small amount of a product that people can try in order to find out what it is like

sample² *v* [T] 1 to ask questions to a group of people chosen from a larger group, in order to get information or opinions from them, so as to better understand the larger group

2 to try a small amount of a product in order to find out what it is like

second *v* [T] to officially support a suggestion, idea etc made by another person at a formal meeting so that it can be discussed or voted on —**seconder** *n* [C]

security *n plural* **securities** 1 [U] actions to keep someone or something safe from being damaged, stolen etc

2 [U] a feeling of being safe and free from worry about what might happen

3 [U] property or other assets that you promise to give someone if you cannot pay back the money that you owe them

4 [C] a financial investment such as a bond or share, or the related certificate showing who owns it

segment¹ *n* [C] 1 a part of the economy of a country or a company's work

2 also **market segment** a group of customers that share similar characteristics, such as age, income, interests, social class etc

3 also **market segment** the products in a particular part of the market

segment² *v* [T] to divide a large group of people into smaller groups of people of a similar age or with similar incomes, interests etc. Companies segment markets so as to be able to sell to each group the products that are most suitable for it —**segmentation** *n* [U]

sell-off *n* [C] when a business, company etc, or part of one, is sold to another company

share *n* [C] one of the parts into which ownership of a company is divided

share capital *n* [U] capital in the form of shares, rather than in the form of loans

shareholder n [C] someone who owns shares in a company

skill *n* [C,U] an ability to do something well, especially because you have learned and practised it

sleaze *n* [U] immoral behaviour, especially involving money or sex **sleazy** *adj*

sleeping partner *n* [C] a partner who invests in a business but does not take an active part in managing it

slip¹ *v past tense and past participle* **slipped** *present participle* **slipping** [I] to become worse or less or fall to a lower amount, standard etc than before

slip² *n* [singular] an occasion when something becomes worse or becomes less or lower

slot *n* [C] a particular time when a television programme or advertisement is shown

slush fund *n* [C usually singular] an amount of money collected for illegal purposes, especially by a politician

sole trader *n* [C] a legal form of company in some countries for someone who has their own business, with no other shareholders

speculate *v* 1 [I] to buy goods, shares, property etc in the hope that their value will increase so that you can sell them at a higher price and make a profit, often quickly

2 [I,T] to think or talk about the possible causes or effects of something without knowing all the facts or details **speculation** *n* [U]

speculative *adj* 1 bought or done in the hope of making a profit

2 based on guessing, not on information or facts

stabilize also **-ise** *BrE v* [I,T] to become firm, steady, or unchanging, or to make something do this

stake *n* [C usually singular] money risked or invested in a business

stand *v past tense and past participle* **stood**
stand at *phr v* [I] to be at a particular level or amount

start-up *n* [C] a new company

stock *n* [C,U] 1 *especially AmE* one of the shares into which ownership of a company is divided, or these shares considered together

2 also **stocks** a supply of a commodity (=oil, metal, farm product etc) that has been produced and is kept to be used when needed

3 *especially BrE* a supply of raw materials or parts before they are used in production, or a supply of finished goods. Stocks of raw materials or parts are usually called inventories in American English

4 a supply of goods, kept for sale by a shop or other retailer. Stocks of goods are usually called inventories in American English

stock control *n* [U] *BrE* making sure that supplies of raw materials, work in progress, and finished goods are managed correctly. Stock control is called inventory control in American English

straight *adj* **be/play straight with sb** to be honest and truthful with someone

strategic *adj* done as part of a plan to gain an advantage or achieve a particular purpose —**strategically** *adv*

strategy *n plural* **strategies** 1 [C] a plan or series of plans for achieving an aim, especially relating to the best way for an organization to develop

2 [U] the process of skilful planning in general

stress *n* [U] continuous feelings of worry about your work or personal life, that prevent you from relaxing — **stressful** *adj*

stressed also **stressed out** *adj* if someone is stressed or stressed out, they are so worried and tired that they cannot relax

subliminal advertising *n* [U] when images appear very quickly during a television or cinema advertisement with effects that people are not conscious of

subsidiary also **subsidiary company** *n plural* **subsidaries** [C] a company that is at least half-owned by another company

subsidize also **-ise** *BrE v* [T] if a government or organization subsidizes a company, activity etc, it pays part of the cost —**subsidized** *adj*

subsidy *n plural* **subsidies** [C] money that is paid by a government or organization to make something cheaper to buy, use, or produce

sweetener *n* [C] 1 something used to make an offer, suggestion etc more attractive

2 a bribe (=illegal or unfair payment made to someone to persuade them to do something)

swindle *v* [T] to get money from someone dishonestly by deceiving them —**swindle** *n* [C], **swindler** *n* [C]

tactic *n* [C usually plural] a method that you use to achieve something

tactical *adj* done in order to achieve what you want at a later time, especially in a large plan

tailor *v* [T] to make something or put something together so that it is exactly right for someone's needs —**tailored** *adj*

take *v past tense* **took** *past participle* **taken**
take over *phr v* [I,T] 1 to take control of something
2 to take control of a company by buying more than half of its shares

takeover *n* [C] the act of getting control of a company by buying more than half of its shares

takeover target *n* [C] a company that may be bought or that is being bought by another company

target¹ *n* [C] 1 an organization, industry, country etc that is deliberately chosen to have something done to it

2 a result such as a total, an amount, or a time which you aim to achieve

target² *v* [T] 1 to make something have an effect on a particular limited group or area

2 to choose someone or something as your target — **targeted** *adj*

tariff *n* [C usually plural] a tax on goods coming into a country or going out of it

teaser *n* [C] an advertisement intended to get people's attention for advertisments that will come later or products that will be available later

total quality management (TQM) *n* [U] the management of systems in a company in order to make sure that each department is working in the most effective way and to improve the quality of the goods the company produces

track record *n* [C usually singular] all the things that a person or organization has done in the past, which shows how good they are at doing their job, dealing with problems etc

trade union also **trades union** *n* [C] *BrE* an organization representing people working in a particular industry or profession, especially in meetings with their employers. Trade unions are called labor unions in American English —**trade unionist** *n* [C]

transaction *n* [C] 1 a business deal, especially one involving the exchange of money

2 the act of paying or receiving money

transition *n* [C,U] *formal* the act or process of changing from one state or form to another

trend *n* [C] the general way in which a particular situation is changing or developing

trial *n* 1 [C] a legal process in which a court of law examines a case to decide whether someone is guilty of a crime

2 [C usually plural] a process of testing a product to see whether it is safe, effective etc **trial** *v* [T], **trialling** *n* [U]

triple¹ *adj* [only before a noun] having three parts or members

triple² *v* [I,T] to become three times as much or as many, or to make something do this

turnaround also **turnround** *BrE n* [C usually singular]

1 the time between receiving an order for goods, dealing with it, and sending the goods to the customer

2 a complete change from a bad situation to a good one

3 a complete change in someone's opinion or ideas

turnover *n* [singular] 1 *BrE* the amount of business done in a particular period, measured by the amount of money obtained from customers for goods or services that have been sold

2 the rate at which workers leave an organization and are replaced by others

3 the rate at which goods are sold

unique selling proposition also **unique selling point** (USP) *n* [C usually singular] the thing that makes a particular product different from all other similar products

unscrupulous *adj* behaving in an unfair or dishonest way —**unscrupulously** *adv*, **unscrupulousness** *n* [U]

upgrade¹ *v* [I,T] 1 to make a computer, machine etc better and able to do more things

2 to buy a new computer, machine etc that is better and able to do more things than your old one

3 to get a better seat on a plane, a better rented car etc than the one you paid for, or give someone a better seat etc than the one they paid for

upgrade² *n* [C] 1 the act of improving a product or service, or one that has been improved

2 new computer software that replaces previous software of the same type

3 an occasion when someone is given a better seat on a plane, a better rented car etc, than the one they paid for

upmarket¹ also **upscale** *AmE adj* involving goods and services that are expensive when compared to others of the same type, or the people that buy them

upmarket² also **upscale** *AmE adv* **go/move upmarket/upscale** to start buying or selling more expensive goods or services

voice mail *n* [U] a system for leaving messages for people by telephone, or the messages themselves

volume *n* [C,U] 1 the amount of space that a substance or object contains or fills

2 the total amount of something

warranty *n plural* **warranties** [C,U] a written promise that a company gives to a customer, stating that it will repair or replace a product they have bought if it breaks during a certain period of time. Warranty is another word for guarantee

welfare *n* [U] help that is given by government to people with social or financial problems because they are unemployed, ill etc

whistleblower *n* [C] someone working for an organization who tells the authorities that people in the organization are doing something illegal, dishonest, or wrong

wholesaler *n* [C] a person or company that sells goods in large quanitities to other businesses, who may then sell them to the general public

withdraw *v past tense* **withdrew** *past participle* **withdrawn** [T] 1 to take money out of a bank account

2 to remove something or take it back, often because of an official decision

3 if a company withdraws a product or service, it stops making it available, either for a period or permanently

withdrawal *n* 1 [C,U] the act of taking money out of a bank account, or the amount you take out

2 [U] the removal or stopping of something such as support, an offer, or a service

3 [C,U] also **product withdrawal** the act of no longer making a product available, either for a period or permanently

4 [U] the act of no longer taking part in an activity or being a member of an organization

workforce *n* [C] all the people who work in a particular country, area, industry, company, or place of work

zero defects *n* [plural] the aim of having no faults at all in products that are produced